THE NATURE OF NORTH CAROLINA'S SOUTHERN COAST

THE UNIVERSITY OF NORTH CAROLINA PRESS   CHAPEL HILL AND LONDON

THE NATURE OF NORTH CAROLINA'S SOUTHERN COAST

BARRIER ISLANDS, COASTAL WATERS, AND WETLANDS

DIRK FRANKENBERG

The paper in this book meets the guidelines for permanence and durability of the Committee on Production Guidelines for Book Longevity of the Council on Library Resources.

01 00 99 98 97

5 4 3 2 1

Unless otherwise indicated, all photographs are by the author.

Display photographs used on pages ii–iii, v, and 219 © Scott Taylor.

Library of Congress Cataloging-in-Publication Data

Frankenberg, Dirk.

The nature of North Carolina's southern coast: barrier islands, coastal waters, and wetlands / Dirk Frankenberg.

p.   cm.

Includes index.

ISBN 0-8078-4655-4 (pbk.: alk. paper)

1. Natural areas — North Carolina.

2. Natural history — North Carolina.

3. North Carolina — Environmental conditions.

I. Title.

QH76.5.N8F73   1997

508.756'2 — dc21   96-46448

CIP

This book is dedicated to my wife,
Susan—

who has been up many creeks with me,
sometimes with, sometimes without benefit
of paddle. Throughout these trips—both
literal and proverbial—her intelligence,
constructive criticism, and unflagging good
humor have gotten us home relatively little
the worse for wear.

CONTENTS

FIGURES AND TABLES

Figures

Tables

PREFACE

This book was written for fun and to serve a useful purpose. The fun came in the fieldwork—fun that I hope will transfer to the reader as you visit the places I describe. The useful purpose is to help you find some wonderful natural areas, and also help you understand their ecology while visiting. There are many ways to enjoy these areas. One is to observe the sheer beauty of them. Longleaf pine savannas can be almost cathedral-like in their quiet verticality; salt marshes are a symphony on a theme of green; and dune shapes sculpted by the wind can be as pleasing as any human sculpture. Natural areas can also be enjoyed for their wildness. While working on this book, I saw an osprey take a great blue heron by diving vertically down on it as it flew across a marsh. I also saw my first red-cockaded woodpeckers, an endangered species of longleaf pine forests, and a large copperhead that swam across a creek in front of my canoe. Natural areas can also be enjoyed for what they teach about adaptation and how natural systems respond to harsh features of their environment. Dunes erode and beaches flatten when subjected to high waves. Dune plants flourish best in areas protected from wind and salt spray, but still survive in exposed locations. Estuarine animals suffer massive die-offs when oxygen depletion and/or parasites affect them, but they recover rapidly as a result of their massive reproductive potential. It is my great hope that readers will find enjoyment from the natural areas along the southern coast, and that this book will be a guide to both the areas and their workings.

The southern coast is being heavily developed to increase the density of human habitation and the intensity of natural resource use. Early stages of this development were often insensitive to the workings of the natural systems and so disrupted them in ways that we have now learned to avoid. Some of our early mistakes remain visible, but the very existence of the natural areas described here is evidence that our society is learning to appreciate, rather than just dominate, nature. Some of our most beautiful areas are places where environmental degradation has been reversed and nature has healed wounds inflicted by insensitive prior use. Such areas are visible along roads, channels, and fields throughout the coastal zone. Other areas remain unmodified despite low economic value and appear much like they did before European contact. These are rare when they once were common, but their existence at the end of four centuries of economic development is cause for hope for their, and our, future.

The book itself is divided into two major chapters and ends with an epilogue describing current development pressure. The first major chapter describes environmental processes that have created and shaped the southern coast. The second chapter is a field guide to natural areas along the southern coast in North Carolina. Together these two chapters are designed to lead the reader to interesting places armed with the understanding needed to appreciate the beauty of the sites as well as the context and environmental controls that have created and sustained them.

Chapter 1 describes the ecological processes that characterize and sustain the natural habitats of the southern coast. The level of technical detail is designed for an interested nonscientist. Each section begins with a synopsis that introduces and explains the importance of the material to follow. Some of the material in Chapter 1 may be difficult reading for nonscientists, but I hope your hard work will be rewarded by deeper understanding. Chapter 1 also identifies the best places to visit the twelve types of natural areas that dominate the landscape. These examples are well-developed natural communities. That is, they have all the species usually found in such areas, and they are dominated by those species most characteristic of the community type.

Chapter 2 describes all major natural areas that I have found along the southern coast of North Carolina. Not all of these sites are as attractive as those mentioned in Chapter 1, but all sites are worth exploring if time and interest allow. I find something interesting and educational in all these areas, but as my students and family will testify, I have never visited a natural area that I didn't like. Not everyone is as simpleminded as I, however, so I have identified the best areas in each coastal section as "five-star natural sites." These are all attractive and characterize full development of the natural community they represent. Unfortunately, since this book was completed in mid-1996, Hurricane Fran devastated several areas of the southern coast of North Carolina. Most of the damage was to beachfront areas, but downed trees will characterize coastal landscapes for many years to come.

The areas described in Chapter 2 can be visited by car, by boat, or on foot. The book provides directions and general maps to the areas described, but driving, boating, and hiking enthusiasts will need to look elsewhere for maps, charts, and books that provide geographic information at the level of detail they may require for specialized plans. Access to all areas begins by road, and maps such as the state transportation map provided free by the North Carolina Department of Transportation or commercially available will be needed for route planning. More detailed maps are also available commercially; a set of state topographic maps produced by DeLorme Mapping of Freeport, Maine, is strongly recommended. County maps of southern states are produced by C. J. Paetz of Lyndon Station, Wisconsin. Charts of southern coastal waters are produced by the National Oceanic and Atmospheric Administration's National Ocean Service and by ADC of Alexandria, Inc., in Virginia. All of these resources are available in bookstores and outdoor or camping supply stores.

Natural areas in North Carolina that must be reached by boat are also described. In most cases these areas are accessible by regular ferry service or by privately arranged water taxis. Sources of information on these services are provided in the text, but since schedules change seasonally and from year to year, readers are encouraged to call ahead for up-to-date information on service that will be available at the time of their visit. Some additional areas are described that are not now served by ferries or nearby water taxis. I have visited all of these areas in a 13-foot canoe, but both smaller and somewhat larger boats could just as easily be used. I have mentioned shallow water and underwater obstructions when they caused problems for me, but I can't promise you won't find some of your own. Boat launching sites are described. All are adequate for kayaks and canoes, and most can serve for small trailered boats as well. The list provided is by no means complete. The state Department of Transportation distributes free copies of the North Carolina Coastal Boating Guide, and commercial chart and map sets are available in bookstores and outdoor supply shops.

The book describes North Carolina hiking and nature trails where they provide access by foot to natural areas worth visiting. I have not personally hiked every trail in the region and therefore welcome advice on overlooked trails and sites that should be included in subsequent editions. A relatively complete list of trails in North Carolina's state parks is included in *State Parks of North Carolina*, by Walter C. Biggs and James F. Parnell, published by John F. Blair in 1993. The geology of these parks and trails is further described in *A Geologic Guide to North Carolina's State Parks*, available from the North Carolina Geological Survey. Trails in national seashores and forests are described in materials available from the National Park Service and the U.S. Forest Service. All of these trails and others are described in *North Carolina Hiking Trails*, a 1988 book by Allen de Hart, published by AMC Press; in *Wild Shores: Exploring the Wilderness Areas of Eastern North Carolina*, by Walter K. Taylor, published by Downhome Press in 1993; and in *Afoot in the South: Walks in Natural Areas of North Carolina*, another 1993 book by Phillip Manning, published by John F. Blair. Finally, coastal natural areas in the state's southern half are described in *A Directory of North Carolina's Natural Areas*, available from the North Carolina Natural Heritage Program. Many of the coastal hiking trails and natural areas mentioned in other books are also described here, but readers with greater interest will find additional and more detailed coverage in the sources listed above.

There are still other guidebooks for those who wish to tour more extensively by automobile or boat. North Carolina tourers should be aware of Daniel Barefoot's series on touring the back roads of North Carolina. The one that applies here is on the "lower coast" and was published by John F. Blair in 1995. Blair also published the excellent *Cruising Guide to Coastal North Carolina*, by Claiborne S. Young, in 1994.

There are also many books for specialized interests. Readers whose interest in the coast focuses on the barrier island beaches should read Glenn Morris's *North Carolina Beaches: A Guide to Coastal Access*, published by UNC Press in 1993. Those who contemplate purchasing coastal property should consult the book by Orrin H. Pilkey, Jr., William Neal, and Orrin H. Pilkey, Sr., *From Currituck to Calabash: Living with North Carolina's Barrier Islands*, published in 1978 by North Carolina Science and Technology Research Center in Research Triangle Park, and/or Wallace Kaufman and Orrin Pilkey's 1983 book, *The Beaches Are Moving: The Drowning of America's Shoreline*, from Duke University Press.

As is the case with all books, many people have helped produce this one, although no one but the author is responsible for errors or omissions. Useful discussions with faculty colleagues have helped me understand the multifaceted complexity of our coastline. At the University of North Carolina at Chapel Hill, Bob Peet helped me understand coastal plant communities, Rick Luettich and Cisco Werner helped me with coastal water circulation, Chris Martens with coastal chemistry, and Conrad Neumann and John Wells with geology. Steve Snyder at North Carolina State University generously shared his insights and data on ancient shorelines with me. Staff biologists at state and national parks as well as those on staff at privately preserved field sites were universally cooperative and helpful. Unsurprisingly, these people are enthusiastic about the sites they oversee and helped immensely by sharing their knowledge and libraries with me. Valuable help was provided by federal employees of national seashores, forests, and military bases; state employees at aquariums, museums, parks, estuarine sanctuaries, gamelands, forests, and the Natural Heritage Program; and private employees of the Nature Conservancy and the North Carolina Coastal Federation. One of the joys of working on a book like this is the enthusiastic support provided by knowledgeable scientists who want to help the public see and appreciate the natural areas they are helping to preserve.

The book owes much to the skill and dedication of the staff at UNC Press, who performed their jobs effectively on its behalf. The illustration program benefited greatly by Jean Wilson Kraus making available her exquisite plant illustrations and by Scott Taylor, who did the same for his photographs. Sharon McBride not only typed and retyped the manuscript without complaint but also constructively criticized the prose and kept things organized against the forces of entropy and the author's own lack of attention to detail.

CHAPTER ONE

ORIGINS, ENVIRONMENTAL PROCESSES, AND COMMUNITIES

Introduction

The nature of the southern coast is determined by its origin, its modification by environmental processes, and the natural communities that now occupy it. Nature is a movie with a plot that develops through time. Observation of a natural field site provides one scene from the movie. That scene, no matter how striking, never tells the whole story. The story depends on what preceded the scene, the background and identity of the characters that appear in it, and the relationship of this scene to events occurring elsewhere. Fiction requires the reader to use imagination and personal experience to enrich and strengthen the plot. Scientific nonfiction is no different; all readers have experienced nature, and this chapter seeks to draw on that experience and provide new information specifically applicable to the southern coast. Your observations of coastal field sites will benefit from your past experience and your knowledge of the origins and temporal development of the area you are observing.

This chapter has been organized into three sections: geologic background, coastal habitats and processes, and natural plant communities. The first section describes geologic processes that formed the southern coast. The second section describes environmental processes that sustain coastal habitats. The third section describes the natural plant communities that occupy the coastal zone and includes drawings by Jean Wilson Kraus to help you identify the most common plants found in them. Because all books must have limits, the communities described here are those that characterize barrier island, coastal water, and wetland habitats that occur within 20 miles of the coastline.

Geologic Background:
Coastal Origins and Sea Level Change

SYNOPSIS

Coastlines exist because the earth's surface has oceans and continents, and coastlines are where they meet. We now know that continents drift across the earth's surface as oceans open and close. Oceans open when new seafloor rocks solidify from molten material along mid-ocean ridges and rises. New oceans can divide a continent by heating it to thin its rocks, then breaking it apart to form new continental margins and coastlines. The nature of the coastline rocks is determined by modification of continental rocks during heating, thinning, and breaking. For the South Atlantic coastline of the United States, the continental breakage was neither smooth nor uniform. As a result, we have deep sediment layers in some areas (Florida and northern North Carolina) and not in others (along the boundary between the Carolinas). We also have weak places (faults) where earthquakes occur (Charleston, for example). But, most importantly for the modern coastal zone, the topography of old continents' rocks was modified when the Atlantic Ocean formed to create a north-to-south series of ridges and basins that have controlled the accumulation of soils and sediments ever since. These sediments have both economic and scientific significance as they contain valuable chemicals (phosphate, carbonate rock, freshwater, and possibly oil and gas) and fossils that can tell us how the earth and its organisms evolved.

Once the ocean opened to produce a coast, environmental processes characteristic of the interface between ocean and continent began to create and shape a coastline. Along the southern coast, these processes worked on sediments — the small pieces of rocks that had eroded out of the Appalachian mountains. Some of these materials were fine-grained clays that stuck together to form sheets in the soil. These fine-grained features inhibit water flow and thereby control drainage patterns. Other particles (sand) were larger, more durable, and more easily moved by wind and waves. The features formed of sand allowed water to drain through them. These porous features accumulated where the ocean met the land. When sea level changed, sand either moved with it, or new sandy features formed at the location of the new coastline. We now know that sea level is as fickle as a teenager in love. We also know, to the sorrow of all oceanfront landowners, that sea level is rising now. What is less obvious is that sea level has fallen over 400 feet since the Atlantic Ocean formed, and that it has risen and fallen repeatedly throughout its history. Where sea level touched the continent, there was a coastline. When sea level fell, some of those coastlines were stranded and are found today as long sandy ridges on the coastal plain. Others disappeared as migrating river channels and wind worked old coastal sands into the surrounding silts and clays.

To understand today's coastal zone, it is important to know something about its origin and the history of sea level changes that have shaped it. The first section of this chapter provides some of that information.

Coastal origins begin before there was a coast. Therefore we begin about 200 million years ago, when almost all continental material on the earth's surface was aggregated into a single continent (Pangea) surrounded by a single ocean (Panthalassa). Eastern North America was somewhere in the middle of that supercontinent, happily connected to continental rocks that were to become Africa and Europe. An earth with only one continent is not unique; aggregation of continental material into a single mass has happened repeatedly during earth's history. Once formed, the supercontinents break apart and come together in a series of continental reunions held about every 600 million years. Geologists call this process of continental assembly and disassembly the Wilson cycle, after the scientist who first proposed it.

Despite what you might be thinking, the Wilson cycle is important to understanding the southern coast because both the formation and the fragmentation of Pangea determined aspects of its coastal zone. During the formation of Pangea, pieces of earlier continents were forced together, creating mountains (the Appalachians), volcanoes (such as those that provided ash to form the southeastern slate belts), and faults between continental fragments (such as that running near the Georgia-Florida line deep beneath the sediment layers now known as the Southeast Georgia Embayment). During the fragmentation of Pangea, the continental crust thinned as it was heated from underneath, then split (in a process called rifting) to open the early Atlantic Ocean. This rift created the antecedents of today's coastlines. As you would suspect, the coastlines have changed greatly over their almost 200-million-year existence. The thinned continental crust off the coast cooled and sank as heavy things such as seawater, sediments from the Appalachians, and limestone coral reefs accumulated on it. Together, these processes created the thick wedge of material that make up today's eastern U.S. coastal plain and continental margin. The geological contents of this margin are illustrated in figure 1, an explanatory cartoon based on one created by my professorial colleague Conrad Neumann. Unfortunately for simplicity of explanation, the processes of continental rifting varied along the southern coast. The thinned continental crust sank to different depths in different places as a result of preexisting continental faults (such as that in the Southeast Georgia Embayment); different rates of heating from below; different loads of seawater, sediment, and coral reefs; and different lateral compression within the crust. As a result, the continental crust of Pangea is now found buried at different depths under the southern coast. It is found only about 500 meters below the surface at the boundary between North and South Carolina, but at depths of over 5,000 meters in south Florida and over 2,500 meters at Cape Hatteras. These differences have had a profound impact not only on the depth of regional sediment accumulations but also on the age and type of these accumulations. The depth and age of sediments accumulated above Pangeal continental rocks between Florida and Cape Hatteras are illustrated in figure 2. As you can see, much older material occurs at the coastal surface near the border of North and South Carolina than in areas to the north or south. Differences in these sediments and the depth of the underlying rock influence the type of surface deposits;

their mineral potential (phosphate content, for example); the erosion rate of the shoreline (fine old sand erodes faster than coarse young sand); the type and age of fossils found along the shore; and, perhaps most surprisingly, even variations in the location of the Gulf Stream. The seaward projection of the Cape Fear Arch produces a topographic ridge that deflects the stream into a wavelike pattern that passes up the coast, moving the stream closer to, and farther from, the coastline.

The reason that old sediments are found where the Pangeal continental rocks are close to the surface is quite simple. In these areas, younger sediments have been eroded away during periods of high sea level. Sea level has risen and fallen repeatedly since the Atlantic continental margin formed (see figure 3). Rising sea levels erode sediment from the shoreface and redistribute it on higher land inland. Falling sea levels move some of this sediment seaward again, but when sea levels fall rapidly, some of the sediment is left behind as an old shoreline. A careful examination of figure 3 shows that such rapid drops in sea level have occurred repeatedly during the last 100 million years. At these times, shorelines were left behind on the coastal plain. Overall, sea level has fallen more than 400 feet in the last 100 million years, but that downward trend has been interrupted many times by periods of sea level rise. Some of these periods of rising sea level lasted 3 to 5 million years (long term); others lasted only a few thousand years (short term). Note, however, that the level reached at the end of each long-term rise was lower than that at the end of the rise that preceded it. The old shorelines stranded at these times of falling sea level occur all across the southeastern coastal plain. They play a major role in determining habitat characteristics of the land, as the shorelines themselves are now sandy ridges, and their associated salt marshes and lagoons are now silty flatlands. Together the shoreline ridges and lagoonal flatlands have formed a seaward succession of topographic terraces known to geologists as "the seven steps to the sea." These steps and their formation by falling sea levels have been interpreted and illustrated by Fred Beyer in his highly readable book *North Carolina: The Years before Man*, published by Carolina Academic Press in 1991. Fred's interpretation is reproduced in figure 4.

The coastal plain terraces formed during highstands of sea level during

Figure 1. Schematic cross section of continental margin of North Carolina. Note (1) sand ridges on coastal plain and sand waves on continental shelf; (2) extensive limestone from ancient coral reefs interlayered with sand and silt/clay deposits (from weathered continental rocks) making up the "sediment wedge" of the margin; (3) blocks of continental rock from Pangea separated by faults; and (4) blocks of continental rock and salt from early stages of Atlantic Ocean.

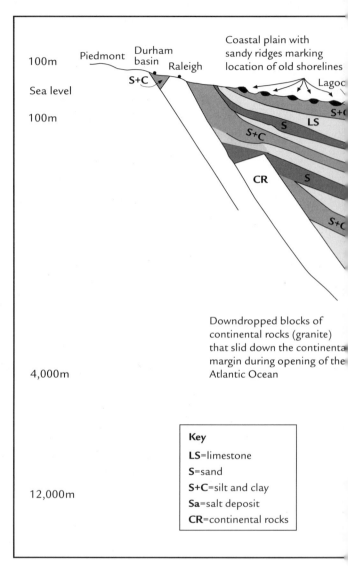

100m

Piedmont

Durham basin

Raleigh

Coastal plain with sandy ridges marking location of old shorelines

S+C

Sea level

Lagoo

100m

S+(

S

LS

S+C

CR

S

S+C

4,000m

Downdropped blocks of continental rocks (granite) that slid down the continental margin during opening of the Atlantic Ocean

12,000m

Key

LS=limestone
S=sand
S+C=silt and clay
Sa=salt deposit
CR=continental rocks

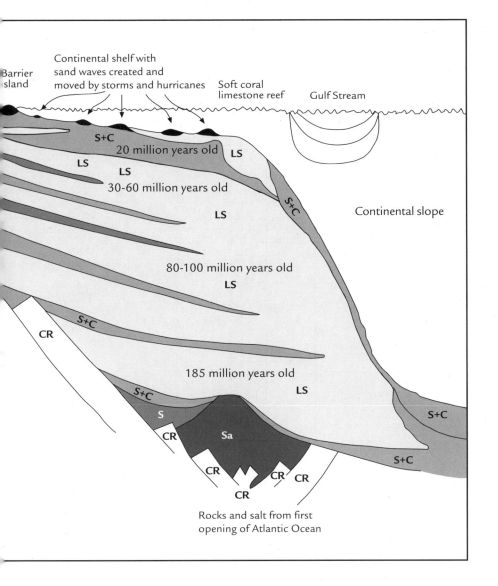

Barrier
island

Continental shelf with
sand waves created and
moved by storms and hurricanes

Soft coral
limestone reef

Gulf Stream

S+C

20 million years old

LS

LS

LS

30-60 million years old

LS

S+C

Continental slope

80-100 million years old

LS

S+C

CR

185 million years old

LS

S+C

S+C

S

S+C

CR

Sa

S+C

CR

CR

CR

CR

Rocks and salt from first
opening of Atlantic Ocean

Figure 2. Stratigraphic cross section along the southern coast from Florida to North Carolina. Note Mid-Carolina Platform High (Cape Fear Arch) with old sediments (ca. 100 million years old) much shallower than in areas to north and south. Redrawn from Gregory S. Gohn, *The Geology of North America* (Colorado Springs, Colo.: Geological Society of America, 1988), chap. 7, fig. 2.

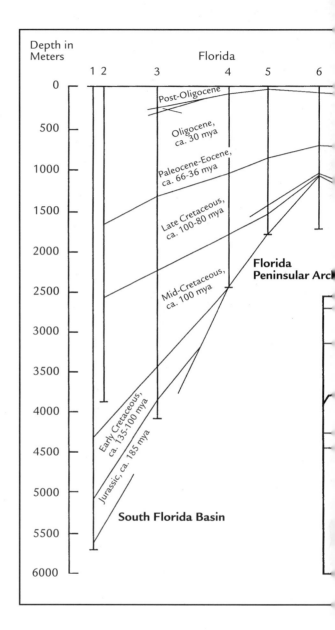

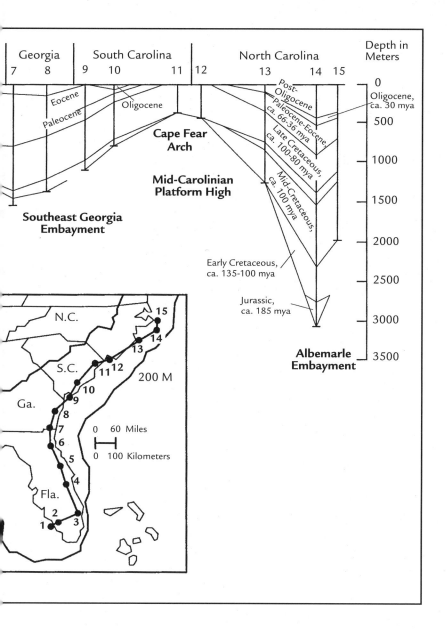

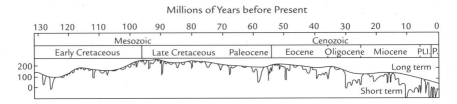

Figure 3. Global sea level changes, 130 million years ago to present. Note long-term decline for last 95 million years and short-term declines and rises throughout the record. The vertical scale shows the differences, in meters, between present and ancient levels. Modified from K. O. Emery and D. G. Aubrey, *Sea Levels, Land Levels, and Tide Gauges* (New York: Springer-Verlag, 1991), fig. 32.

the last 100 million years have had controlling impact on distribution of soil types and drainage patterns on the modern coastal plain. These distributions underlie current land use patterns. The high, well-drained sandy deposits of the old beach ridges have been selected for transportation routes and settlement sites throughout human history. The most striking example of this role is found with the Suffolk Scarp. This scarp is the most recent of the stranded shorelines. It served as seacoast between 140,000 and 120,000 years ago. Its name comes from the town of Suffolk, Virginia, where it was first described. The scarp stretches south into North Carolina near Edenton on Albemarle Sound. The same feature — a sandy ridge or ridges with a relatively steep east side leading down to land at lower elevation — continues south across the Albemarle-Pamlico peninsula as the Pinetown and Chapel Scarps. Readers familiar with the peninsula may have already seen these scarps south of Plymouth, as Long Ridge Road (NC Bike Trail 3) is built on the Pinetown Scarp, and NC 32 is built on the Chapel Scarp. The same shoreline system extends farther south between the Pamlico and Neuse Rivers, although there geologists call it Grantsboro Scarp or Minnesott Ridge. Highway NC 306 is built on it from Aurora to Minnesott Beach. This system formed over a period of 20,000 years. As a result, it is made up of multiple sand ridges, as are today's barrier islands. The old shoreline is quite a long way from the current shore (65 miles for the Pinetown/Chapel Scarp system and 35 miles for the Grantsboro Scarp/Minnesott Ridge system).

Other old shorelines occur throughout the southern coastal zone (see figure 4). An important one called Bogue Scarp parallels the present shoreline from Harkers Island to Morehead City before disappearing under Bogue Sound. In keeping with the age of subsurface sediments west of Bogue Sound, other, much older, shorelines continue to the south and east to form the shoreline behind the nearshore barrier islands (that is, less than a mile from the mainland). Farther south, this system extends past Wilmington to Fort Fisher. In fact, Snow's Cut—the canal between Carolina Beach and the Cape Fear River—cuts through the coquina rock of this old shoreline (figure 56). The same system appears to continue on the west side of the Cape Fear River from Brunswick Town to Southport to Holden Beach.

The age of these old shorelines has been (is?) an ongoing source of controversy among coastal geologists. Early data suggested ages of a few tens of thousands of years based on carbon isotope dating. More recent data on global sea level changes and geological studies using a new dating technique based on amino acid racemization rates suggest dates between 100,000 and 140,000 years for even the most recent features. The section of old shoreline facing the back of the modern barrier islands south of Swansboro is generally called Pleistocene—meaning it formed less than 1.5 million years ago. The landward shorelines illustrated in figure 4 are older than that, but there is little agreement about ages until you get to the earliest (Orangeburg) scarp, which is generally viewed as having formed during the sea level highstand that occurred about 90 million years ago (see figure 3).

Figure 3 presents a moderately detailed description of past sea level changes, but it now appears that both sea level change and the features formed by these changes are more complex than illustrated. Geologists Stan Riggs and Steve Snyder have found evidence of 18 sequences of sea level rise and fall during the last 1.5 million years, and 18 more during the 20-million-year period known as the Miocene. This multitude of sea level changes has left a rich fossil and shoreline record in the southern coastal

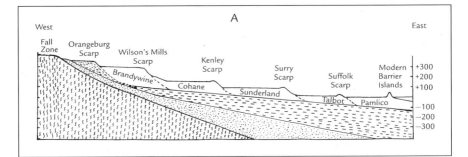

Figure 4. Old shorelines on the southern coastal plain. (A) Schematic cross section with names of scarps (old shorelines) and sedimentary formations between them. From Fred Beyer, *North Carolina: The Years before Man* (Durham, N.C.: Carolina Academic Press, 1991). (B) Map view of five most recent shorelines—four stranded on the coastal plain in times of declining sea level and the modern one that is eroding in the current period of sea level rise.

plain. One can, and some professors do, make a case that every sandy ridge is an old shoreline of some sort. Fortunately not all readers have to listen to, and take notes on, such interpretations while traveling seaward at the crack of dawn on some college field trip.

Many coastal residents are unaware of the long period of falling sea level that followed the opening of the Atlantic Ocean, but everyone is well aware that sea level is rising now. During the depth of the Wisconsinian glaciation (about 17,000 years ago), sea level was about 300 feet lower than at present. As climate warmed and the glaciers melted, sea level rose rapidly for about 13,000 years and has continued to rise at a slower pace to the present. This rise is almost obscured by the long timescale of figure 3 but is very apparent in shorter records.

It is certainly true that sea level is rising against the southern coast. This rise is eroding the shoreface and flooding our estuaries and river valleys with saltwater that kills trees in our coastal forests. Thus sea level change controls many aspects of the nature of the southern coast.

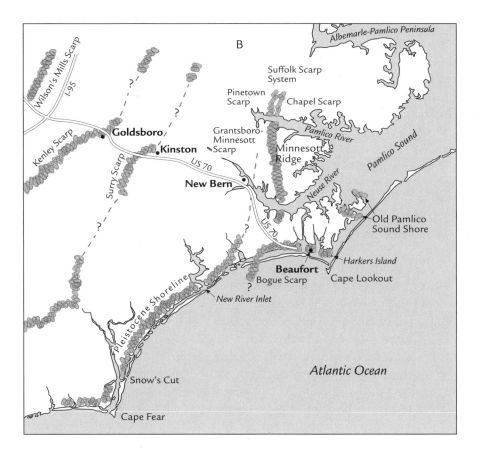

Coastal Processes and Habitats: Conditions That Sustain the Southern Coast

SYNOPSIS

Coastal habitats are formed and sustained by environmental forces focused at the boundary between sea and land. Some of these forces (tides, waves, and major storms) come from the sea; others (sediment supply, freshwater, and rocks) come from the continents. The unique features of each coastline come from the ways in which these forces interact. The major features of the southern coast are barrier islands (low-lying sandy ridges that occur offshore of the mainland) separated from one another by openings called inlets and backed by bodies of open water called sounds, estuaries, or lagoons. The land surface along the southern coast generally lies close to sea level, resulting in areas of this coast being referred to by terms such as "tidewater" and "the low country."

Environmental controls of coastal habitats are relatively simple in comparison with those that influence habitat differences in the open ocean or noncoastal land areas. For example, it is only a modest oversimplification to say that the major features of barrier island morphology — beaches and inlets — are controlled by tides, waves, and sediment supply. Similarly, one could say that the natural communities of barrier islands are controlled by the way in which plants stabilize sand that otherwise would be moved by currents of air and water, and that most characteristics of coastal waters are controlled by the way in which freshwater running off land interacts with ocean water.

The following section of this chapter explains how environmental factors exert their influence to create and sustain the coastal habitats of the southern coast. This explanation is based on understanding coastal processes such as tides, breaking waves, alongshore currents, storm effects, sand stabilization by plants, and water circulation in sounds and estuaries. This material is not simple, but once grasped, it will deepen your understanding of coastal habitats and the problems they face as a result of human development.

How Barrier Islands, Inlets, and Beaches Are Controlled by Tides, Waves, and Sediment Supply

Barrier Islands

Tides and waves are two of the most obvious coastal processes (remember, a process is "any phenomenon which shows continuing change with time"). Tides and the waves caused by wind blowing over the ocean surface have obvious impacts on coastal activities from boating to swimming to surfing. What is less obvious, but probably more important, is that tides and waves control the shape of seacoast barrier islands and the stability of beaches, dunes, and inlets. Tidal range (distance between high and low tide) is so important to coastal morphology that scientists classify coasts on that basis. Microtidal coasts, with tidal ranges less than 6.5 feet, are characterized by long, thin, frequently overwashed barrier islands and few inlets. Mesotidal coasts, with tidal ranges of 6.5 to 13 feet (2–4 meters), are characterized by barrier islands that are shorter, less frequently overwashed, and backed by large areas of sand flats, salt marshes, and tidal deltas. Along the southeastern coast, microtidal conditions exist from Virginia to Charleston, and mesotidal conditions occur from Charleston to Florida (see table 1). Tidal ranges of less than 3.3 feet (1 meter) occur from Cape Hatteras to Swansboro. This coast is characterized by long, thin barrier islands that are dominated by ocean overwash. The barrier islands along this section of coast average over 20 miles in length and are separated from the mainland by large expanses of open water. South of Swansboro, tidal ranges are larger, and barrier islands average less than 9 miles in length and have more extensive tidal deltas as well as better-developed intertidal habitats such as salt marshes and sand flats. The difference in tidal range illustrated in table 1 dominates the environment of the southern coast.

The reason for the difference in tidal range along this coast relates both to the primary tide-producing forces (gravitational attraction and centripetal force generated by the rotating earth-moon and earth-sun astronomical systems) and the secondary forces generated by oscillation of offshore tidal basins. A full explanation of these relationships is more complicated than needed here, but, in brief, tidal waves generated in the circumglobal ocean around Antarctica travel north up the Atlantic Ocean and cause water in offshore basins to oscillate toward land and away from land. The currents generated by this oscillation are the familiar flood and ebb tides that we observe near shore. The height of the tide from high to low is related to one's position along the side of the oscillating tidal basin. If you are close to the center of oscillation, the tidal range is small (Bermuda's tidal range is less than half that of Cape Hatteras). The farther

Table 1. Astronomical Tidal Ranges, Capes and Inlets, North Carolina to Florida

Place	Average Tidal Range (ft.)	Spring Tidal Range (ft.)
Capes		
Cape Hatteras	3.6	4.3
Cape Lookout	3.7	4.4
Cape Fear	4.5	5.1
Cape Romaine (S.C.)	4.7	5.5
Inlets		
Ocracoke Inlet	1.9	2.3
Beaufort Inlet	3.2	3.8
New River Inlet	3.0	3.5
Masonboro Inlet	3.8	4.5
Lockwoods Folly Inlet	4.2	4.8
Little River Inlet (N.C./S.C.)	4.6	5.2
Charleston Harbor Entrance (S.C.)	5.1	5.9
Savannah River Entrance (Ga./S.C.)	6.9	8.0
North Newport River (Ga.)	7.6	8.9
South Brunswick River (Ga.)	7.6	8.9
Cumberland River (Ga.)	6.8	7.9
Saint Mary's River (Ga./Fla.)	5.8	6.7
Saint John's River Entrance (Fla.)	4.5	5.3

Source: Data from 1994 Tide Tables, East Coast of North and South America, U.S. Department of Commerce.

you are from the center, the larger the tidal range becomes (as do the ranges from Cape Hatteras to Georgia [see table 1]). The tidal range reaches its maximum at the end of the tidal basin. In the southeastern United States, the basin reaches its greatest distance from the center on the coast of Georgia, where tidal amplitudes can be almost 9 feet.

Other tidal features warrant a few words of explanation. One of these is the term "spring tidal range" and its difference from average tidal range (see table 1). Average tidal range is fairly obvious—it is the average difference between high and low tide over all tidal cycles. Spring tidal range is the difference between high and low tides for the periods when tides reach their highest and lowest extremes. These periods are called spring tides from use of the German word *Springen* (to leap up) to describe them. Large tidal ranges occur when the gravitation effect of moon and sun reinforce each other—that is, when the objects are on opposite sides of the earth (full moon) or when both are on the same side of the earth (no moon). These periods each occur once a month, so tidal ranges are high near full moon and no moon conditions. When the moon is one-quarter full (when you can see one-half of its circumference reflecting sunlight to earth), the sun and moon are at right angles to each other when viewed from earth. This arrangement causes the gravitational effect of the sun to cancel part of that caused by the moon and produce periods of low tidal range called neap tide periods. There are two such periods each month, near first and last quarter moons. Thus tidal ranges can be predicted to vary regularly throughout the lunar month, with high ranges (and fast tidal currents) near full- and no-moon periods and small tidal ranges at quarter-moon periods.

Unfortunately, such predictions of tidal ranges and currents cannot include the effects of winds and storms. The impact of these phenomena on tides is called meteorological tide, and it can be very important, especially along microtidal coasts such as North Carolina's. Winds can blow water into and out of areas to produce effective tides much higher or lower than predicted from astronomical data alone. Storms surrounding centers of low atmospheric pressure (hurricanes, cyclones, typhoons, and thunderstorms) create a bulge of water under the area of low pressure. This bulge can pile up against the coast when storms come ashore and flood coastal areas with what is called a "storm surge." These surges of water are commonly 6–10 feet high and can be as high as 23 feet under extraordinary circumstances (Hurricane Camille in Mississippi in 1971). In September 1996 the storm surge was 12 to 16 feet high during Hurricane Fran's arrival along southern North Carolina. Fortunately the height of these surges can now be predicted from knowledge of atmospheric pressure distribution within storms, the shape of the coast, and its offshore topography. These predictions are a common feature of news reports on hurricanes.

Tides and waves have the power to shift sediment to create and alter barrier islands, but their effect is controlled by the supply of sediment available to be moved. When sediment supply is large (as it appears to have been at the end of the last glaciation), extensive island chains can form. When the sediment supply is small and/or finite, islands must thin and migrate landward in response to rising sea level. Thinning and landward migrating islands characterize today's southern coastline, because little new sandy sediment is reaching the coastline.

Inlets

Water driven by tidal forces must pass between or over coastal features as it moves toward and away from land. During normal tide ranges, water passes between barrier islands through openings called tidal inlets. As already described, the spatial distribution of inlets is related to tidal range. Where tidal ranges are low, inlets occur infrequently (there are only five between Beaufort, N.C., and Virginia). Where tidal range is high, inlets occur more frequently (there are fourteen between Beaufort and South Carolina). Inlets are kept open by the flow of tidal water through them. Inlets close when more sand enters than can be swept away by tidal currents. Inlets on coastlines with low tidal ranges are therefore susceptible to closure; between Beaufort and Virginia a total of twenty different inlets are known to have closed since colonial times.

Tidal flows through inlets move sand in ways that are generally, but not specifically, predictable. The strongest flows occur in the narrowest part of the channel (the throat) and erode sand from both bottom and sides of the inlet. The currents slow quickly when they reach less confined waters beyond the throat. Sand suspended in these currents settles to the bottom to form complex sandbars and shoals called ebb tide deltas when they form seaward of an inlet on ebbing (falling) tides and (predictably enough) flood-tide deltas when they form landward of the inlet on flooding tides. The tidal currents and delta structures of inlets are illustrated in figure 5.

As is the case with tidal range predictions, the old axiom "nothing is simple" applies to inlet processes. Scientists who study inlets classify them as wave dominated, tide dominated, and transitional and also as ebb dominated or flood dominated. The first of these classifications refers to the relative role of waves and tides. Where tidal range is small, inlet processes are dominated by waves and the alongshore sediment transport they drive. Drum Inlet (see figure 5) is wave dominated. Where tidal range and current are large, inlets are dominated by tidal processes. Inlets from Carolina Beach to Georgia are such inlets. Ebb and flood dominated inlets refer to those where more water leaves than enters (ebb dominated) or vice-versa (flood dominated). These terms apply to inlets that are hydraulically linked—for example, Beaufort and Bogue Inlets in North Carolina are linked by Bogue Sound. When winds blow from the northeast, much flood tidal water enters Beaufort Inlet, flows the length of Bogue Sound, and exits through Bogue Inlet. As a result, Beaufort Inlet functions as a flood dominated inlet and Bogue as an ebb dominated inlet. The role of prevailing winds in establishing ebb or flood domination of inlets is always important and makes predicting inlet type difficult.

The most important practical aspect of inlets is the dynamism of their channels. Channels change with each tide. The change is smallest in tidal dominated inlets because large tidal prisms (the volume of water entering and leaving an inlet on a low-high-low tidal cycle) keep deep channels open through the ebb- and flood-tide deltas. Wave dominated inlets are another matter. Change in wind or alongshore transport can result in dramatic changes in channel location. You can see how that could be the case in Drum Inlet (see figure 5). It is unnavigable unless dredged. The same is even more true for the infamous Oregon Inlet, where dredging is constantly needed to keep the channel open and jetties have been proposed to "stabilize" the channel. Stable, deep channels through inlets are much admired by navigators. The analogy of death to "crossing the bar" draws its point from the fear navigators feel when preparing to cross a wave-swept ebb tide delta. We now know, in general terms, why natural channels through inlets shift so much, but this knowledge can be classified as small consolation when you are hard aground on a regrettably specific lobe of a tidal delta.

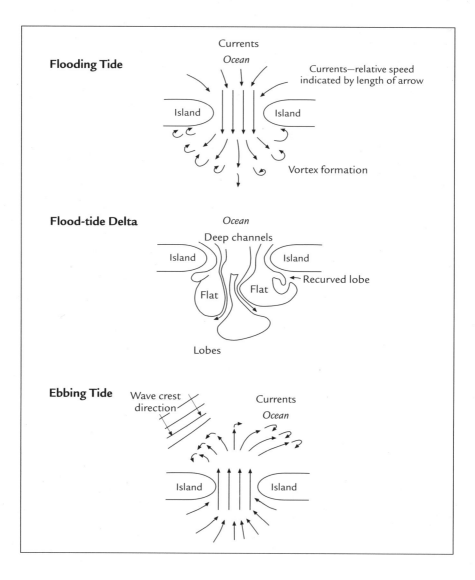

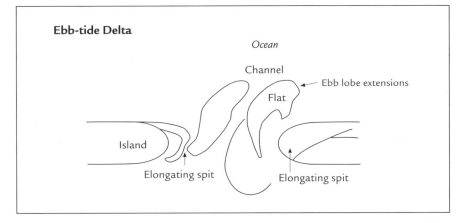

Ebb-tide Delta

Ocean

Channel

Ebb lobe extensions

Flat

Island

Elongating spit

Elongating spit

Figure 5. Tidal currents and sand deposits (tidal deltas) in inlets. Photograph of Drum Inlet, summer 1995. Note (1) sand accretion from both sides—the inlet is closing; (2) flood-tide delta exposed at low tide; and (3) ebb-tide delta marked by whitecaps offshore.

Beaches

The open ocean shoreline of the southern coast is almost all sandy beach. The beaches usually are the seaward face of barrier islands — islands that occur offshore of the mainland and form a barrier to the energy of ocean waves. Barrier islands form along sedimentary coastlines when three conditions are met: (1) sea level is rising against the coast; (2) there is a supply of sand sufficient to form islands; and (3) there are winds and waves with sufficient energy to move the sand around. It appears that these conditions have been present along the southern coast for millions of years. The habitats that form on and behind these barrier islands seem to have an equally long history, although some controversy exists about how well developed these habitats were during periods of rapidly rising sea level, such as that which occurred 17,000 to 5,000 years ago. Be that as it may, today's barrier islands exist in an era of slowly rising sea level, and their habitats reflect a history of almost 5,000 years of this relatively slow rise. Unfortunately, even slow rates of sea level rise can erode barrier island beaches when there is little new sand available to supply them. That appears to be the case along the southern coast today.

From ocean to sound, barrier islands typically have a sequence of habitats from offshore sandbar, to beach and berm (the flat area between high-tide line and the primary dune), to dunefield, to interdune flat, to salt marsh, to sand flat, to grass flat, to sound or estuary on the landward side (figure 6). Five of these habitats are regularly covered with water (sandbar, beach, salt marsh, sand flat, and grass flat). Four of the habitats are linked together by erosion-deposition cycles to form a shoreface "sand-sharing system" (sandbar, beach, berm, and primary dune). Dunefields and interdune flats are variably vegetated, sometimes supporting only pioneer plants that tolerate salt spray, sometimes maritime grasslands, sometimes thickets, and sometimes maritime forests. The most important environmental processes on barrier islands are sand transport by wind and water, and sand stabilization by plants.

Wind, Waves, and Sand Transport

Currents of air and water move sand on, off, and over barrier islands. This movement is easiest to see when wind moves sand within or into a dune-field. Air is less dense than water, so even relatively strong winds usually move particles no larger than very fine sand. You can see fine sand being transported when wind speeds exceed about 25 miles per hour (see figure 64). During storms and hurricanes, enough sand is moved rapidly enough to sand your feet and ankles raw while you walk along the beach. The sand being moved is always fine, however, so dune sands are almost always made of smaller-sized grains than are beach sands. Exceptions occur when local sand is uniformly fine. In these cases, both beach and dune will have similarly sized grains.

Less obvious than wind transport of sand, but quantitatively more important to barrier islands, is sand picked up and moved by breaking waves and coastal currents. Waves on the sea surface are created when something disturbs that surface. The most common waves are caused by wind, although less common waves can be caused by earthquakes (tsunamis) and differences in atmospheric pressure around storms (storm surges). All waves (including tides) are physically similar to one another but differ in length, speed, and frequency.

Common wind waves are the main sand movers. Waves created by wind blowing across the sea surface move sand on and off the beach when they move into shallow water and break. Waves formed by wind over the ocean bring energy to shore and release it in friction and turbulence. Breaking begins when waves interact with the seafloor as they approach the beach. Friction from this interaction slows the wave's forward progress, causing the wave to shorten and steepen. When the height-to-length ratio exceeds 1 to 7, waves break and release energy in the surf zone of the beach.

Not all waves break in the same way. Spend some time watching waves break, and you will see that this is true. In some waves, the wave crest is thrown forward and plunges down the wave front in a curl of water that traps a "tube" of air in front of the breaker. Scientists, literal-minded souls that they are, call these "plunging" waves. Other waves break less dramatically, when the crest just spills down the front of the wave as

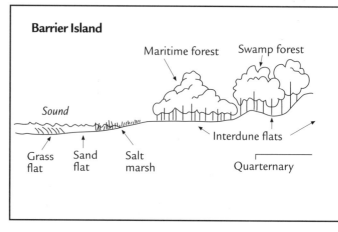

Figure 6. Schematic cross section of a barrier island of the southern coast.

Barrier Island

Maritime forest   Swamp forest

Sound

Grass   Sand   Salt   Interdune flats
flat   flat   marsh   Quarternary

a froth of water and air bubbles. These are called "spilling" breakers. Both spilling and plunging breakers erode sand from the beach. They and their beach-accreting cousin, the collapsing breaker, are diagramed in figure 7.

Spilling and plunging breakers are quite easy to see and identify, at least in contrast to the third important type, the collapsing breaker. Collapsing waves are worth some effort to see because they move sand onto the beach rather than off the beach. The mechanics of this difference are easily appreciated by those who swim or stand in the surf zone. Those experiencing plunging and spilling breakers can feel a landward rush of water against their upper body as the break moves past them; as the wave recedes, a seaward rush of water undermines the sand from beneath their feet. In other words, the water contained in the broken part of the wave is moving toward shore across the surface, sometimes even while backwash from the previous breaker is still moving seaward along the seafloor. This two-layer flow pattern in the wave — landward in the broken wave crest on top and seaward in the backwash along the bottom — means that the water in direct contact with the beach sediment is moving seaward. Any sand transported by such water will be carried off the beach, resulting in beach erosion and formation of an offshore sandbar. A collapsing breaker

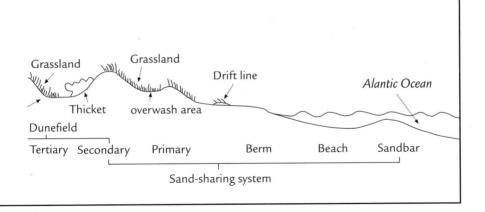

Grassland   Grassland   Drift line   Alantic Ocean   Thicket   overwash area   Dunefield   Tertiary   Secondary   Primary   Berm   Beach   Sandbar   Sand-sharing system

is quite different: water moves toward land throughout the breaking process. All the water in the wave moves landward until it reaches its maximum run up on the beach; then all the water moves back toward the sea. The movement up the beach is powered by the energy of wave collapse, but the subsequent backwash is not; therefore, the landward surge is more powerful. That surge picks up sand and carries it up the beach; the less powerful backwash does not carry it as far back toward the sea. Sand moved by collapsing breakers accumulates on the beach, causing the beach to grow or "accrete." Evidence of beach accretion is usually provided by ridge and runnel systems. These systems consist of sand ridges separated by lower areas (runnels) through which water from wave crests runs off. Figure 8 is a photograph of such a system.

The slope of the beach is also important to the type of breaker as well as the number of breakers in the surf zone at any one time. A group of scientists known as the Australian School of Beach Morphodynamics has developed a beach classification system that ranges from reflective beaches (steep beaches that reflect wave energy from their narrow surf zone) to dissipative beaches (flat beaches that dissipate wave energy within a broad surf zone). There are several intermediate types with features that grade into one another, but the end members are easy to recognize. True reflec-

Figure 7. Types of breakers: plunging, spilling, and collapsing. Plunging and spilling breakers move sand off the beach; water moves landward at the top of the breaker and seaward along the submerged beachface, carrying sand offshore. Collapsing breakers move sand up the beach toward land; the collapse of the wave face causes a surge of water up the beach that has more power to move sand than does its backwash.

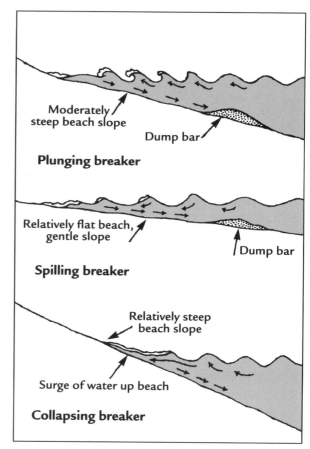

tive beaches have only one breaker in the surf zone at a time, whereas dissipative beaches have at least three.

Waves and breakers move sand on all types of beaches. As a result, beaches are constantly shifting features whose future position can be predicted only as well as we can predict the size and direction of the waves that break on them — that is, not very well. However, we can predict three things: (1) beach sands will move; (2) beach erosion will be more common

Figure 8. Beach accretion on Shackleford Banks. Sand is moved onshore (right to left in photo) by breaking waves and tidal currents. Photograph by Scott Taylor.

than beach accretion when sea level is rising; and (3) sand will be transported along the shore in a direction controlled in the long term (weeks to years) by prevailing winds and in the short term (hours to weeks) by the wind and waves occurring at the time.

Sand moves along the shore whenever waves approach the beach at any angle other than 90°. This movement of sand is called alongshore transport. Sand also moves on and off the beach. This movement of sand is called the coastal sand-sharing system. It operates from the oceanfront dune to the offshore sandbars. Sand eroded from the beach or dune by plunging or spilling breakers moves offshore to depths greater than those in which it can be transported by prevailing waves. Beyond this depth, the moving sand settles to the bottom and becomes part of an offshore bar.

Later, when shoreward tidal currents and collapsing waves return, the sands of the offshore bar are moved back onto the beach. This movement onto the beach occurs so slowly and under such calm conditions that it can be seen best by time-lapse photography. Beachgoers can see evidence of the process, however, by watching for sandbars that appear stranded on the beach. Usually these bars create long, narrow runnels on their landward side (see figure 8). Repeated visits to the same location will show that the stranded bar moves up the beach until it disappears as its sand is incorporated into the beachface.

The beachfront sand-sharing system operates all the time, but during storms it broadens to include more offshore bars and more of the coastal dunefield. Storm waves move sand over amazingly large areas. The bigger the wave, the farther seaward its influence is felt. Large offshore bars occur all across the continental shelf; these bars or "sand waves" remain stationary for long periods and move only in the largest storms (see figure 1). Coastal dunefields may also be stable for long periods before being eroded away during a storm such as Hurricane Fran. Figure 9 illustrates both the "normal" sand-sharing system and its extension during storm conditions.

The sand-sharing system diagramed in figure 9 seems quite benign, but there are parts of the system that trap sand for long periods, thereby reducing the sand supply to other parts of the system. Figure 9 gives a hint of one of those sand-holding parts of the system. Washover deposits are formed when sand washes over the dunes and settles on the island or in the sound behind it. The importance of washover events to maintaining island height and position during periods of rising sea level was first described on Core Banks. The process and its results are described in the Core Banks section of Chapter 2.

The combined effects of wind, waves, tides, and currents move sand to alter beaches, elongate barrier island beaches, and form dangerous offshore shoals. They also sustain the beaches by moving sand from one barrier island to another. Scientists call this sand movement an inlet bypass system (see figure 10). These inlet bypass systems are important to maintaining barrier islands because they transport sand from one side of the inlet to the other, thereby maintaining the sand supply to downstream is-

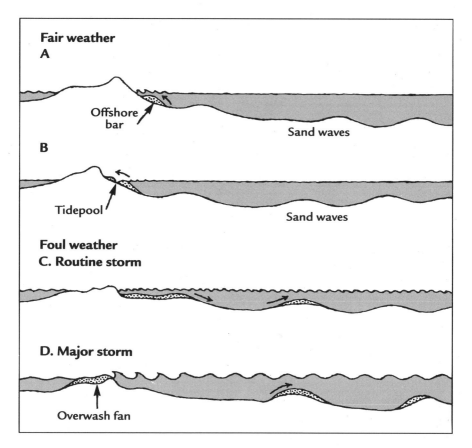

Figure 9. The coastal sand-sharing system, fair weather and foul. In fair weather, collapsing breakers and tides move sand onto the beach from offshore bars (A), sometimes creating a narrow tidepool on the beach (B). In foul weather, spilling and plunging breakers erode sand from the beach and carry it offshore to form sandbars (C). In major storms, high waves and tides move sand over and between sand dunes to form overwash fans behind the dunes (D). Overwash events often carry sand onto roads and buildings built close to the beach.

lands and beaches. The importance of natural inlet bypass systems to the maintenance and survival of downstream lands requires that those who try to "stabilize" these dynamic inlets must include features comparable to the system in their designs. If not, they will face continuing expense for dredging sand from where it is not wanted (navigation channels) to where it is urgently needed (beaches downstream from the inlet).

Sand Stabilization by Plants

Both visitors to and residents of barrier islands have reason to display the bumper sticker that asks "Have you thanked a green plant today?" Everyone has to thank green plants for the food and oxygen that let us survive on earth, but inhabitants of barrier islands also need to thank plants for stabilizing the landforms they live on. Sand moved by wind, waves, and currents is stopped and held in place by plants. Obviously there are limits to their ability to do so; the bare sand in overwash deposits, active dunefaces, and elongating sand spits testifies to those limits. But the natural processes that create bare sand are almost always overcome by plants that gradually cover the exposed surface. Vegetation develops in a sequence of stages, each of which prepares for the next. These stages can easily be observed as one walks across a barrier island from the ocean to the sounds. The first plants to become established are those one sees first on such a transect: sea oats and beach grass. These plants trap sand because they interrupt the smooth flow of wind across the beach and cause any sand being transported to be deposited among them. In this way they operate like a natural sand fence.

Behind the first (primary) dune, sea oats, beach grass, and other dune plants create a maritime grassland that covers the sand with low vegetation. These plants are well adapted to the direct sunlight, high soil temperatures, and porous soils that occur in dunes. The plants hold the sand in place with both above-ground and below-ground structures. Above the ground the upright stems create a zone that gentle winds do not penetrate (the no-wind zone; see figure 11), and as winds increase, the stems bend parallel to the sand surface, further protecting it from the direct effect of the wind. Below-ground structures become involved in sand stabilization when winds expose the extensive network of roots and rhizomes

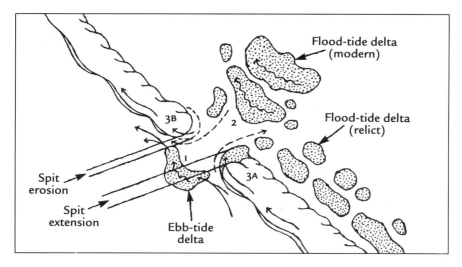

Figure 10. Sand transport across inlets. Sand moving alongshore can be carried to the downstream side of an inlet by 3 processes: (1) it can be carried to the ebb-tide delta and be moved across the inlet mouth by alongshore current, waves, and tidal currents; (2) it can be carried through the inlet to the flood-tide delta and be moved to the downstream side by waves and currents; or (3) it can activate the inlet by being deposited on the upstream sand spit (3A), thereby focusing tidal currents on the downstream side of the inlet, where they erode sand (3B) and carry it to downstream beaches. Modified from D. L. Inman and R. Dolan, "The Outer Banks of North Carolina: Budget of Sediment and Inlet Dynamics along a Migrating Barrier Island System," *Journal of Coastal Research* 5, no. 2 (1989): 219.

to produce an almost continuous blanket of plant matter over the sand. Sometimes, of course, storm winds overwhelm the natural protection that plants provide. Dunes "blow out" and migrate; primary dunes become "cliffed" as waves wash sand from under their plant cover; overwashed sand covers plants to provide a new, bare sand surface. Nevertheless, plants provide the only natural protection for the sand surface. Disturbing these plants is an invitation to dune migration and island maintenance problems.

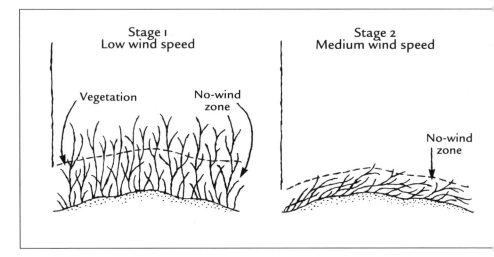

Figure II. Dune plants trap and hold sand. Dune plants disrupt the windfield by creating turbulence. This results in a zone of no wind within the plant zone (stage I). Sand blown into this no-wind zone will settle there. As winds increase, plants respond in ways that hold the settled sand in place. First, the plants are blown flat against the sand, thereby protecting as much sand as possible from

Dune plants are the first vegetated stage in a continuum that culminates as a full-fledged maritime forest. In protected areas downwind from dunes visitors will find shrubs, thickets, trees, and forests. The plant life that grows in island interiors is also affected by wind speed, salt spray exposure, organic matter in the soil, and constancy of water supply, but none of these comes into play until the sand is stabilized. Grasslands, thickets, and maritime forests occur where there are different combinations of environmental factors. The plants that live in these different communities alter the factors by their very existence (see figure 12). As a result, conditions change to improve the survival of plants characteristic of other stages of the sand stabilization sequence. Some plants — sea oats, for example — tolerate salt spray exposure better than other dune plants, such as salt meadow cordgrass or dune broomsedge. As a result, cordgrass

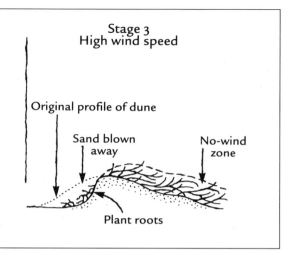

Stage 3
High wind speed

Original profile of dune

Sand blown away

No-wind zone

Plant roots

the erosive effect of the wind (stage 2). In the event that sand is blown from beneath the plants, the roots of the plants are exposed to further protect the sand that remains (stage 3).

and sedge only grow in areas protected from salt spray by dense stands of sea oats or by frontal dunes.

Thicket and forest communities grow only in unusually protected areas of the dunefield. Salt spray exposure often keeps these pioneers from extending much above the top of the dune behind which they grow. Farther back from the ocean, where wind speed and salt spray have been reduced by passage over dunes and sea oats, thicket plants such as red cedar, marsh elder, and yaupon holly grow successfully. Thickets (also called maritime shrub communities) can be so dense that it is hard for humans to make their way through them. I hope you will try, for once inside, you will see just how well these plant communities shield the sand from the effect of wind and salt spray. You will also see that the ground has a layer of leaves on it. If you dig a hole, you will see that the decay products of the leaf layer have worked their way down into the sand to create layers of dark brown and yellow soil above the white sand that is the original material.

The impact of wind-driven salt spray alters the growth form of individual thicket plants and the shape of the canopies that they combine to form. Individual plants are shaped when salt-laden winds stunt the branches on the windward side. On the leeward side, branches are normally developed. The net effect of this differential growth is that the plants look like flags, with the trunk on the upwind side and most of the branches and foliage on the downwind side. This phenomenon, called "flagging" by botanists, is best seen in cedars, live oaks, and thicket shrubs. In addition, salt spray exposure controls the shape of thicket and forest canopies. These show ground-hugging growth on their windward side, gradually getting taller farther downwind (see figure 42). The windward plants absorb the brunt of salt spray exposure, thereby stunting their own growth but protecting the plants behind them. The top of the canopy is also shaped by salt spray, as twigs growing upward beyond the canopy in summer are killed by salt spray during subsequent storms. The almost impenetrable network of branches at the top of the canopy keeps the salt-laden air from entering the interior. As a result, the sand under thickets is relatively undisturbed and develops organic-rich layers. Soil development sustains increasingly complex plant communities as moisture, nutrients, and organic matter increase and exposure to salt spray and blown sand decreases.

Landward of the thicket is the maritime forest. The patches of natural forest that remain undeveloped are dominated by loblolly pine and live oaks but differ from one another in their diversity, age, and subdominant species. The common species found in maritime forests are illustrated in the plant guide provided below. The ecological conditions of barrier island dunefields that characterize grasslands, thickets, and maritime forests are illustrated in figure 12. As you can see, the differences in vegetation reflect changing levels of sand stabilization as well as differences in soil nutrients, organic matter, salt spray exposure, blowout frequency, and depth of the freshwater table.

How Freshwater Runoff and Tidal Circulation
Control Coastal Waters

The aquatic habitats landward of the barrier islands along the southern coast are varied in size and extent but similar in the general environmental processes that occur in them. These coastal water habitats are sometimes called estuaries or lagoons, although most systems do not fit accepted definitions very well. Estuaries are defined as semienclosed coastal water bodies in which the salt content of the water is measurably reduced by land runoff. There is no doubt that the lower reaches of the Cape Fear River and the South Carolina and Georgia rivers meet that definition. In a similar fashion, large sounds such as North Carolina's Bogue, Core, and Pamlico clearly meet the definition of a shallow coastal body of water connected to the sea but with a relatively constant salt content—the definition of a lagoon. Many smaller coastal water bodies, however, fit the definition of estuary during periods of high runoff and the definition of lagoon when runoff is low. One should not worry much when natural systems fail to fit scientific definitions, but in this case the failure is useful because it illustrates the complexity found when small streams drain areas of variable rainfall into microtidal coastal water bodies. It is quite common for southern sounds to be completely filled with ocean water when runoff is low, and completely filled with freshwater runoff during spring rains or after storms. This seasonal variation can significantly affect the reproductive success of important fisheries species such as striped bass, mullet, blue crabs, shrimp, and oysters as well as other commercially important species that are "estuarine dependent" during some part of their life cycle.

Salt content of southern coastal waters can also vary substantially over periods as short as a few hours. Summer thunderstorms can drop inches of rain on a watercourse filled with water almost as salty as the ocean. When this happens, coastal waters "stratify" as a freshwater layer floats on top of the heavier saltwater underneath. During such periods, oxygen in the air does not reach the salty bottom waters. This results in bottom waters with no oxygen (anoxic) and eventually leads to asphyxiation of oxygen-requiring animals, plants, and microbes—that is, "fish kills." Re-

Figure 12. Ecological conditions in dune-fields. Wind strength, salt spray exposure, soil moisture and nutrients, dune blowout frequency, and plant cover all differ at different points in a dunefield. This figure illustrates a cross section of a dunefield showing the shape of the primary, secondary, and tertiary dunes, the types of plants that grow near them, the depth of the water table, and the direction in which freshwater flows after reaching the dune as rainfall. It also shows the relative level of soil nutrients, soil moisture, and dune blowout frequency at different points in such a dunefield.

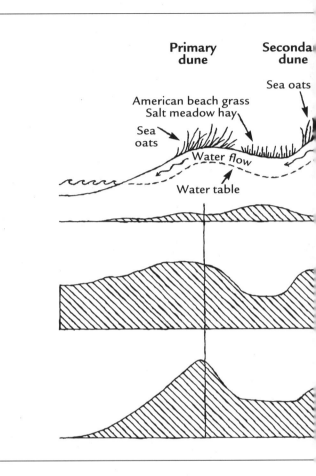

gretfully, additions of oxygen-consuming waste materials always make the situation worse, and fish kills appear to be becoming more common, even without stratification events. The summer of 1995 and the period of post-Fran runoff demonstrated that fact for coastal rivers in North Carolina.

The movement of saltwater and freshwater with coastal watercourses

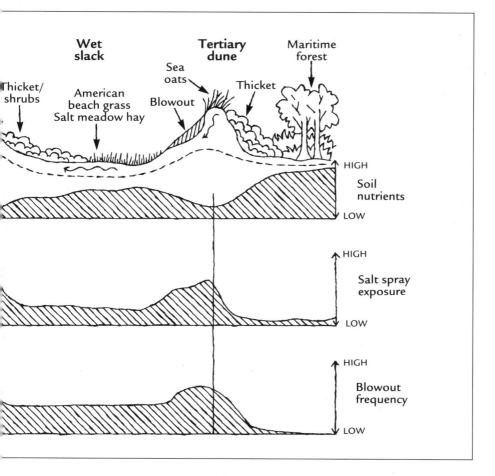

has profound effects on sedimentation, biological diversity and production, and environmental chemistry of coastal waters (see figure 13). Sedimentation and biological diversity are greatly influenced by the transition between freshwater and saltwater. Environmental chemistry is influenced by the difference in chemical composition of the two water types. All three of these phenomena move up and down the estuary when the freshwater section extends seaward with runoff or contracts landward during droughts.

Sedimentation events at the freshwater/saltwater interface are driven by the increase in electrical conductivity that comes with chemicals dissolved in salty water (Na^+ and Cl^-, for example). The conductivity of the salty water draws electrical charges from sediment particles that had been kept apart by the repelling effect of like charges (negative charge repels negative charge). The particles with lesser charges aggregate together until they become heavy enough to settle to the floor of the estuary (figure 13A). This settling of particles produces estuarine floor sediment that is carried by currents into areas where it forms mudflats and the soil of salt marshes. Marsh and mudflat sediments are rich in organic matter, in part because organic matter coats the particles that settle in response to change in conductivity across the freshwater/saltwater boundary, and in part because upper estuarine waters are biologically productive.

Biological productivity in coastal waters is a result of nutrients such as nitrogen and phosphorous being brought downstream by rivers and held for long periods in coastal waters by oscillating tidal currents. The plant photosynthesis stimulated by these nutrients is converted to fisheries. Coastal fisheries are very productive and are focused in the relatively few species that can tolerate the great variability of coastal water habitats. Both biological diversity and production are affected by the transition from freshwater to saltwater (figure 13B). Biological diversity (essentially the number of species per unit area) is always lowest just downstream of a freshwater/saltwater interface. The reason is quite simple: the water is too salty to be tolerated by freshwater species and too fresh to be tolerated by ocean species. This area is therefore inhabited only by the small number of species adapted to a mixture of the two water types (brackish-water species). The high harvest rates of coastal fisheries reflect the fact that the organisms that are adapted to estuarine conditions often occur in great abundance. A single species of salt marsh grass covers acres. Shrimp, crabs, clams, oysters, mullet, menhaden, spot, and croaker occur in such large numbers they have supported productive fisheries for centuries. These fisheries owe their existence to the great biological production of the coastal zone. Rivers bring sediment, organic matter, and nu-

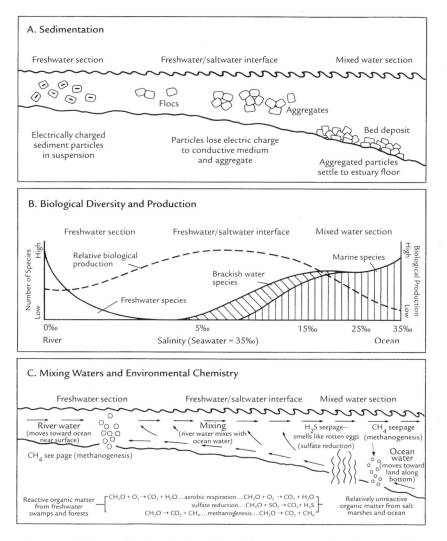

Figure 13. Sedimentation, biotic diversity, mixing waters, and environmental chemistry along an estuary. (See explanation in text.)

trient chemicals to the upstream end of estuaries. Tidal energy comes from the ocean to cause reversing flows (upstream on rising tides, downstream on falling) that trap nutrients and estuarine organisms in the same water mass long enough for photosynthesis and feeding to occur. Together, the aquatic and attached plants of estuaries produce a rate of photosynthesis as great as that found anyplace on earth.

Photosynthesis is the process that makes life as we know it possible. Understanding what controls photosynthesis tells us much about the nature of coastal environments and their susceptibility to additions of excess nutrients and organic matter. In photosynthesis, chemical compounds containing carbon, nitrogen, phosphorous, and other chemicals are taken out of the environment and combined to form plant tissue. The energy to drive this conversion is provided by the sun. The combined chemicals forming plant tissues contain only about 1 percent of the sun's energy that reached the plant surface, but that 1 percent supplies the needs of the plants with enough left over to support all the animals as well. Both plants and animals extract energy from plant tissue by metabolic processes (respiration) that have the effect of reversing photosynthesis. Photosynthesis traps energy in organic chemicals, while respiration releases energy for use by plants and animals in maintaining themselves, growing larger, and reproducing. Plants depend on respiration to meet their metabolic requirements when there is no light for photosynthesis (at night, for example). Animals depend on respiration all the time. Thus the process of photosynthesis supports the food chain that leads to observable natural communities and the harvests that humans extract from them.

Photosynthesis also has important chemical effects on the environment. Most strikingly, photosynthesis produces oxygen for the ocean and the atmosphere. This oxygen is needed for breathing, but the ultimate use for it chemically is as a participant in the processes of respiration. The most energy-efficient respiration (aerobic respiration) utilizes oxygen in its free or chemically uncombined form, that is, as a pure gas rather than combined with some other chemical. During respiration based on free oxygen, the pure gas is either taken out of the air (which is about 20 percent oxygen) or from that dissolved in water. Regrettably, water contains less than 0.1 percent oxygen. As a result, aquatic systems frequently lack the amount of dissolved oxygen needed for organisms to efficiently respire all available organic matter. Insufficient oxygen for respiration is rarely a problem in terrestrial systems because air holds a lot of oxygen, and it is circulated rapidly by winds to areas where it is needed. Neither of these things is true of aquatic systems. In addition, oxygen is a gas that can bubble up and out of a water body after oxygen is formed by photosynthesis. The rate of oxygen loss by bubbles far exceeds the rate at which oxygen from air dissolves back into the water. As a result, low oxygen conditions often occur in photosynthetically productive coastal waters. Sometimes these conditions become so severe that fish, shellfish, and even some plants die from lack of dissolved oxygen.

The importance of photosynthesis and oxygen-based respiration justifies an effort to understand the chemical equations that describe them. One equation summarizes what is said in the two preceding paragraphs (is that equation worth a thousand words?). The equation also provides information on the ratios in which different chemicals react to form compounds and/or organic matter. This knowledge is summarized in the boxed equation.

The rate of photosynthesis is defined as the rate at which carbon is transformed into plant material. Photosynthesis rates can be measured on an areal basis. When this is done across a river-to-ocean transect, we discover that coastal waters are about ten times as productive as the ocean and three times as productive as rivers (see figure 13B). The organic matter of coastal plants is eaten by fish and shellfish, which in turn are eaten by humans. Thus, coastal plants support humans by providing food for the table and, sometimes, oxygen for the air we breathe. Such plants also provide shelter for juvenile forms of many species eaten directly or indirectly by humans. Scientists estimate that over 85 percent of commercially important coastal animals are dependent on estuaries during some significant part of their life cycle. For these reasons, estuarine communities are protected by the Coastal Area Management Act as areas of environmental concern, and both plant communities and the waters nearby are protected as nursery areas by coastal fishing regulations.

The rate of production of food, fisheries, and dissolved oxygen is not

Energy + 106 CO_2 + 90 H_2O + 16 NO_3 + 1 PO_4 yields organic matter + 177 O_2 + heat

(from (in (in (in (in   containing energy   (in air

sunlight) air) estuary) runoff) rocks)   as well   or

    as major   dissolved

    chemicals in   in

    the following   estuary)

    ratio:

    106 C : 15 N : 1 P

Photosynthesis occurs when energy from sunlight is trapped by bio-chemically active plants to produce organic matter in plant tissues, driving the equation from reactants on the left to yield the products listed on the right. Aerobic respiration occurs when organic matter and free oxygen react biochemically, driving the equation from reactants on the right to energy and chemical products on the left.

the only aspect of environmental chemistry that changes across the river-to-ocean transition. This transition is characterized by underlying changes in the sedimentation rate, reactivity of organic matter, and chemicals dissolved in the water. Figure 13C provides a simplified version of these re-lationships. The chemical reactions on this figure refer to the use of or-ganic matter (CH_2O) to provide energy for the metabolic needs of organ-isms that respire it to meet metabolic needs. A simplified equation for aerobic respiration is $CH_2O + O_2 \rightarrow CO_2 + H_2O$ + energy; that is, organic matter reacts with dissolved oxygen to form carbon dioxide and water. This equation leaves out the nitrogen and phosphorous transformations contained in the equation presented above but captures the relationship between organic matter and oxygen. As already mentioned, this rela-tionship is critically important in productive coastal waters. Aerobic res-piration often uses up all the dissolved oxygen. Coastal ecosystems do not stop when oxygen is gone; they simply shift to respiration processes based on oxygen bound to other chemicals. Bacteria have evolved ways to use bound oxygen in their metabolic processes. Some of these bacteria (methanogens) can break up organic matter into carbon dioxide and methane ($CH_2O \rightarrow CH_4 + CO_2$). This reaction goes on with great vigor at the upstream end of estuaries where reactive organic matter from freshwater marshes and swamp forests is incorporated into the estuarine sediments. The process is described by the equation in figure 13C. Organic matter from marshes and forests actually contains many kinds of oxygen-containing chemicals. Bacteria have evolved ways to use most of these, but the two examples described above give the idea. Aerobic respiration and methanogenesis both produce energy for metabolism, but methanogenesis produces only 10 percent as much energy because most of the energy is used in breaking down the organic matter to get at the oxygen. At the ocean end of coastal waters, aerobic respiration and methanogenesis are joined by respiration based on chemicals from seawater. Prime among these is sulfate (SO_4). Sulfate is the fourth most abundant compound in seawater. It contains lots of oxygen — a fact not lost on bacteria in need of some for their metabolic processes. Bacteria have evolved an ability to combine hydrogen from organic matter with sulfur from sulfate to form hydrogen sulfide (H_2S), a gas with the smell of rotten eggs that combines with iron to form a common black form of iron sulfide as well as a rarer, crystalline, gold-colored form. The black, smelly form of iron sulfide gives salt marsh and mudflat sediments near the ocean their characteristic color and (as my grandfather used to say) makes them smell "like dead fish." The golden crystal is iron pyrite — the "fool's gold" made famous by western movies.

The chemical reactions diagramed in figure 13C do more than account for the composition, color, and smell of estuarine sediments. Methane is the major component of natural gas. This gas is produced anywhere that organic matter is broken down by methanogenic bacteria. Sometimes this gas is trapped for potential human use as an energy supply. This is thought to be the case in sediments on the continental slope off Cape Hatteras. Mobil Oil Company would like to drill an exploratory well to see if that is true. So far, they have not been given permission to do so, even though they paid the United States several million dollars to lease the area for exploratory drilling. Most often, however, methane is not trapped in seafloor sediments. Usually it escapes in the form of bubbles (see figure 13C). When it reaches the atmosphere, this escaped methane becomes a potential contributor to global climate change, because methane in the atmosphere allows short wavelengths of light from the sun to reach the earth's surface but prevents reflected long wavelengths from getting out. Such gases act just like the glass of a greenhouse; as a result, environmental scientists refer to them as "greenhouse gases." Coastal marshes and wetlands are a significant source of global methane production and thus contribute to greenhouse gas concentrations that may cause warming of the global climate. Other greenhouse gases include CO_2, which results from burning of fossil fuels (like methane) and from burning organic matter of cleared tropical forests as well as that produced when organic matter is respired by organisms to provide energy for their metabolism.

The processes illustrated in figure 13 have led coastal scientists to refer to estuaries and coastal waters as environmental filters, because suspended particles are removed from estuarine water by the chemical processes illustrated in figure 13A and by feeding activities of estuarine animals. These two processes are called the geochemical and biochemical filters, respectively. Both types of filters trap and store mineral and organic matter in the coastal zone. Bacteria process the organic matter to produce compounds such as carbon dioxide, hydrogen sulfide, and methane, which move into the air rather than continuing downstream toward the ocean, but chemicals that cannot be metabolized by plants, animals, or bacteria are stored in coastal sediments. These sediments trap materials in a way that is similar to that of a filter in a coffee maker. Unfortunately, like all filters, the estuarine filter can get dirty and/or be clogged if too much of the wrong things reach it. Toxic materials are also trapped by estuaries; pesticides, herbicides, heavy metals, and an array of industrial compounds are caught in estuarine filters and sometimes reach concentrations almost 1,000 times the natural background level. Even natural products such as hog or chicken manure can clog an estuarine filter if too much reaches the estuary at one time. Waste spills in the early summer of 1995 demonstrated this in the New River when 25 million gallons of hog waste escaped a treatment lagoon, removing oxygen from the upper estuary and killing thousands of fish.

Natural Plant Communities:
Twelve Examples from the Southern Coast

SYNOPSIS

Natural plant communities along the southern coast are controlled by earth, fire, and water. Earth is represented by soils that result when particles of underlying rock (described above in the section on geologic background) are modified by additions of plant material (described above for barrier island communities) and losses resulting from dissolution and erosion by rain and runoff. Fire is a major control of southern plant communities, as fires from lightning and the activities of human beings have been part of the natural setting for thousands of years. Water's control of plant communities is important because southern coastal communities are essentially wetlands, and their ecology depends on flooding and immersion.

Specific distribution patterns of plants in the southern coastal landscape remain a matter of scientific controversy. This is more a matter of ecological theory than of the plants themselves. It is not a purely academic concern, however, because land management decisions are based on ecological theory, and bad theory begets bad decisions. In essence, the controversy revolves around whether southern plant distributions represent natural communities (defined as "a distinct and reoccurring assemblage of plants, animals, bacteria and fungi naturally associated with each other and their physical environment") or, as one prominent ecologist maintains, these distributions represent "nothing more than physiological characteristics and chance." The controversy embedded in these two views of plant ecology has raged for over 120 years and will not be solved here. But, as a matter of organization of this book, I have adopted the "community approach" in the presentation that follows. In large part, I am blindly following the lead of two scientists who have done most to describe plant distributions in North Carolina: Michael P. Schafele and Alan S. Weakley. Schafele and Weakley work for North Carolina's Natural Heritage Program and together have produced three sequential "approximations" of the "natural communities" of the state; the latest was in 1990. The books are available from the North Carolina

Natural Heritage Program, P.O. Box 27687 in Raleigh (27611), for those who wish their own copies of this useful and important work. I have also chosen to follow Schafele and Weakley in focusing on plants rather than animals. Animals unquestionably live among the plants and, arguably, may form natural communities of their own in most settings; but plants, bless their little heartwoods, stay in the same place long enough so that they will be as I describe them when you visit. Animals, on the other hand, will assuredly have gone on to wherever animals go when not being watched by scientists.

Twelve of the more than forty natural communities described as "coastal" by Schafele and Weakley are examined here. These all occur within 20 miles of the seacoast throughout the Southeast. The distribution of the twelve communities is related to soil composition (mineral, organic, or a mixture); frequency and duration of flooding (submergence) in fresh or salty water; and, for the communities closest to the coast, exposure to salt spray. All of these factors are related to environmental processes already described. Soil type is related to old shorelines and lagoonal terraces of the coastal plain (see figure 4). Flooding (submergence) is related to rising sea level (long term) (see figure 3) and tides, storm surges, rainfall, and land runoff (short term). Salt spray exposure is related to breaking waves and prevailing winds. The extent of the influence of these factors on the twelve natural communities described here is presented in table 2. As you can see, the communities are listed in a sequence of increasing distance inland from the beachface.

Soil type is the most complexly distributed ecological feature of coastal habitats, as it is related to geology, drainage patterns, and vegetation history. The author's interpretation of the processes involved is presented in figure 14.

The geological contribution to modern soil distributions is in providing the original mineral that makes up the soils of the shorelines. As described earlier, the southeastern coastal plain has been occupied by shorelines several times since the Atlantic Ocean opened. The beach and dune ridges of these shorelines were as sandy as current shorelines, and the mineral soils referred to in table 2 trace their origin to these shoreline fea-

Table 2. Coastal Plant Communities and Their Habitat Characteristics

Community	Soil Type	Flooding Frequency Salt (S), Brackish (B), or Fresh (F) Water	Salt Spray Exposure
Dune grass	Sand	Common S	Heavy
Maritime grassland	Sand	Occasional S	Heavy
Maritime shrub (thicket)	Sand	Occasional S	Moderate
Maritime evergreen forest	Sand	Rare B	Light
Salt marsh	Mineral/organic	Common S–B	Moderate
Estuarine fringe forest	Organic/mineral	Rare B–F	Light
Tidal freshwater marsh	Organic	Common F	Nil
Maritime swamp forest	Organic/mineral	Common F	Nil
Bottomland hardwood	Mineral/organic	Occasional F	Nil
Longleaf pine savanna	Mineral	Common F	Nil
Pond pine woodland	Surface: organic Deep: mineral	Occasional F	Nil
Pocosin	Organic	Common F (rainfall)	Nil

tures. Most of these mineral soils have been modified for farming and forestry and so do not appear in the listing of natural communities in table 2. Lower-lying areas between the ancient sand ridges and on river floodplains have finer-grained sediments typical of lagoon and estuary floors, where they were first deposited. Often these fine sediments have high concentrations of organic matter accumulated from plants that have

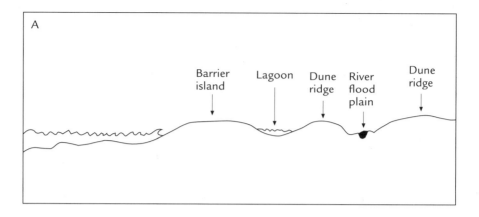

A

Barrier island   Lagoon   Dune ridge   River flood plain   Dune ridge

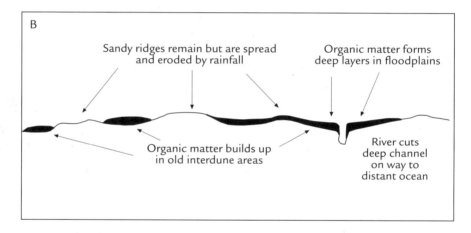

B

Sandy ridges remain but are spread and eroded by rainfall

Organic matter forms deep layers in floodplains

Organic matter builds up in old interdune areas

River cuts deep channel on way to distant ocean

lived and died there. In some places the organic layer is thin, as under grasslands and thickets; in others it can become deep, as under marshes and swamps. In addition, some rarely flooded organic soils have developed on isolated interridge areas far removed from developing drainage (and hence flooding) patterns. These highly organic soils support some of the most unusual communities in the southeastern coastal zone — the pocosins. Pocosins are low forest or shrub communities that emerge on

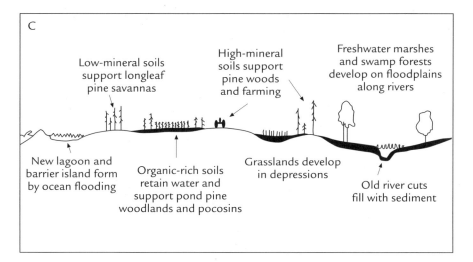

Figure 14. Origins of coastal zone soils and plant communities — a hypothesis. (A) Ca. 100,000 years before present (YBP). Barrier islands, dune ridges, and lagoons form on coastal plain when sea level was higher than at present. These features are preserved as the Suffolk Scarp. (B) 100,000 to 17,000 YBP. Sea level falls, wind and rivers erode the land surface, and plant organic matter is added to form soils. The ocean is far to the east as a result of the fall in its level during glaciation. (C) Present. Sea level rises, estuaries form and flood low areas, and land areas far from rivers develop water-retaining organic-rich but nutrient-poor soils and support pond pine woodlands and pocosins.

self-developed peaty soils formed by accumulation of leaves, stems, and roots of previous vegetation. The peat holds moisture, so pocosins are seasonally wet; but unfortunately for them, they are easily drained because of their elevation above surrounding land. Much of the original pocosin area has been drained and converted to farm and forest land. Those that remain are usually surrounded by pond pine and pine savannas that are also prime candidates for draining.

The complex interactions between soil type, flooding regime, and drainage characteristics of coastal areas result in plant distributions that sometimes fit community theory and sometimes do not. The plants themselves are unlikely to know this; they just grow wherever their seeds can reach that has environmental conditions suitable for germination and growth. As a result, readers will find areas that have plants from several communities. These transitional areas should not confuse you. They are admittedly exceptions to community theory, but, as emphasized above, that concept is controversial and questionably applicable to dynamic coastal habitats. The transitional areas you see will provide data from which you can form your own opinion about this scientific controversy.

The twelve natural communities listed in table 2 and their most common plant species are described below. The plants that occur abundantly in these communities have been illustrated by Jean Wilson Kraus to help you identify them. I have included scientific names for the species illustrated but only common names for other species that might occur. A brief description of environmental factors that control the ecology of the community and a few good sites where the community can be found are also included in each description.

Dune Grass Communities

Sand dunes closest to the sea along the southern coast are occupied by a dune grass community. The most characteristic dune plant is sea oats (*Uniola paniculata*), with sea rocket (*Cakile harperi*) and dune spurge (*Euphorbia polygonifolia*) nearer the beach and dune panic (or running beach) grass (*Panicum amarum*), salt meadow hay (*Spartina patens*), and bluestem (*Andropogon scoparius*) behind the primary dune. These plants are illustrated in figure 15. American beach grass (*Ammophila breviligulata*) (figure 16) normally occurs only north of Hatteras but has been planted farther south to help stabilize dunes.

The most important factor in the ecology of a dune grass community is wind-driven salt spray. Sea oats tolerate the greatest continuous exposure. As a result, it is the only perennial plant found on the seaward face of the primary dune and at the tops of high dunes farther inland (see figures 12 and 47). The other plants that occupy these salt-spray–dominated habitats are annuals (sea rocket, dune spurge, and, less commonly, Russian thistle and orach). Other perennial grasses (salt meadow hay, dune panic grass, and bluestem) occupy habitats with less intense salt spray exposure, such as on the landward side of the primary dune and in interdune swales and low elevation settings on secondary and tertiary dunes. The perennial plants have extensive root systems that take up water from rainfall as it percolates swiftly down through the porous sand. These root systems bind the sand and help stabilize it against being moved by wind. The shoots of dune plants disrupt the windfield, causing turbulence and markedly reduced wind speed within their stands (see figure 11). Together, the roots and shoots of dune grasses slow, trap, and stabilize sand, thereby building the dunes higher and reducing their tendency to migrate. In many places, sensible local ordinances or state laws prohibit disturbing these plants so as to maintain their dune building and stabilizing capacities.

Sites to Visit

The dune grass community is fairly easy to find and observe because primary dune areas are protected as an area of environmental concern by North Carolina's Coastal Area Management Act. As a result, almost any beach access area has a relatively natural dune grass community between the parking area and the beach. Totally natural dune grass communities are widespread along the seawardmost dunes of the national seashores, state parks, and estuarine research reserves described in Chapter 2.

Maritime Grassland Communities

Maritime grasslands occur within dunefields and on overwash terraces behind the seaward dunes. The plant cover can be sparse in the aftermath of an overwash or quite dense when the community is fully developed a few years later. The most common plant is salt meadow hay (*Spartina patens*), but flowering plants such as seaside goldenrod (*Solidago sempervirens*), fire-wheel (*Gaillardia pulchella*), and croton (*Croton punctatus*) occur, as do species of sedge such as *Fimbristylis* spp. and grasses such as finger grass (*Chloris petraea*) (see figure 16).

The most important factor in the ecology of maritime grassland communities is ocean overwash (see figure 9). These aperiodic events bring sand and seawater into interdune areas and often bury the grassland com-

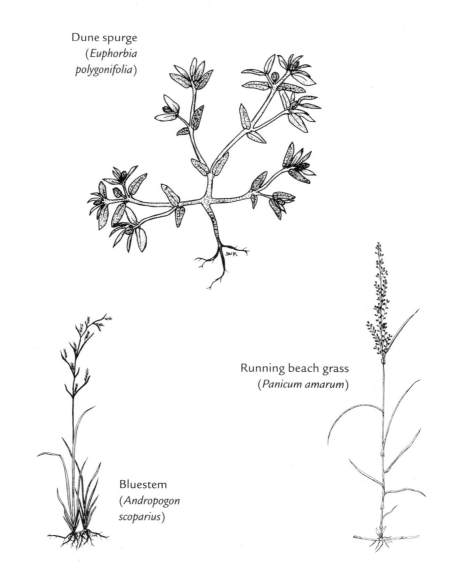

Dune spurge
(*Euphorbia
polygonifolia*)

Running beach grass
(*Panicum amarum*)

Bluestem
(*Andropogon
scoparius*)

Figure 15. Common plants of dune grass communities. From E. Jean Wilson Kraus, *A Guide to Ocean Dune Plants Common to North Carolina* (Chapel Hill: University of North Carolina Press, 1988).

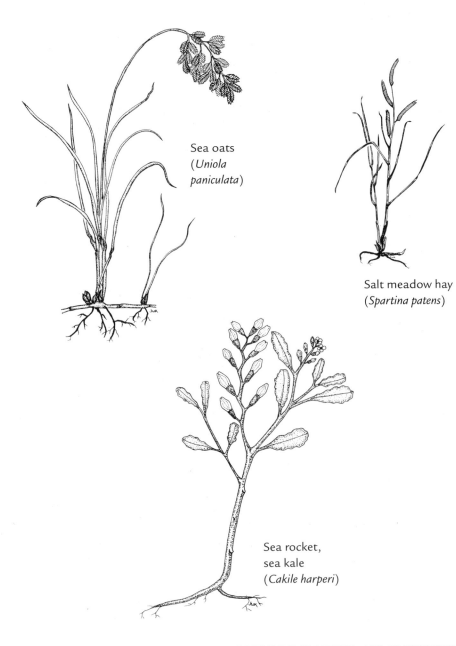

Sea oats
(*Uniola paniculata*)

Salt meadow hay
(*Spartina patens*)

Sea rocket,
sea kale
(*Cakile harperi*)

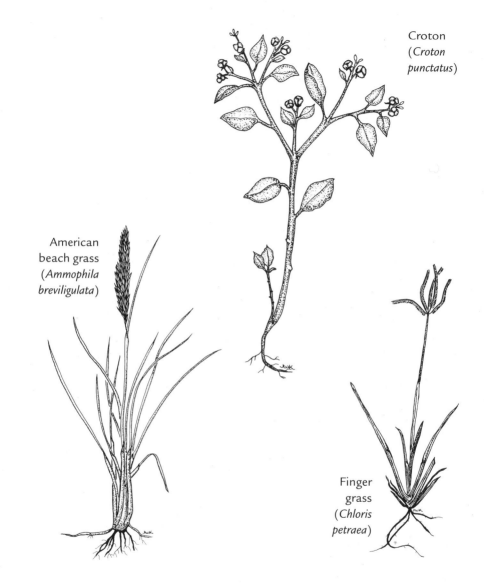

Croton
(*Croton
punctatus*)

American
beach grass
(*Ammophila
breviligulata*)

Finger
grass
(*Chloris
petraea*)

Figure 16. Common plants of maritime grasslands. From E. Jean Wilson Kraus, *A Guide to Ocean Dune Plants Common to North Carolina* (Chapel Hill: University of North Carolina Press, 1988).

Fire-wheel, Indian blanket
(*Gaillardia pulchella*)

Marsh
sedge
(*Fimbristylis
spadicea*)

Seaside goldenrod
(*Solidago sempervirens*)

munities beneath several inches (tens of centimeters) of new sand. Maritime grassland plants tolerate these additions, however, and simply grow up through the new sand layer. Their ability to do this is prodigious, as is their ability to sprout new shoots from deeply buried roots when sand is removed from their habitat. The movement of sand into and out of maritime grassland areas alters local drainage patterns, leading to a well-drained, dry surface on recently added sand and a wet, even seasonally flooded surface when sand has been removed (by overwash or wind blowouts — see figure 12). Wet or dry conditions support different types of maritime grasslands. The dry grassland community is dominated by salt meadow hay and contains the other species illustrated in figure 16 as well as obviously dry-habitat species such as prickly pear cactus (*Opuntia* spp.) and yucca. Dry grassland is more common than wet grassland, but where wet maritime grassland communities do occur, they are dominated by salt meadow hay and contain *Fimbristylis*. Wet maritime grassland communities also have wet-habitat plants such as black needlerush (usually found in salt marshes) as well as several other species of sedge, rushes, grass, and shrubs that are not found in areas with the plants illustrated in figure 16. Wet maritime grasslands often have very flat surfaces indicative of the seasonal water table and its ability to hold sand in place while drier sand near the surface is washed or blown away (see figure 34).

Sites to Visit

Since grassland communities on most residentially developed barrier islands have been converted to housing areas, the best places to see these communities is in preserved areas such as on Shackleford or Core Banks in Cape Lookout National Seashore, at Fort Macon or Hammock's Beach State Parks, or in the Zeke's Island Estuarine Research Reserve east of Wilmington. These sites all have good examples of dry maritime grassland. Wet maritime grassland is found on Core and Shackleford Banks (see figure 34) and reportedly also occurs on Hutaff Island in Pender County south of Topsail Island.

Maritime Shrub Communities

Maritime shrub communities occur in places that are protected from the full exposure to salt spray. They are found in patches behind individual dunes, in dense stands on interdune lows, and as an almost solid band on the ocean side of maritime forests. Many of the same plants are found at the upland fringe of salt marshes, although Schafele and Weakley classify that grouping as a salt shrub community. The most common large plants are wax myrtle (*Myrica cerifera*), yaupon (*Ilex vomitoria*), red cedar (*Juniperus virginiana*), Hercules club (*Zanthoxylum clava-herculis*), and stunted live oaks (*Quercus virginiana*) (figure 17), but thicket plants are often bound together by poison ivy, Virginia creeper, and other vines.

The most important factor in the ecology of maritime shrub communities is usually salt spray exposure, but shrub communities are widespread and relatively hardy as well as being a stage in the successional process by which dune habitats develop into maritime forests. As a result, although salt spray is important in exposed habitats, shrub communities may also be importantly affected by overwash, dune blowouts, storm surge flooding, inlet migration, and other aspects of their barrier island location. Shrub communities do much to change their own habitat. Once established, they form an almost impenetrable thicket that isolates the sand surface from the wind and thereby stabilizes it far more effectively than grasses do. Shrub species also drop their leaves and thereby begin the process of soil humus formation. Thickets also develop a dense canopy that is shaped by salt-laden winds into a form that forces winds up and over the thicket. This airfoil protects individual plants within the thicket from salt spray, which reaches only the topmost branches. As a result, once a thicket develops, it can maintain itself even if salt spray increases to levels that could not be tolerated by a solitary plant. All of these features make shrub communities highly adaptable. This is illustrated in developed areas where conditions behind artificial dunes, walkways, and buildings often result in shrub communities displacing maritime grasslands and leading the way to survival of live oaks and pines. Thus, maritime shrub communities occur in a spectrum of developmental stages ranging from

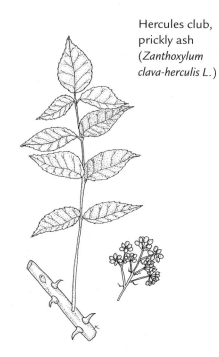

Hercules club,
prickly ash
(*Zanthoxylum
clava-herculis L.*)

Live oak
(*Quercus
virginiana*)

Wax myrtle
(*Myrica
cerifera*)

Yaupon
(*Ilex vomitoria*)

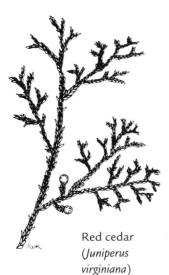

Red cedar
(*Juniperus
virginiana*)

Figure 17. Common plants of maritime shrub communities. From E. Jean Wilson Kraus, *A Guide to Ocean Dune Plants Common to North Carolina* (Chapel Hill: University of North Carolina Press, 1988).

early stages dominated by bayberries to late stages in which live oaks and pines can be found.

Sites to Visit

Maritime shrub communities at some stage of development are almost ubiquitous on the barrier islands of the southern coast. As a result, they, like dune grass communities, can be found near almost every beach access site. Well-developed, late-stage shrub communities can be found in protected areas such as Fort Macon State Park and Hammock's Beach State Park, on Shackleford Banks in Cape Lookout National Seashore, and in Zeke's Island Estuarine Research Reserve and Bald Head Island near Wilmington.

Maritime Evergreen Forests

Maritime evergreen forests occur in relatively protected areas on barrier islands and in well-drained areas on the inland shore of sounds and estuaries. The plants in these communities not only tolerate light exposure to salt spray; they appear to require the nutrients provided by the spray. They, like the shrub communities described above, often have a canopy that is "streamlined" by salt spray to extend dune or thicket shapes that occur seaward of the forest. The most common trees in these forests are illustrated in figure 18, although live oak, one of the dominant species, is in figure 17. Figure 18 illustrates the codominant laurel oak (*Quercus laurifolia*) as well as the characteristic loblolly pine (*Pinus taeda*) and the understory shrubs dogwood (*Cornus florida*), red bay (*Persea borbonia*), and wild olive (*Osmanthus americana*). Another common understory plant, Hercules club, is illustrated in figure 17.

The most important factors in the ecology of evergreen maritime forests are salt spray exposure, windstorm damage, dune migration, and soil drainage characteristics. Windstorm damage and human development of forested areas have similar impacts in that both create gaps in the canopy that may expand catastrophically as trees within the stand are killed by increased salt spray concentrations. This process is called forest fragmentation, and it has resulted in major disruptions of maritime forest communities along roads and other open areas all along the southern coast. Dune migration can also destroy maritime forests. On Shackleford Banks the overgrazing of maritime grasslands by livestock set the stage for dunes to migrate during hurricanes. The dunes migrated through and over the maritime forests, leaving behind dead trunks of a "ghost forest" that are still visible(see figure 34). The same process continues today on Shackleford Banks as well as on Bear Island and elsewhere. Salt spray exposure sculpts the canopy of maritime forests, sometimes in quite dramatic ways (see figure 42).

"The Ecology of Maritime Forests of the Southern Atlantic Coast" is an excellent community profile by Dr. Vincent J. Bellis of East Carolina University. Bellis describes the community and its environment in detail and analyzes current and improved management practices for these increasingly developed habitats. Bellis's 1995 report can be read and understood by nonspecialists. It is available from the National Biological Service, 700 Cajundome Boulevard, Lafayette, Louisiana 70506.

Sites to Visit

Excellent relatively natural evergreen maritime forests are found on Shackleford Banks (see figure 33), Bear Island, Theodore Roosevelt State Natural Area, and the Bald Head–Smith Island complex south of Wilmington (see figure 62). The latter community is particularly interesting for its huge live oaks and the Sabal palms that reach the northern end of their range in this forest.

Salt Marsh Communities

Salt marshes occur in the intertidal zones along the edges of sounds, estuaries, and lagoons. In North Carolina, salt marshes are best developed in the upstream and downstream ends of estuaries. This is because salt marshes need sediment to form the intertidal landforms that support them. The upstream marsh sediments come down the rivers and settle near the salt line (see figure 13); the downstream sediments come mostly from fine-grained material winnowed from offshore deposits and brought into inshore waters by waves and tides operating in a period of rising sea

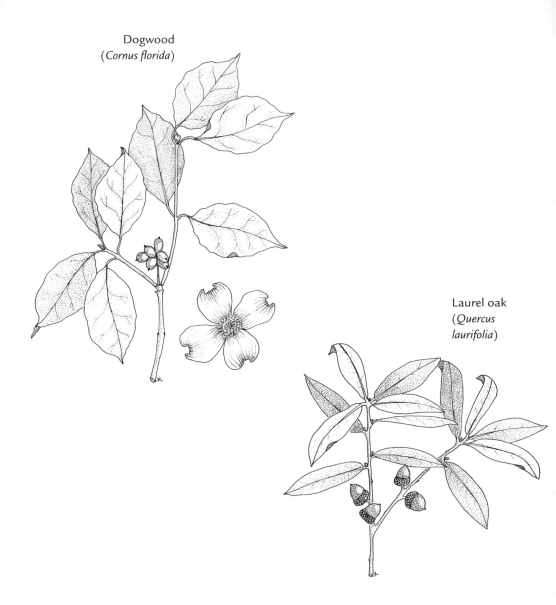

Dogwood
(*Cornus florida*)

Laurel oak
(*Quercus laurifolia*)

Figure 18. Common plants of maritime evergreen forests. Illustrations by Jean Wilson Kraus.

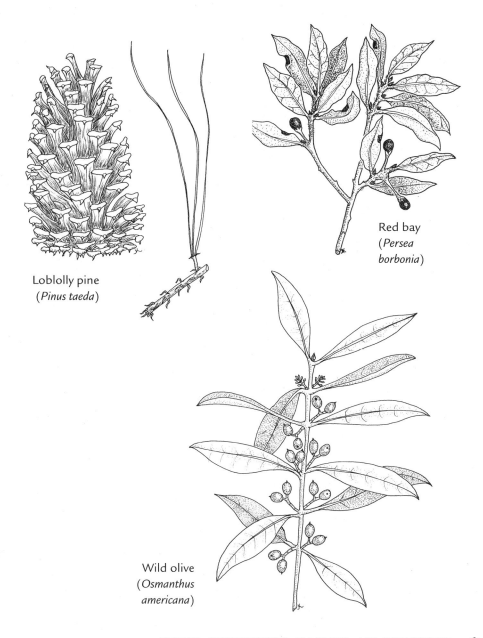

Loblolly pine
(*Pinus taeda*)

Red bay
(*Persea borbonia*)

Wild olive
(*Osmanthus americana*)

level. These two sources have not supplied enough sediment to build intertidal areas in the mid-reaches of the Newport, White Oak, New, and other smaller rivers or the large, open-water sounds that characterize North Carolina's coast. This situation differs greatly from that farther south, where salt marshes fill such areas completely. The large rivers in South Carolina and Georgia carry much more marsh-building sediment to the coast than do the smaller rivers (Cape Fear River excepted) of North Carolina. Once at the coast, these riverine sediments are formed into marshes by the stronger tidal currents associated with the higher tidal ranges found farther south (see table 1). What may be bad for salt marsh development rebounds to the advantage of recreational water sports. The lower sediment load of North Carolina rivers results in coastal waters much less turbid than those farther south.

The most common plants of salt marshes are similar throughout the southeastern United States. The characteristic species is salt marsh cordgrass (*Spartina alterniflora*), in the regularly flooded low- to mid-tide level, and a series of plants in distinct zones in higher areas. The zoned species include black needlerush (*Juncus roemerianus*), spike grass (*Distichlis spicata*), several species of salt-laden succulents called glassworts (*Salicornia* spp.), and at the upper fringe, the sea ox-eye (*Borrichia frutescens*), which has striking, daisylike flowers in the early summer (figure 19).

The most important factors in the ecology of salt marshes are sediment supply and the height of the marsh surface in relation to tidal range. Sediment supply determines if marshes form. Relative height of marsh surface and tidal height determine plant distribution and productivity. Tidal events bring water, sediments, nutrients, and dissolved oxygen to the plants and animals of the marsh. Those that live closest to the creeks get first and best access to those resources and therefore grow best. This is easily seen along a transect across a marsh from creek to neighboring high ground. The marsh grass closest to the creek is tallest, greenest, and most vigorous. The creek bank plants get first exposure to waters flooding the marsh, and because the velocity drops as waters move from the confined area of the creek to the unconfined area of the marsh surface, the creek bank marsh gets the sediments that settle out of suspension when the currents slow down. The deposition of sediment forms a natural levee along the edge of the creeks. Marsh areas farther back from the creek get decreasing periods of inundation and decreasing loads of sediments and nutrients. Marsh grass far from the creek is often only one-third to one-fourth as productive as that next to the creek. At some distance from creeks, marsh surfaces may be flooded only at extreme high tides, once or twice a month. These areas are often bare sand because, when the sun evaporates the flood tide water, the salts remain to create soil water concentrations that can be twice that of full-strength seawater. No common plants can tolerate these salinity levels, so none grow. Above these bare areas (salt-pannes), freshwater drainage from neighboring uplands dilutes the salty soil water, allowing salicornia, spike grass, sea ox-eye, and other marsh-edge species to survive.

Sites to Visit

Southern salt marshes have soft sediments that make walking difficult. As a result, it is easiest to visit those that are bridged by boardwalks. One of the best is the tideland trail at Cedar Point in Croatan National Forest (see figure 46), although its boardwalks will have to be rebuilt after Fran. Other salt marshes occur near roads and bridges throughout the area described in Chapter 2. A good place to visit an unbridged salt marsh is on the nature trail near the North Carolina Aquarium at Fort Fisher (see figure 54). The trail exits from the aquarium parking lot and traverses marsh and grassland habitats along its 1-mile loop.

Estuarine Fringe Loblolly Pine Forests

Unsurprisingly, estuarine fringe forests occur between salt marshes and the less disturbance-tolerant forests of the uplands. It is possible that the group of plants found here simply represents a stage in the recovery of more permanent communities that have been killed by fire (common in the uplands) or flooding with saltwater (common in the marshes). Most of the plants that occur in these systems are also found elsewhere. Most experts believe that this community is dominated by disturbances that prevent permanent establishment of communities on either side of it. Nonetheless, the community is newly described and well represented in

Sea ox-eye
(*Borrichia frutescens*)

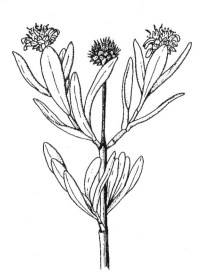

Black
needlerush
(*Juncus roemerianus*)

Figure 19. Common plants of salt marshes. From Elizabeth Jean Wilson, *A Guide to Salt Marsh Plants of North Carolina* (UNC Sea Grant Publication, UNC-SG-81-04, 1981).

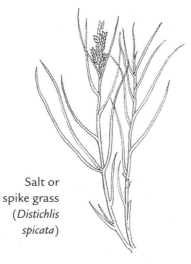

Salt marsh cordgrass,
saltwater cordgrass
(*Spartina alterniflora*)

Glasswort
(*Salicornia*)

Salt or
spike grass
(*Distichlis
spicata*)

Croatan National Forest. The most common species in these areas are loblolly pine (see figure 18), red maple (*Acer rubrum*), sweet gum (*Liquid-amber styraciflua*), and swamp tupelo (*Nyssa biflora*) (see figure 20). The understory usually contains red bay (see figure 18) and wax myrtle (see figure 17).

Site to Visit

The tideland trail at Cedar Point in Croatan National Forest.

Tidal Freshwater Marshes

Tidal freshwater marshes grade into salt marshes along many streams and rivers. They also vary in species composition depending on tidal range (see table 1), soil type, and latitude. Common species that occur in these marshes are cattails (*Typha* spp.); several sedges, including saw grass (*Cladium jamaicense*), common three-square (*Scirpus pungens*), and white top (*Dichromena colorata*); and an array of wildflowers such as lance-leaved arrowhead (*Sagittaria lancifolia*), pickerel weed (*Pontedaria cordata*), and southern blue flag (*Iris virginica*) (see figure 21).

The most important environmental factors in the ecology of tidal freshwater marshes are salinity, sediment supply, and flooding regime. The importance of sediment supply and flooding regime to freshwater marshes is essentially similar to the importance of those two factors to the ecology of salt marshes as described above. The importance of salinity to freshwater marshes relates to differences in salt tolerance of plants that characterize these habitats. Schafele and Weakley describe two variants of tidal freshwater marsh: an oligohaline (low salt) variant that occurs where salt influences the habitats even though the salinity remains below 0.5 parts per thousand (that is, unmeasurable except with electronic instruments), and a freshwater variant where salt is absent even at the highest high tides. The species illustrated in figure 21 are all found in the oligohaline variant. The freshwater variant has only salt-intolerant species and is not further described here. Freshwater tidal marshes have been studied less than salt marshes, but those studies that have been done suggest that these systems are as productive as salt marshes (that is, as productive as any natural systems known). It is easy to believe that freshwater marshes

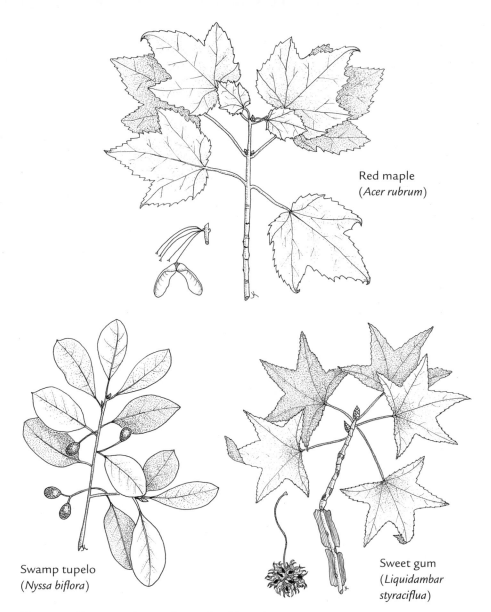

Red maple
(*Acer rubrum*)

Swamp tupelo
(*Nyssa biflora*)

Sweet gum
(*Liquidambar
styraciflua*)

Figure 20. Common plants of estuarine fringe forests.
Illustrations by Jean Wilson Kraus.

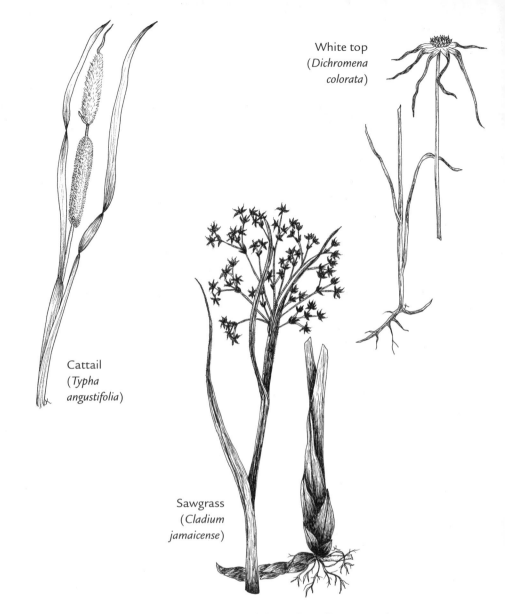

White top
(*Dichromena colorata*)

Cattail
(*Typha angustifolia*)

Sawgrass
(*Cladium jamaicense*)

Figure 21. Common plants of freshwater tidal marshes. Illustrations by Jean Wilson Kraus.

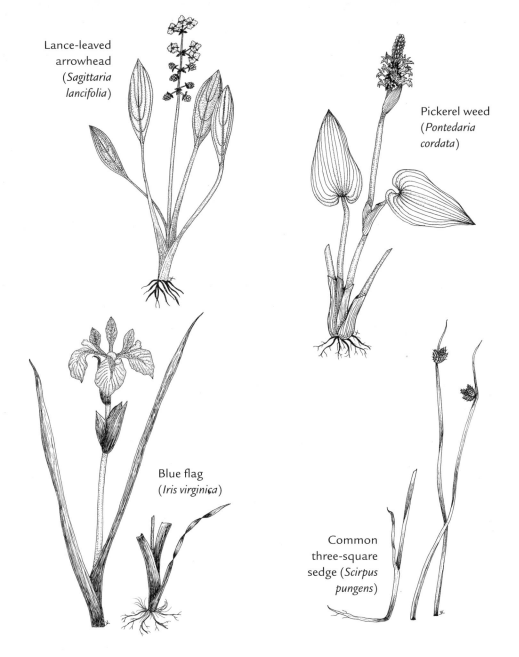

Lance-leaved arrowhead (*Sagittaria lancifolia*)

Pickerel weed (*Pontedaria cordata*)

Blue flag (*Iris virginica*)

Common three-square sedge (*Scirpus pungens*)

are productive when one observes the tall, dense, and diverse plant material that characterizes them. Needless to say, salt marshes, oligohaline marshes, and freshwater marshes grade into one another along the lower reaches of coastal rivers. This diversity of marshes and the abundance of wildflowers within them leads me to urge plant enthusiasts to get a relatively complete identification guide (such as Ralph Tiners's *Fieldguide to Coastal Wetland Plants*, published by the University of Massachusetts Press in 1991) and head up the creeks and rivers of the southern coast. The marshes and forests are primeval, the botanizing is excellent, the birds are diverse and abundant, and you rarely see a jet ski. A thoroughly pleasant way to spend a day.

Sites to Visit

In general, any river will do, but I recommend the Newport (see figure 36), the White Oak (see figure 45), the Cape Fear, and the Lockwoods Folly (see figure 60) as well as Town Creek (see figure 61) in Brunswick County.

Swamp Forests

Swamp forests are diverse and interesting communities that are frequently flooded with freshwater. As in freshwater marshes, they contain several community types that grade into one another and jointly contain too many species to be fully described here. A recent review of these systems listed twelve types of swamp forests in the Southeast, and Schafele and Weakley list eleven communities in North Carolina alone. Anyone who has seen the movie *Cape Fear* will recognize the general swamp forest type as looking like the forest primeval, with open wet soil underlying tall trees festooned with Spanish moss and supporting themselves with broadly spreading roots, some of which (bald cypress and swamp tupelo) have "knees" that penetrate upward through the soil into the air above. Common trees in swamp forests of all types are swamp tupelo, red maple, sweet gum (all illustrated in figure 20), bald cypress (*Taxodium distichum*), water oak (*Quercus nigra*), and Carolina ash (*Fraxinus caroliniana*). Understory plants often include swamp dogwood (*Cornus foemina*) and ironwood (*Carpinus caroliniana*) (see figure 22).

The most important factors controlling the ecology of swamp forests are the dynamics of the river channel and the flooding/immersion regime (hydroperiod). There are two types of rivers on the lower coastal plain: brownwater rivers, whose headwaters occur outside the coastal plain, and blackwater rivers, with headwaters that originate within the coastal plain. Both types are dynamic, with eroding and depositing bends that gradually cause river channels to migrate across floodplains. This meandering behavior sometimes cuts off river bends to form oxbow lakes and constantly creates new, bare soil areas where erosion cuts into the riverbank or where deposition produces a sand or mud bar. These freshly exposed, bare soils provide fresh habitat on which a series of communities establish themselves in a pattern of temporal succession. These continuous habitat and community changes cause most experts to question whether the concept of a stable community applies to these swamp systems. Flooding frequency of coastal plain rivers also varies, although blackwater rivers flood more frequently than brownwater rivers, in keeping with their small drainage areas being flooded by local rainstorms. Flooding regime is important because flooding alters many features of swamp forest soils by bringing sediments to them from the river and altering soil chemistry by initiating periods of reduced to absent oxygen. Anaerobic (zero oxygen) conditions develop rapidly after soils are flooded. Oxygenated conditions are reestablished almost as rapidly after the floodwaters recede. Most rooted plants cannot function properly when soil oxygen is reduced; some, however, have specialized structural features (knees) that aid in gas exchange to the roots, albeit at a rate that is less than 1 percent of total respiration of the tree. Flooding changes more features of soil chemistry than just oxygen availability because once oxygen is gone, the omnipresent bacteria quickly initiate anaerobic reactions to decompose the abundant organic matter in the soil (see figure 13). All of these flood-related effects vary within the forests because flooding generally decreases in depth and frequency with increasing distance from the river (except on the streamside levees that characterize many brownwater rivers).

The aggregate effect of different river types, channel meanders, and flooding regime is to create a multifaceted mosaic of environments across which swamp and bottomland forest plants grow. As a result, the distri-

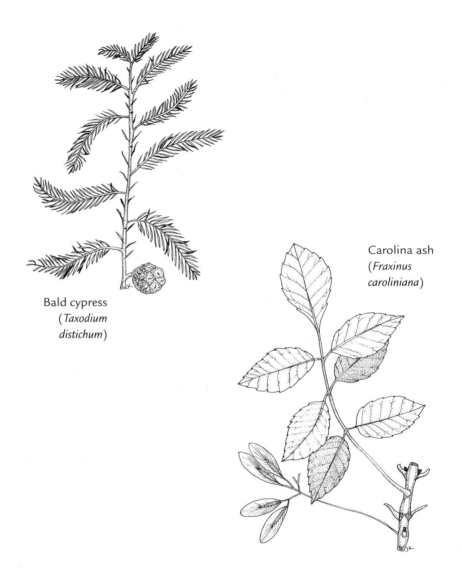

Bald cypress
(*Taxodium
distichum*)

Carolina ash
(*Fraxinus
caroliniana*)

Figure 22. Common plants of maritime swamp forests.
Illustrations by Jean Wilson Kraus.

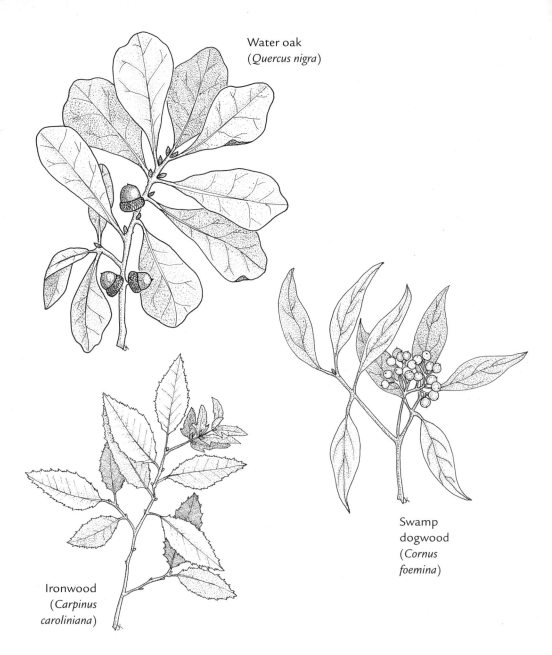

Water oak
(*Quercus nigra*)

Swamp
dogwood
(*Cornus
foemina*)

Ironwood
(*Carpinus
caroliniana*)

bution of forest types, community intergrades, and individual species is patchy and difficult to generalize. Map views of these distributions show complex patterns of community type with little regularity or consistency from place to place.

Sites to Visit

White Oak River near Haywood Landing (see figure 45), Cape Fear River north of Wilmington, Waccamaw River (see figure 59), and Town Creek in eastern Brunswick County (see figure 61).

Coastal Plain Bottomland Hardwood Communities

Bottomland hardwood communities are divided into blackwater and brownwater types by Schafele and Weakley. The two community types are generally similar, with only subtle floristic differences between them. Both types of communities are dominated by a diverse array of oaks, including laurel (see figure 18), water (see figure 22), and willow (*Quercus phellos*), along with loblolly pine and swamp bay (see figure 18), red maple and sweet gum (see figure 20), and Atlantic white cedar (*Chamaecyparis thyoides*) (now rare). The understory is usually better developed than in swamp forests and often includes swamp magnolia (*Magnolia virginiana*) (see figure 23), swamp bay (*Persea borbonia*), and red maple. The shrub layer is often a dense and diverse assemblage of thicket plants.

The most important factors in the ecology of bottomland hardwood forests are similar to those that influence plant distributions and productivity in swamp forests. Bottomland hardwood systems are flooded less frequently than swamps, and succession is initiated after storm damage or logging rather than by river meanders; but the net effect is to create a mosaic of plant distributions almost as complex as that of swamp forests. Bottomland hardwood forests almost always have uneven-aged canopies as a result of similar successional changes filling different aged gaps in the canopy. Bottomland hardwoods along the Waccamaw River seem to be an exception to this uneven-aged canopy generalization, although no one seems to know exactly why.

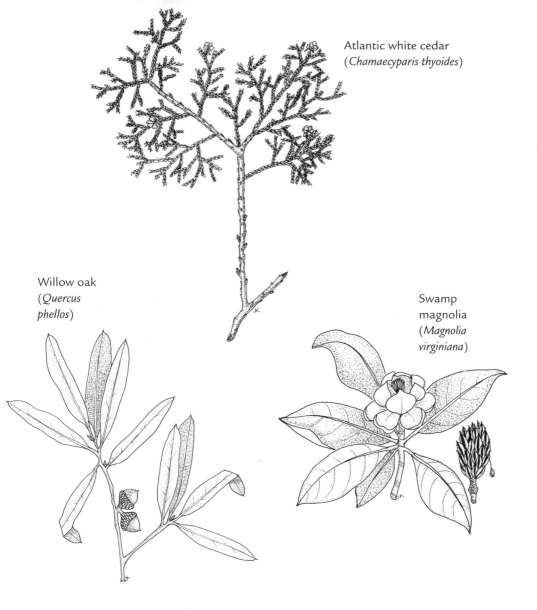

Atlantic white cedar
(*Chamaecyparis thyoides*)

Willow oak
(*Quercus
phellos*)

Swamp
magnolia
(*Magnolia
virginiana*)

Figure 23. Common plants of bottomland hardwood forests.
Illustrations by Jean Wilson Kraus.

Sites to Visit

The same as those for swamp forests: White Oak, Cape Fear, and Wacca-maw Rivers and Town Creek.

The final three communities originally occupied the nearshore flatlands of the coastal plain. These communities are not flooded by rising rivers but are appropriately classified as wetlands since they all have surface standing water during wet summer months and following rainstorms. There are mineral soils on these flatlands throughout the region, but where natural wildfires have been suppressed and plant material (leaves, branches, roots, etc.) has accumulated, there is a surface layer of organic-rich peat. The peat layer may be as much as 4 meters thick in some places. Soil modification by peat buildup often results in increased elevation of land surface, thereby increasing water retention and creating opportunities for ditch and drain projects. The natural setting produces an unusual situation in which the tallest community canopy (longleaf pine savanna) occurs on land of slightly lower elevation than the shorter canopies of the peaty-soiled pond pine woodlands and pocosins.

Longleaf Pine Savanna Communities

Pine savannas develop on seasonally wet, but rarely flooded, mineral soils on flats between rivers or sometimes on islands of higher ground within pocosins or swamps. They are generally open forests (as the term "savanna" suggests) dominated by longleaf pine (*Pinus palustris*), although pond pine also occurs in wet places and at the edges of the savanna. An underlying shrub layer commonly includes wax myrtle (see figure 17), huckleberries (*Gaylussacia frondosa*), and inkberry (*Ilex glabra*). A vinelike blueberry (*Vaccinium crassifolium*) is also common (see figure 24). One of the most important members of this community is the common wire grass (*Aristida stricta*) (see figure 24). This grass dominates the herb layer and provides most of the fuel for the frequent, but not very intense fires that characterize this community.

The forest floor is a diverse collection of grasses, sedges, and wildflowers (orchids, lilies, and composites). Longleaf pine savannas are among the most diverse forest communities known from the southeastern United States.

The most important factor in the ecology of longleaf pine savannas is fire. It is now clear that longleaf pine is the only tree in the region with seedlings that can survive in a frequent fire regime — the natural regime in the southeastern coastal plain. In these days of Smokey the Bear, we tend to think of wildfires as both bad for forest environments and a result of human carelessness. Both of these generalizations are untrue when applied to longleaf pine savannas. Field studies have shown that natural lightning can start up to sixty-five fires in a single day. Fires have, of course, also been started by man. Native Americans apparently set fire to the landscapes each fall as part of their deer hunting techniques. In flat, uniform areas such as the Pamlico Terrace (see figure 4), there are few natural firebreaks, and a single fire can extend over hundreds of square miles. In these situations a few fires per state would be sufficient to burn the whole area. We know that something of this sort must have happened because longleaf pine savannas cannot be sustained without frequent fire, and in the precolonial era this community stretched from Virginia to mid-Florida to Texas, covering an estimated 55 million acres. As European settlement, naval store industries, and logging moved through the Southeast, fires were suppressed, longleaf pines were killed and/or harvested, and the area regrew not in longleaf pine but in the now nearly ubiquitous southern mixed forest of oak, hickory, beech, gums, maples, and loblolly pines. Less than 1 percent of the area once occupied by longleaf pine supports that forest today. An interesting description of the longleaf pine savanna, the southern mixed forest, and the ecological changes that drove the transition of one to the other is found in chapter 10 of *Biodiversity of the Southeastern United States: Lowland Terrestrial Communities*, edited by William H. Martin, Stephan C. Boyce, and Arthur C. Echternacht and published by John Wiley and Sons in 1993. Chapter 10 is written by Stewart Ware, Cecil Frost, and Phillip D. Doerr and bears the provocative title "Southern Mixed Hardwood Forest: The Former Longleaf Pine Forest."

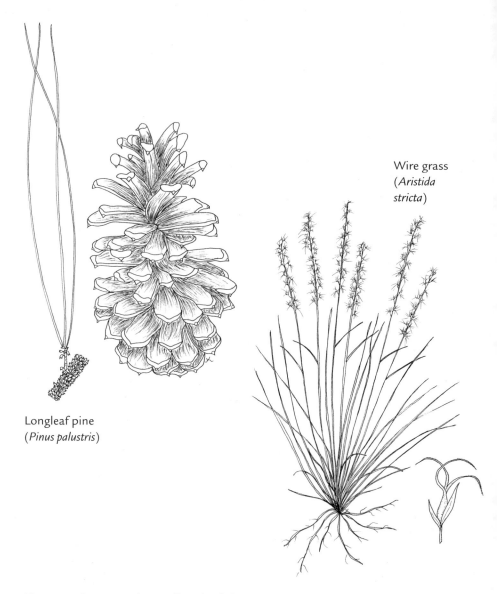

Longleaf pine
(*Pinus palustris*)

Wire grass
(*Aristida stricta*)

Figure 24. Common plants of longleaf pine savannas.
Illustrations by Jean Wilson Kraus.

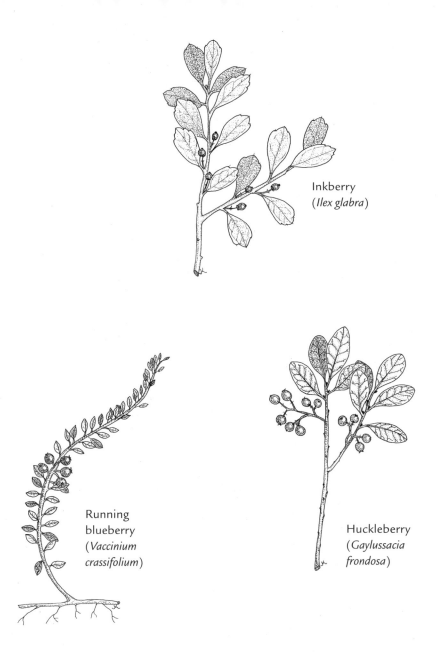

Inkberry
(*Ilex glabra*)

Running
blueberry
(*Vaccinium
crassifolium*)

Huckleberry
(*Gaylussacia
frondosa*)

Sites to Visit

There are three excellent places to see remnants of the once-dominant southeastern longleaf pine forest. These are the Nature Conservancy tract in Brunswick County's Green Swamp (see figure 58), Holly Shelter Game Management Area, and off Millis Road in Carteret County (see figure 37). These areas are all worth visiting, but I have arranged them here in the order that most visitors find most appealing.

Pond Pine Woodland Communities

Pond pine woodlands often occur at the edge of longleaf pine forests and surround pocosins. Pond pine woodlands separate the high, peaty-soiled areas of pocosins from the lower, mineral soils occupied by pine savannas. Soils in pond pine woodlands are intermediate between those on either side — usually with deep mineral layers overlain by relatively shallow organic-rich surface layers. More surprising is the fact that these woodlands, although usually dominated by pond pine (*Pinus serotina*) (see figure 25), sometimes have hardwoods, such as loblolly bay (*Gordonia lasianthus*), equally abundant. Other trees may include Atlantic white cedar, swamp bay, and swamp magnolia (see figure 23), red maple (see figure 20), and loblolly pine (see figure 18). This list indicates the transitional nature of pond pine woodlands. Only one of these seven trees is not found in other communities as well. The most important unusual feature of pond pine woodlands is the tall, dense shrub layer that creates a thicket-like mass of vegetation under the trees. These include a number of plants also found in pocosins, including titi (*Cyrilla racemiflora*), fetterbush (*Lyonia lucida*), sweet gallberry (*Ilex coriacea*), hollies, and other gallberries, all bound together with spiny vines — especially the laurel-leaved greenbrier (*Smilax laurifolia*) (see figure 25).

The most important factors in the ecology of pond pine woodlands are fire and flooding. This seeming paradox is a function of their peaty soils and proximity to the frequent fire regimes of longleaf pine forests. Peat soils absorb and store water. When wet, they can serve as firebreaks, but when dry, the peat itself can burn. Pond pine woodland plants have highly combustible wood and leaves. The high pitch content of pond pine led early botanists to classify it as a subspecies of pitch pine — a notoriously hot-burning species of the northeastern United States that extends to Georgia along the Appalachian mountains. Pond pine is adapted to fire, as it can sprout both from its base and from underground as well as reproduce by seed from its fire-resistant cones that drop seeds only after being heated by fire. Pond pine woodland soils are flooded seasonally and in downpours, but in subsequent dry periods the water drains through the peaty surface layers and is lost to the underlying mineral soils. This drainage carries nutrients out of the reach of most plants — a condition that limits the height and productivity of the forest.

Pond pine woodlands are clearly transitional communities controlled by conditions and disturbances that dominate the communities on either side of them. In this regard they are similar to the estuarine fringe loblolly pine forests described earlier. Their transitional nature also affects their distribution in both space and time. Pond pine can be found within complex mosaics of communities on peatlands formed by various processes and after logging of swamp forests as well as between pocosins and longleaf pine forests. Pond pine woodlands also develop under specific fire regimes that, if changed, can result in their replacement by communities as different as canebrakes, swamp forests, pine savannas, pocosins, and estuarine fringe loblolly pine forests. The common understory plants of pond pine woodlands are those that characterize pocosins. If fire is suppressed for long periods, pocosin vegetation may take over the area, and if a hot fire destroys both the pond pine and the tallest shrubs, pocosin plants may reestablish themselves earlier than the pines. Some experts believe that many areas that are now pocosins will, if left under natural fire regimes, turn into pond pine woodlands.

Sites to Visit

Holly Shelter Game Management Area (see figure 49), Croatan National Forest, Carolina Beach State Park (see figure 52), and Green Swamp.

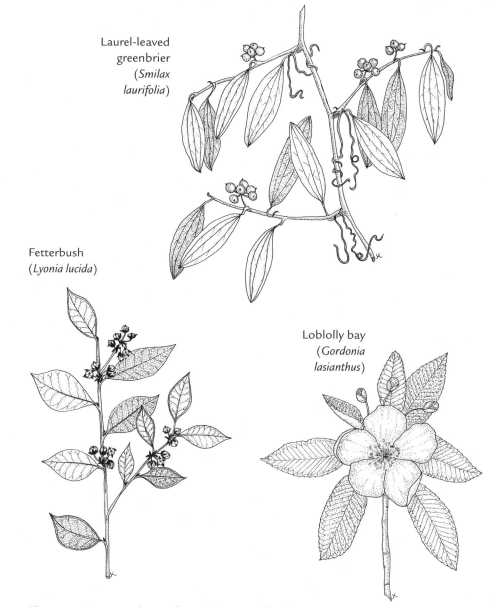

Laurel-leaved greenbrier (*Smilax laurifolia*)

Fetterbush (*Lyonia lucida*)

Loblolly bay (*Gordonia lasianthus*)

Figure 25. Common plants of pond pine woodlands. Illustrations by Jean Wilson Kraus.

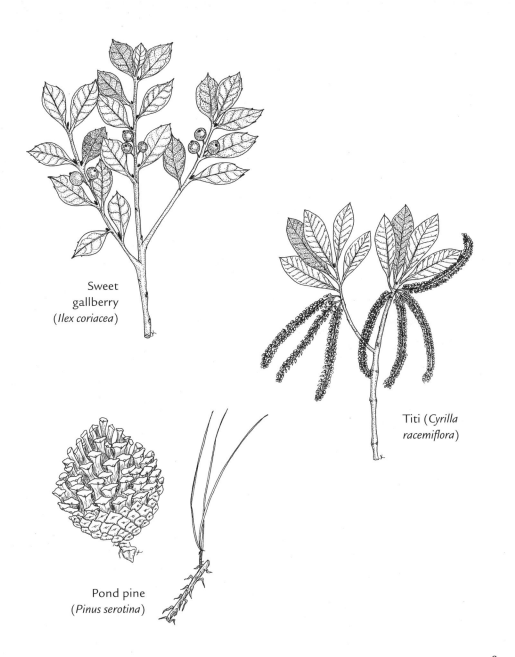

Sweet
gallberry
(*Ilex coriacea*)

Titi (*Cyrilla
racemiflora*)

Pond pine
(*Pinus serotina*)

Butterwort
(*Pinguicula caerulca*)

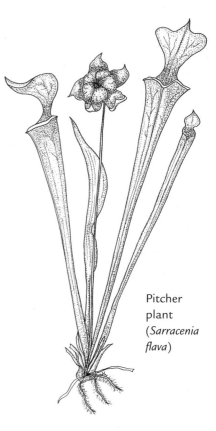

Pitcher
plant
(*Sarracenia
flava*)

Figure 26. Carnivorous plants of pocosins. Illustrations by Jean Wilson Kraus.

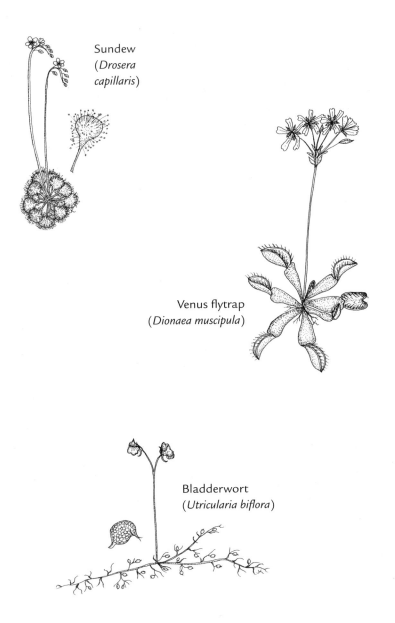

Sundew
(*Drosera capillaris*)

Venus flytrap
(*Dionaea muscipula*)

Bladderwort
(*Utricularia biflora*)

Pocosin Communities

Pocosins are nontidal wetlands in which trees, shrubs, and other emergent plants cover more than 30 percent of the area and open water is rare. The word "pocosin" is traceable to an Algonquin Indian word translatable as "swamp-on-a-hill." Apparently the Algonquins used this word to describe a variety of bogs and swamps, not a single type of wetland. This is still true, because the plants typical of pocosin communities frequently occur elsewhere, sometimes even in peat-filled depressions of Carolina Bays quite unlike the domed peatlands once thought characteristic of classic pocosins. The classic pocosins are self-made ecosystems like other types of bogs; that is, they have changed the nature of their habitat by their own growth to produce a self-perpetuating wetland system that appears remarkably stable until drained. The original habitat had a mineral soil like the soil that pine savannas occupy now, but through gradual accumulation of organic matter from previous generations, an organic layer like that at the surface of pond pine communities has developed. In fully developed pocosins the peat layers are deep and actually extend above the surrounding landscape as low, dome-shaped features. This, of course, makes them surpassingly easy to drain, and much drainage has been done — so much so, that large unmodified pocosins are mostly found in Camp Lejeune, Croatan National Forest, and other publicly held or preserved wildernesses.

As is the case in pond pine woodlands, the organic-rich soils of these communities are nutrient poor, as they receive no sustenance from rivers or runoff. Their only source of water and nutrients is rain. They dry out almost completely during droughts, making them susceptible to fire — a feature that has historically been a natural part of their ecology. Most authors subdivide pocosin communities into low and high variants based on the height of the vegetation (shorter or taller than about 5 feet (1.5 meters). Everyone agrees that these two variants grade into one another and into pond pine woodlands at their drier extremities.

Pocosins are covered with extremely dense shrub vegetation made up of species that occur less abundantly in other communities. The most common ones are fetterbush, titi (see figure 25), and inkberry (see figure 24), always with abundant smilax and greenbrier binding things together. The shrubs rarely are more than 10 feet high, although, as you already know, pond pines, swamp bays and magnolias, and loblolly bays may sometimes occur at the edge of the shrub communities. Thus the highest ground in the coastal plain flatlands supports the shortest plant community. This, of course, is just a reflection of the nutrient situation, which is so poor that several small plants that live between flooding regimes of pocosins and fire regimes of pine forests have evolved ways to get nitrogen by trapping and digesting insects. The ecotone regions where flooding and fire conditions are mixed support at least five types of insectivorous plants, including the famous Venus flytraps, sundews, and pitcher plants, but also the less well known butterworts and bladderworts (see figure 26).

The most important factors in the ecology of pocosins are fire, flooding regime, and soil nutrient limitation. These factors are basically the same as those that control distribution and productivity of pond pine woodlands, but since pocosins are the wettest end of the dry-wet spectrum in these communities, the role of nutrient removal looms largest here. There is no doubt that the peaty soils of pocosins are very low in dissolved nutrients; several studies have shown that phosphorous additions dramatically stimulate the growth rate of pocosin plants. The availability of soil nutrients obviously increases after fires. These same studies have shown that within a year of burning, some pocosin communities have regrown more than 20 percent as much plant material as existed before the fire.

Sites to Visit

Holly Shelter Game Management Area (see figure 49), Croatan National Forest, Carolina Beach State Park, and Green Swamp — the same areas to observe pond pine woodlands.

CHAPTER TWO

FIELD GUIDE TO COASTAL NATURAL AREAS

OUTER BANKS TO SOUTH CAROLINA

Introduction

This field guide covers the North Carolina coast between Ocracoke and South Carolina. It is divided into seven sections. Some sections are largely undeveloped (Ocracoke to Beaufort); others are almost completely developed along the shoreface but have impressive natural areas farther inland (Topsail Island and Brunswick County). Irrespective of development, good natural sites remain all along this coast. Some are small, some have restricted access, some are hard to find, but all are worth visiting. All sections also have more natural areas than some readers will wish to visit. Therefore, I have identified those that I think are most attractive and informative and have listed them as five-star features in the text and on the maps at the beginning of each section. This field guide was current in 1996. Things do change, however, with Hurricane Fran being the primary agent of change in 1996. Reader advice on changes and resultant inaccuracies will be appreciated.

Comfort in the Field

One thing that is consistent in all sections and times is the benefit derived from being comfortable and safe during field study. None of the places listed in this guidebook is inherently uncomfortable or dangerous, but people who venture into natural areas expose themselves to situations that may become unsafe and/or uncomfortable. The level of danger and discomfort to be found in areas covered by this book is modest, but it is not zero. Proximity to coastal waters carries with it the potential risk of drowning or hypothermia. All open areas pose the risk of being struck by lightning. Proximity to natural areas all but assures greater exposure to sunburn, animals that bite, and prickly or rash-inducing plants. These risks do not justify staying home, but they do need to be recognized, planned for, and minimized. Almost all trail and camping guides provide sensible cautions. For more extensive outdoor exposures, books on wilderness survival and outdoor medicine should be consulted. The most basic rules are both simple and obvious: do not go alone; make sure others know where you are going and when you will return; dress for conditions you are likely to encounter; make use of predicted changes in weather or tidal conditions; and remain alert to your surroundings. If further assurance would make you or your companions more comfortable, a book available from Menasha Ridge Press (3169 Cahaha Heights Road, Birmingham, Ala. 35243), *Emergency Medical Procedures for the Outdoors*, provides a well-organized and copiously illustrated guide to diagnosing and providing initial care for practically any medical problem that might arise.

The most likely problems that summer visitors to southern coastal areas face are those related to heat, sun, and irritating or poisonous plants and animals. Solving all three problems at once is hard. The clothes you wear to protect you from sun, mosquitoes, and poison ivy make the heat less bearable, and vice versa. The trick, of course, is to make intelligent compromises. Dress for present and predicted weather, wear sun block, carry insect repellent, and bring some water and food for emergencies. The natural areas described in this book can be visited in half-day trips, but their isolation and lack of development make it likely you will have little protection from changing weather, plants that scratch, and animals that bite and sting. It is a sad fact of southern natural areas that warm-season visitors are almost certain to encounter mosquitoes and other biting insects, so take extra precautions (tuck your pants into your socks, wear long-sleeved shirts, and look for chiggers or ticks on your skin after returning). You are also likely to see snakes while in the field. Some can be poisonous, so keep your eyes and ears open for their presence. The State

Museum of Natural Sciences provides a helpful booklet titled *Poisonous Snakes of North Carolina* that will allay your concerns about the snakes you meet—most are harmless to you and helpful to the workings of nature.

Wading and swimming in coastal waters exposes you to additional dangers, the most important of which is shallow water itself. Follow the orthopedist's adage — "feet first, first time" — when jumping into water from boat or dock. Once in the water, be aware that shells and fish have sharp edges and spines that can cut and puncture. It is a good idea to wear shoes to avoid cuts. Learn no more about the sharp features of seafloor dwellers by painful experience than is absolutely necessary.

There are other cautions that should be taken into account when boating. These are covered completely in boating safety books, but the most germane warning regarding small boats is be aware of weather, location, and surroundings. Weather can change rapidly along the southern coast. Winds can develop and create large waves in a surprisingly short time if they blow along the length of a sound. Even more dangerous are the "stealth" thunderstorms that can approach unseen behind the humid haze of summer. Lightning in these storms is dangerous to anyone in a high or exposed position. It is best to be off the water, marsh, or beach when lightning threatens. Do not be fooled by air moving toward the storm — it *does not necessarily* mean that the storm is moving away from you. The air may simply be flowing into an updraft within the thunderstorm.

Location is always important. Bring a map or chart and at least a compass. Once one becomes confused about location, I can promise that all marshes and watercourses will look alike. Reinforce location and identification of landmarks as you go out so you can recognize them easily on your return trip. If you plan to spend a lot of time in the field, consider buying a handheld GPS system and a cellular telephone. These miraculous inventions fit in a pack and can give you peace of mind that far outweighs their cost or likelihood of use.

Stay sharply aware of your surroundings so you can keep unpleasant surprises to a minimum. Tides along the southern coast are of relatively small range, but that does not mean tidal currents can be ignored. Sailing or paddling against a 2-knot current can be frustrating — and frightening if it is washing you out to sea. Keep tidal stage in mind when you plan your trip. Our shores are relatively free of toxic or biting sea life, but we do have jellyfish and other stinging animals as well as sharks, bluefish, and other carnivores. Avoid them if you can. Do not attract them with bait or disturbance if you plan to swim. It is good practice to give all wildlife enough space to escape if they want to. Even affable and good-natured creatures will bite or strike if threatened.

Finally, be aware that cold water and air are a potentially deadly aspect of the field environment. Together they are more dangerous than snakes, sharks, and "things that go bump in the night." Hypothermia kills — even in the South. If you are going out in a boat, prepare to keep yourself dry, warm, and afloat by bringing clothing and flotation devices appropriate to your setting. Even wet suits and/or survival suits are appropriate if you expect to be in small boats in winter.

Identifying Plants and Animals

This book's focus on natural areas requires that most common plants be identifiable from information in the book itself. This book emphasizes plants because they are rooted to their habitat and hence are always there to be observed and identified. That characteristic is, of course, why they are important components of natural areas. Readers will, however, see many plants that are not identified in Chapter 1. Other books that can be used to identify them are listed below. The books cover a wide range of completeness of coverage and technicality of plant descriptions. Those listed first are relatively easy to use without formal botanical training. Those listed later are more technical but also more complete in their coverage.

Easily used books include E. Jean Wilson Kraus, *A Guide to Ocean Dune Plants Common to North Carolina* (Chapel Hill: University of North Carolina Press, 1988); *Wildflowers of the Outer Banks*, compiled by the Dunes of Dare Garden Club (Chapel Hill: University of North Carolina Press, 1980); and Ralph W. Tiner, *Field Guide to Coastal Wetland Plants of the Southeastern United States* (Amherst: University of Massachusetts Press, 1993).

More technical books without coastal or wetland focus are William S.

Justice and C. Ritchie Bell, *Wild Flowers of North Carolina* (Chapel Hill: University of North Carolina Press, 1987); Albert E. Radford, Harry E. Ahles, and C. Ritchie Bell, *Manual of the Vascular Flora of the Carolinas* (Chapel Hill: University of North Carolina Press, 1968); and W. T. Batson, *Wildflowers of the Carolinas* (Columbia: University of South Carolina Press, 1987).

Useful books on animal identification include E. E. Ruppert, and R. S. Fox, *Seashore Animals of the Southeast: A Guide to Common Shallow-Water Invertebrates of the Southeastern Atlantic Coast* (Columbia: University of South Carolina Press, 1988); P. Meyer, *Nature Guide to the Carolina Coast: Common Birds, Crabs, Shells, Fish, and Other Entities of the Coastal Environment* (Wilmington, N.C.: Avian-Cetacean Press, 1991; C. S. Manooch, *Fishes of the Southeastern United States* (Raleigh: North Carolina Museum of Natural Science, 1984); W. M. Palmer and A. L. Braswell, *Reptiles of North Carolina* (Chapel Hill: University of North Carolina Press, 1995); Eloise F. Potter, James F. Parnell, and Robert P. Teulings, *Birds of the Carolinas* (Chapel Hill: University of North Carolina Press, 1986); and Wm. David Webster, James F. Parnell, and Walter C. Biggs, Jr., *Mammals of the Carolinas, Virginia, and Maryland* (Chapel Hill: University of North Carolina Press, 1985).

Interpretive Centers

One of the most effective ways to extend this book's treatment of environmental processes and natural areas is to visit the museums, aquariums, and field sites that describe and interpret coastal processes. There are at least five that are unquestionably worth visiting. From north to south, these are the North Carolina Maritime Museum in Beaufort, the North Carolina Aquarium in Pine Knoll Shores on Bogue Banks, the North Carolina Coastal Federation headquarters near Ocean on NC 24 between Morehead City and Cape Carteret, the Cape Fear Museum in Wilmington, and the North Carolina Aquarium at Fort Fisher, south of Kure Beach on US 421. All of these centers have both permanent and changing exhibits that describe, explain, and interpret coastal environments, organisms, and culture. All offer programs of lectures and field trips. All but the Cape Fear Museum have interpretive nature trails on-site or nearby.

All have friends programs through which interested people can help support and operate the facilities and educational programs. Some have specialized programs, such as the wooden boat building courses at the North Carolina Maritime Museum. For those interested in coastal phenomena, I strongly recommend visiting all these centers, and for those who live near them, I encourage participation in the friends organizations. Lots of interesting things are planned and provided by these interpretive centers. For more information on specifics, call or write the centers at the following addresses:

North Carolina Maritime Museum
315 Front Street
Beaufort, NC 28516-2125
(919) 728-7317

North Carolina Aquarium/Pine Knoll Shores
P.O. Box 967
Atlantic Beach, NC 28512
(919) 247-4003

North Carolina Coastal Federation
3609 Highway 24 (Ocean)
Newport, NC 28570
(919) 393-8185

Cape Fear Museum
814 Market Street
Wilmington, NC 27401
(910) 341-4350

North Carolina Aquarium/Fort Fisher
P.O. Box 130
Kure Beach, NC 28447
(910) 458-8257

A visit to these interpretive centers will get you oriented to the section of the coast you are visiting and prepare you for further explorations on your own. The field guide that begins below describes the coast from north to south, but there is no need whatsoever to follow that organization in exploring. Each of the seven sections should stand alone and provide equally useful places to see and study the natural processes that sustain the dynamic southern coastal zone.

Ocracoke Inlet to Beaufort: The Undeveloped Shore

The shoreline of the United States has few large areas that remain undeveloped. One of these extends for more than 50 miles between Ocracoke and Beaufort Inlets (see figure 27). The barrier islands along this shoreline are all part of Cape Lookout National Seashore. As a result, the only residential structures are in Portsmouth Village at the northeast, a few concession cabins along Core Banks, and a cluster of leased residences near Cape Lookout. Few, if any, East Coast shorelines can boast such an undeveloped status. There are no maintained roads, campgrounds, or lifeguarded beaches. Even shade, shelter, and potable water are scarce. The barrier islands that make up this shoreline (Portsmouth Island, Core Banks, and Shackleford Banks) are separated from the mainland by Core and Back Sounds; of these, natives say, "There's a lot of water in them sounds, but it's spread mighty thin." The sounds are so shallow that water depths of less than 1 foot at low tide make up 40 percent of those recorded on navigation charts in Back Sound and over 75 percent of those east of the channel up Core Sound. It is literally true, as *Esquire* magazine once said, that you can swim for as long as you want in these sounds and still stop whenever you are tired and walk home.

The mainland side of Core Sound is known as the "downeast" section of Carteret County. Eleven small villages dot the 50-mile shore of the sounds, but much of the sound-side shore remains residentially undeveloped. This cannot be said for Harkers Island or Beaufort, the towns nearest Back Sound. The difference in development status is a function of drainage. Harkers Island and Beaufort are built on barrier islands formed in the Pleistocene. The land is relatively high and sandy and drains well. The rest of the downeast section was once seafloor or salt marsh, and the resultant low-lying muddy soils drain slowly. The low-lying lands of the

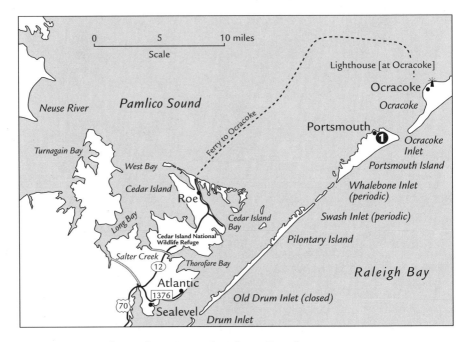

Figure 27. Coastal zone from Ocracoke Inlet to Beaufort.
Base map from North Carolina Coastal Boating Guide.

downeast shore are penetrated by four bays and fifteen named creeks, but none of these has any major freshwater source, so all can best be thought of as inshore extensions of the sounds.

Five-Star Features. There are five sites that impress me as worthy of special mention along the undeveloped coast. Unsurprisingly, four are in Cape Lookout National Seashore. From north to south, my five are (1) Portsmouth Island, with its village, salt marshes, and gigantic sand flat; (2) Cape Lookout, with its lighthouse, inlet, and uncrowded beaches; (3) Shackleford Banks, with its excellent examples of dune, thicket, grassland, and maritime forest communities; (4) Rachel Carson Estuarine Reserve, with its salt marsh and sand flat habitats; and (5) the suite of creeks and roadside marshes crossed on the highway (US 70 and NC 12) between

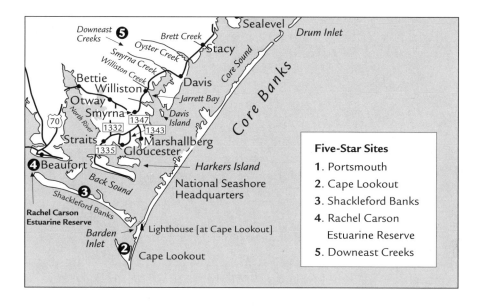

Beaufort and Cedar Island. Unfortunately, the first four of these five-star features must be reached by boat, but the boat trip is part of the fun of visiting, as well as much of the reason why the sites remain as natural as they are. To partially atone for beginning the field guide section by recommending five-star features that require boat trips, the site descriptions will begin with the highway-accessible creeks and move seaward to describe the bays, sounds, barrier islands, and inlets found between Ocracoke and Beaufort.

Access to natural areas in the downeast section is manageable by car and ferry and easy by small boat. Highway US 70 extends to the town of Atlantic (about three-quarters of the way up the peninsula), and highway NC 12 extends the remainder of the way to Cedar Island. Here roads end where the ferry provides an option of a 2-hour ride to Ocracoke Island farther north. There are toll ferries to the barrier islands from the towns of Atlantic, Davis, Harkers Island, and Beaufort. Portsmouth Village, a 250-acre historic district that was the largest human settlement on the Outer Banks in 1770, is reachable by public ferry only from Ocracoke. It is at the northern tip of Portsmouth Island. Access to creeks, bays, and sounds is achievable from US 70 and NC 12; access to bays, sounds, barrier islands, and inlets requires the use of a boat.

Creeks

The creeks of the downeast mainland are interesting for three major reasons: (1) the salt content of the water stays almost constant from mouth to head; (2) the marsh plants occur in zones up along the length of the creek as well as the more common zonation across the marsh from creekside to upland; and (3) the headwaters of these creeks are extending into, and killing off, the upland pine forests as sea level rises and storms push salty water inland. All three of these phenomena can be seen from roads and highways.

Observations from highways can be made to simulate an upstream transect along a creek by synthesizing information from creeks bridged at different distances from the mouth. Oyster Creek (just north of Davis) and Ward Creek (between Bettie and Otway) are crossed by US 70 at about 25 percent of the distance from mouth to head. Williston Creek (just north of Williston) is crossed about halfway between mouth and head. Wade Creek (north of Smyrna) is crossed as close to the upstream end as could be reached by most small boats. Observations at these points can be integrated mentally to produce a picture of zonation along downeast creeks. Near the mouths the creeks are bordered by typically zoned salt marshes. Salt marsh cordgrass occurs close to the creek, with clumps of black needlerush in irregularly flooded areas farther back from the creek. If you observe these areas at low tide, you will also see the tops of oyster reefs in the creeks themselves. At areas midway between mouth and headwaters of these creeks, you will see some additional plants, such as spike grass, glasswort, and sea ox-eye.

The upstream ends of the creeks are characterized by black needlerush marshes (sometimes with patches of spike grass on the creek bank) intermixed with dead and dying pine forests (see figure 28).

These creek heads are obvious and dramatic evidence of rising sea level. The marsh is invading the forest as storms push seawater into forests

Figure 28. Upstream end of downeast creeks; head of Smyrna Creek.
Note salt marsh, thicket, and dying forest.

with increasing frequency and duration as sea level rises. The trees take years to die, but the stumps of earlier forests are easily seen farther downstream and serve as mute testimony to the continuing landward movement of ocean waters. The invasion is well illustrated in the downeast section of this coast because the land is both low and poorly drained, resulting in frequent flooding with salty coastal waters little diluted with runoff from land.

This salt marsh invasion of coastal forests is most obvious where sea level is rising relatively rapidly, as it is in northern North Carolina and tidewater Virginia, but the invasion goes on inexorably all along the East Coast. The impact of rising sea level on beach erosion and landward recession of barrier islands is well known and well publicized. The invasion of coastal forests by salt marsh plants is less well known but affects a greater area than beach erosion does.

Detailed observations of creeks are easily made from small boats. Unofficial but effective launching ramps are located at almost every highway crossing between Ward Creek and Cedar Island. Official and improved launching ramps are located in North River off SR (state road) 1300 north of East Carteret High School, off Ward Creek west of Otway, in Davis, in Atlantic, under the high bridges over Salter's Creek and Thorofare Bay, at Lewis Creek near the Cedar Island National Wildlife Refuge Headquarters in Lola, at Landing Road in Roe, and near the ferry landing in Cedar Island. I suggest you ask someone before leaving vehicles on property that may be privately owned (at the fish handling plant at Williston Creek, for example). One can assume that leaving vehicles is acceptable at official ramps, but recent incidents of cars being broken into suggest securing valuables in trunks or out of sight. Most of the downeast creeks and bays can be explored by boat in a few hours; thus cars do not have to be left long.

All of the creeks I have explored are quite similar, and each has the features described above for the composite creek transect. Beauty is always in the eyes of the beholder, but my personal choice for most attractive creek is Smyrna Creek west of Davis. Here the most common salt marsh plants are sequentially arranged as you move upstream, with smooth cordgrass, black needlerush, glassworts, spike grass, and sea ox-eye all easily observed from the comfort of your boat. The creek teems with fish; they are likely to jump all around your boat as you head upstream. The creek banks are heavily burrowed by fiddler crabs. The males will demonstrate their myopia (or sexual frustration) by trying to lure you into their burrows with come-hither waving of their large claws (female crabs presumably find this much less resistible than humans). You will also see ribbed mussels attached to the creek bank peat. These animals are less demonstrative than the crabs but are known to be important contributors to marsh productivity. They filter nutrient-rich particles from seawater and deposit them on the marsh surface, thereby enriching the soil to stimulate plant growth and photosynthesis rates. The upstream end of Smyrna Creek is particularly attractive, as the creek ends in a U-shaped opening in the forest, with patches of spike grass, black needlerush, cattails, and salt marsh cordgrass progressively closer to the source of freshwater seepage from a forest of pines, live oak, maples, and gums. The edge of the forest is a thicket of cedars, marsh elder, yaupon, and wax myrtle. The marsh and thicket areas grow under and around dead pine and hardwood trees, demonstrating that salt marsh has invaded the forest. Damaged and dying trees occur at the margin of the forest. Many of these trees have been burrowed into by woodpeckers and other birds, and ospreys have built a nest in a large dead pine on the forest margin. All in all, it is an interesting place to visit.

All the creeks in this coastal section are navigable by small boat. Several are worth visiting for bird-watching. The southwest branch of Oyster Creek parallels a dike beyond which the marsh is fresh and much visited by wading birds (egrets and herons of many types) and other waterfowl. Ospreys have nests in several of these creeks, and pelicans fish in most of them.

Two downeast creeks have been extended and deepened to provide navigable connections between Core and Pamlico Sounds. The well-marked creek is called Thorofare and connects Core Sound's Thorofare Bay with Pamlico Sound's Long Bay. The less well marked creek connects Core Sound's Nelson Bay with Pamlico Sound's Long and Turnagain Bays. Both canals have high bridges over them and boat launching ramps. Boats of moderately deep draft can make a circuit through the marshes of Thorofare and the forests of Salter Creek, although parts of several channels are narrow, so good navigation charts are essential. The water throughout this circuit is relatively salty. In explorations of this area I have seen little wildlife other than birds, but my enthusiasm for exploring the forests firsthand was reduced after I saw a copperhead swimming across the Salter Creek canal.

Bays

There are four major bays between Beaufort and Cedar Island: Jarrett, Nelson, Thorofare, and Cedar Island. All are shallow arms of Core Sound with sand bottoms that are sometimes covered with sea grass flats. These bays are well suited to wading, swimming, and other water sports. All but Nelson Bay support shellfish leases, indicating bacterial water quality levels more than fourteen times as restrictive as is required for approved swimmable waters.

The most obvious natural habitats in the bays are the salt marsh borders and the sea grass flats. The salt marsh areas have already been described, as they do not differ greatly from those near the mouths of creeks; they consist of smooth cordgrass near the water's edge, backed by black needlerush, with spike grass and sea ox-eye at the upper fringe. The sea grass beds are usually found in monospecific stands of one of three species: eel grass, widgeon grass, or shoal grass. These represent three of only twelve known genera of plants in the world that can function normally and complete their life cycle while fully submerged in saltwater. Some of the grass beds that appear to be of a single species may actually have two or more, as eel grass usually dominates North Carolina beds in winter and spring, while shoal grass often dominates the same bed in summer and fall. Sometimes all three species occur together on the same bed. Fortunately for those who wish to identify them, the leaves of these plants are quite different from one another. The easiest to identify is eel grass. It has a wide ($\frac{1}{8}$–$\frac{1}{4}$ in. [1.5–3.0 mm]) leaf with a rounded tip that comes to a point in the middle, like a parenthesis mark. Widgeon grass is the next easiest to recognize. It has narrow leaves (less than $\frac{1}{16}$ in. [1 mm] wide) alternately arranged along the stem, with a sheath at the base and a tip that narrows to a single point. Shoal grass is hardest to distinguish. It has a narrow leaf like widgeon grass; but there are two to three leaves per sheath, and the tip may have two or three points (see figure 29).

The ecological roles of marshes and sea grass beds have some features in common. Both are important producers of plant material, much of which remains uneaten by herbivores throughout the life of the plant. The uneaten leaves generate turbulence in the waters flowing through them, causing suspended particles of organic and inorganic matter to settle to the seafloor, thereby increasing sedimentation rates to levels higher than those for nearby unvegetated substrate. Both marsh and sea grass systems provide habitats for animals and plants that do not occur as abundantly in unvegetated habitats. Both systems appear to export organic matter (both living and dead) to be eaten by omnivorous animals in surrounding creeks and bays. There are some differences between salt marsh and sea grass flats, however. The subtidal nature of grass flats makes them more important than marshes as a habitat for other aquatic species. Recent summaries have shown that over 350 species of algae and more than 120 species of animals are found on the sea grass leaves, and four to five times as many species live in the sediment under sea grasses as live in the unvegetated sand nearby. Salt marshes do not support a diversity of life nearly as great. Also, much of the productivity of salt marshes, particularly that of the irregularly flooded needlerush marshes, is incorporated into the marsh soil to produce organic-rich peat rather than food for animals in the surrounding waters. Scientists now recognize that sea grass beds are even more important to coastal ecosystems than salt marshes, and that increased efforts to preserve sea grass flats will be directly reflected in increased harvest of fish and shellfish nearby.

Sand flats and sandy seafloor are less striking than the vegetated areas of downeast bays (see figure 29), but they, too, play an important role in the natural system. Human seafood harvesters and other predators focus their efforts on these sandy bottoms, thereby reducing the number of species and number of individuals to levels below those of vegetated areas. These areas provide habitats where bottom-feeding fish, crustaceans, and molluscs settle, develop, grow, and are harvested by man and the aquatic food chain.

Access. Downeast bays are relatively similar to one another. Several are worth visiting, and if you are touring them by small boat, your choice may be determined by prevailing winds and waves. Cedar Island Bay is well protected from southeast winds (the most frequent direction in the summer) but is fairly exposed to northeast winds (usually the direction from which the strongest winds blow). Cedar Island Bay has many islands, tidal flats, and shoals that can serve as picnic or camping spots, and there is swimmably deep water relatively close. For automobile visitors, Cedar Island Bay is accessible by walking east along the beach near the ferry dock. Visitors with boats can put in at Landing Road in Roe.

My personal favorite downeast bay is Jarrett Bay near Williston. Jarrett Bay has all the typical features (salt marsh, sea grass beds, sandy seafloor, and tidal flats) and is protected from waves from all directions. It also has a sand ridge extending from the north shore for two miles to Davis Is-

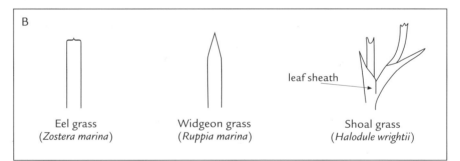

Eel grass
(*Zostera marina*)

Widgeon grass
(*Ruppia marina*)

leaf sheath

Shoal grass
(*Halodule wrightii*)

Figure 29. Core Banks, Core Sound, and sea grasses. (A) Maritime grassland, salt marsh, sandy seafloor, and sea grass habitats (dark bottom) in Core Sound. (B) Characteristic leaf shapes of sea grasses common to North Carolina.

land. This ridge is built on a base of hardening sand (not quite sandstone) that forms excellent picnic spots at the edge of swimmable water. All of Jarrett Bay is accessible from US 70 — good news if you are arriving by car, but bad news if the sight of a distant roadway detracts from your enjoyment of the natural setting.

Sounds

Ecologically, downeast sounds are much like the bays. They are shallow, high-salinity areas with sandy bottoms, some with grass beds and some without (see figure 29). Sounds are bigger than bays in downeast usage. Core Sound is almost 25 miles long and ranges from 2 to 6 miles wide. Back Sound is 6 miles long and 2 miles wide. Altogether, these sounds make up about 140 of North Carolina's 2,500 square miles of inshore estuarine and lagoonal waters. The large size and clean waters of the sounds give them huge recreational potential for all types of water sports as well as for their current use, which is largely commercial and recreational fishing.

The large size of the sounds and the undeveloped barrier islands between Beaufort and Cedar Island makes a complete description of them beyond this book. The characteristic habitats of these areas can be described in general terms, and a few good areas will be described in detail; but visitors may well find other areas even more interesting and attractive. I encourage readers to explore the vast natural recreational area of this shoreline to discover their own favorite spots, even as I describe mine for you to consider visiting.

The vegetated habitats of the sounds have already been described. They are essentially the same as those of the coastal bays — grass flats and salt marshes (see figure 29). Unvegetated sand flats and sandy seafloor areas are better represented in the sounds than in the bays. These unvegetated areas seem like biological deserts when compared with salt marshes and sea grass beds, but careful research shows that they play important roles in transferring the energy fixed by salt marshes and sea grasses into the fish, birds, and fishermen that characterize the coastal zone.

Sand flats and mudflats form when sediments are carried into shallow coastal areas by tidal or storm currents. Tidal currents enter coastal waters through inlets between barrier islands. The heavy, sandy sediments carried in by flooding tides are deposited in areas close to the inlets, where currents slow as they spread out into the sounds. As a result, sand flats are best developed inside major inlets. Examples are found inside Beaufort Inlet and Drum Inlet (see figures 30 and 5) and, to a lesser extent, inside Old Drum Inlet (now closed), three miles north of the current Drum Inlet. Sand flats also develop where high tides and waves wash over the barrier islands and carry sand into shallow areas on the landward side. Examples of sand flats formed on the inshore side of overwash deposits are common all along Core Banks. In fact, most of the tidal flats and extensive shallows of eastern Core Sound have all been formed by sand transported during washover events.

Fine-grained sediment particles—the silts and clays that make up "mud"—are carried farther by tidal and washover currents than are the larger, sand-sized particles. As a result, muddy sediments occur relatively far from inlets and overwash areas. In Core and Back Sounds, intertidal mudflats and mud bottoms are rare and occur mostly behind marshy areas in open water or in the upstream areas of bays and creeks.

There is much life on sand flats and mudflats, but most of it hides beneath the surface to avoid being eaten. Any plant or animal that lives exposed is ready prey for birds at low tide and fish at high tide. As a result, successful colonizers of sand flats burrow below the surface of the flat. Evidence of these buried plants and animals is subtle and requires close observation. Charles and Nancy Peterson's *The Ecology of Intertidal Flats of North Carolina* is a community profile published by the U.S. Fish and Wildlife Service in 1979. The Petersons list few animals that live above the surface but many that live beneath it. Many, but not all, of the burrowing animals are small. Some feed by filtering food from tidal waters above the flat (suspension feeders). Others ingest the sediments themselves and digest the living plants, small animals, and detritus contained therein (deposit feeders). Clams are the most common suspension feeders; many types of worms are deposit feeders. Buried clams and worms are difficult but not impossible to see. Clams have fleshy extensions called siphons

Figure 30. Intertidal sand flats, salt marshes, and forests of Rachel Carson Estuarine Reserve near Beaufort.

that extend to the surface. Worms have burrows, sometimes with funnel-like depressions caused by their ingestion of sediment, but more often worm burrows are marked by the undigested fecal matter they leave on the surface of the flat. Some of these deposit feeders process surprising volumes of sediments. Large seaworms can pass as much as 8.5 cubic inches of sand per day through their digestive tract.

Many species of fish and birds feed on intertidal sand flats and mudflats. Peterson and Peterson list over 150 species of fish and 50 species of birds that feed directly on tidal flats, and another 16 fish species and 5 bird species that prey on the tidal-flat feeders.

My favorite place to visit sand flats is on the Carrot Island/Bird Shoal complex that makes up the 2,600-acre Rachel Carson Estuarine Reserve (see figure 30). This area is large, varied, and easily accessible by boat, ferry, or water taxi from the Beaufort waterfront. The reserve is home to a herd of picturesque horses, roosting areas for heron, and small patches of cedar, pine, and oak maritime forest.

The best place to enter the Rachel Carson Estuarine Reserve is near its northwest corner, directly across Taylor's Creek from the docks of the North Carolina Maritime Museum and two private ferry services. For those visiting the reserve in their own boats, there is a public launching ramp near the east end of Front Street (about three miles from the North Carolina Maritime Museum). The northwest corner of the reserve has a twenty-stop, half-mile nature trail that leads you through oak forests to the thickets and salt marshes that border the flats. Brochures describing the nature trail are available at the Maritime Museum and in a box on the large white sign that marks the entrance to the trail. The brochure does a good job of describing the habitats through which it passes, and its illustrations will help you identify some of the most common plants and animals you are likely to encounter. The brochure directs you to the tidal flats and Bird Shoal after stop 11. Bird Shoal comes by its name honestly, so bring binoculars and a bird guide if you enjoy birding.

The tidal flats near Bird Shoal extend over two miles from Beaufort Inlet to Horse Island. Much of what you would expect to find on a tidal flat is here. Birds are always present. Waders (egrets, herons, and ibises), surface searchers/probers (sandpipers, plovers, and dowitchers) and aerial searchers (terns, gulls, and pelicans) are always present, although the species and numbers will differ throughout the year. Burrowing animals will also be seen. Most obvious are the fiddler and hermit crabs that occur in great abundance. In early summer there are so many fiddler crabs that they make a noise like wind as they rustle through the grass on the edges of the flats. Deeper-burrowing worms and wormlike animals are less obvious, but their presence is signaled by the volcano- and funnel-shaped mounds and cavities they build while feeding, and by the piles of fecal material they leave behind (these are *not* fastidious beasts).

The food chain that supports the abundant wildlife of intertidal flats is even harder to see. We now know from studies of isotope chemistry that many commercially important estuarine animals (such as clams, oysters, and crabs) do not rely on marsh grass for their food supply. Instead, they eat algae. If you look carefully, you can find their food. The brown, golden, or green coating on the sand surface is algae. These plants bind the sand grains together and serve as food for many herbivores. Sometimes you can actually catch an animal eating this stuff. Snails do it constantly, but careful observations of fiddler crabs will show that they, too, eat algae. They scrape up surface sand with their claws, roll it around with the mouthparts extracting the algae, and leave behind the little barrel-shaped sand lumps you see around their burrows. The algae that compose the base of this food chain form fairly obvious mats on the surface of the flats. The mats are complex, as they contain many different species and types of microscopic algae, protozoans, crustaceans, and worms, but together these make a nutritious food source for the tidal-flat animals. The tidal-flat animals themselves make nutritious food for birds, fish, and humans. We do not eat many hermit crabs, but blue crabs feed on the flats along with oysters, clams, and frequently eaten finfish such as spot, croaker, sea bass, sea trout, bluefish, red drum, and flounder. If you visit the flats at high tide, you may see some of these animals "doing lunch" together. I saw a large black sea bass feeding on the flats on my last visit there.

Rachel Carson Estuarine Reserve is by no means the only place to visit intertidal and shallow seafloor habitats along this coast. Together, salt marshes, intertidal sand flats, sea grass beds, and sandy unvegetated seafloor occupy nearly all of the edge and bottom areas of Core and Back Sounds. There are some oyster reefs in the creeks and at the periphery of some marshes, but they are visible only at low tides. The distribution of the major habitat types is different in different areas. Salt marshes are abundant in Back Sound, where one complex called Middle Marsh occupies an area 1.5 miles long and ¾ mile wide. Extensive marshes also occur behind old inlet sites on Shackleford Banks. Similarly, extensive marshes extend from Core Sound into the sound east of Harkers Island, Davis, Stacy, and Cedar Island. Tidal flats are most common near present and recent inlets, but they occur in some bays as well. Sea grass beds and sandy seafloors occur together throughout the region. Sea grass beds are more common in Core Sound than in Back Sound, but the reverse is true for sandy seafloor. All of these areas are accessible to waders.

Core Banks

Core Banks is the longest unmodified section of shoreline in North Carolina. It has never been "improved" by construction of man-made dunes along its beach. Core Banks is also one of the lowest, thinnest, and most frequently overwashed barrier island complexes along our coast (see figure 29). Core Banks looks today like the Outer Banks must have looked in the late 1920s, before the Civilian Conservation Corps began constructing the palisade dunes that protect most of these banks now. The habitats on Core Banks tend to be quite similar from one end to the other. Someone familiar with Core Banks has told me that "when you've seen 50 feet of this bank, you've seen it all." That may not *quite* be true, but it is more true than one might think of the 40-plus miles of island between Cape Lookout and Ocracoke Inlet. Drum Inlet separates Core Banks into northern and southern halves, with the northern half further subdivided by two periodic inlets (Swash and Whalebone) into three named islands (Pilontary, Sand, and Portsmouth). Portsmouth Island has habitable land and an abandoned village facing Ocracoke Inlet.

The major habitat types on Core Banks are beach and berm, dune, maritime grassland, and salt marsh. The beach and berm have all the features described in Chapter 1. The sand-sharing system is well developed all along Core Banks. Nearshore bars are almost always present off the beach, and ridge and runnel systems indicative of onshore sand transport are common throughout spring and summer. Eroded dunefaces and interdune overwash deposits are as common as offshore bars, indicating that sand moves landward from the beach as well as seaward. The dunes are low, except in a few areas where taller experimental dunes were made by humans earlier in this century. The dunes are usually only sparsely vegetated. Between and behind the dunes are overwash deposits colonized by maritime grasslands that can be subdivided into several overlapping types. Woodlands and fresh marsh areas occur in only a few places, but salt marsh occupies the intertidal zone on the sound side all along the banks.

The plant communities of Core Banks have been the subject of a classic study of barrier island dynamics carried out by Paul and Melinda Godfrey and published by the U.S. Park Service in 1976. Although twenty years old, this work remains important because few unmodified barrier islands have been studied, and the Godfreys were able to document the previously unappreciated role of overwash events in sustaining barrier islands under both normal and storm conditions. At first it seems surprising that sand washing over and across an island can preserve it from destruction by hurricane winds and waves, yet that is what happens on Core Banks.

The Godfreys analyzed old navigation charts and aerial photographs to describe the changing shape of Core Banks over a century. They found that the island had remained low, thin, and surprisingly constant in position throughout that time. The Godfreys also conducted their fieldwork soon after the U.S. Army Corps of Engineers first surveyed the banks and thus were able to use survey benchmarks to assess the vertical changes in land height above sea level during a decade that had both "typical" weather and several major storms (both hurricanes and northeasters). The Godfreys found that a single major storm could erode as much as 120 feet of sand from the beach by high tides and waves overwashing the dunes and spreading sand over backdune grasslands to depths of as much as a foot (see figure 29). They found that the plants that lived on these grasslands were fully capable of growing through the added sand to recolonize the surface and restore the grasslands. They also found that normal weather conditions gradually brought sand back to the beach, thereby restoring it to its original position. The island was found to absorb storms as sand moved from beach to grassland, but it regained its wide beach after a storm. The grassland, however, retained some of its newly overwashed sand—an unquestionable advantage for island stability in a period of rising sea level. Core Banks has retreated landward relatively little in the last century—quite a difference from the situation on the stabilized Outer

Banks farther north, where beach recession rates can be up to 7 feet per year.

The plants of Core Banks are less diverse and often cover the soil less completely than do those in other, less frequently overwashed barrier islands, such as nearby Shackleford Banks. The beach berm vegetation is widely scattered but includes sea rocket, dune spurge, and the rare seabeach amaranth, all of which grow through lines of drift stranded on the berm. The only perennial plant that occurs on the beach berm is sea oats, and even it occurs more abundantly in the dunes. The dunes also contain plants that spread widely across the maritime grasslands that occupy interdune overwash deposits. These plants include salt meadow cordgrass and pennywort. The maritime grasslands that develop on overwash deposits are widely colonized by salt meadow cordgrass, seaside goldenrod, pennywort, and broomsedge. These four plants also occur in "closed" grasslands where plants cover more than 50 percent of the sand surface. The Godfreys found that these closed grasslands have the largest amount of plant material among the dunes and marshes of Core Banks — an average of over 3 pounds per square yard. In most areas the maritime grasslands grade into high salt marsh, where salt meadow cordgrass and seaside goldenrod are found mixed with sea ox-eye and black needlerush. None of these plants extends into the low, regularly flooded salt marsh that occurs along the edge of the sound. Here, the typical salt marsh plants dominate — smooth cordgrass, spike grass, glasswort, and marsh lavender.

Less frequent plant associations on Core Banks include thickets, fresh marshes, and woodlands. Thickets are fairly typical in being formed primarily of marsh elder, wax myrtle, silverling, and red cedar. Fresh marshes are rare, but when they occur, they include cattails and saw grass, along with black needlerush, sedges, and seaside mallow. Woodlands on Core Banks are rarely fully developed maritime forests, such as those on Ocracoke and Hatteras Islands to the north or Shackleford and Bogue Banks to the south. Most woodlands on Core Banks are comprised of cedar and pine and lack the oaks, persimmons, hollies, bays, and dogwoods that often occur in forests on less overwashed barrier islands in the southeast.

My two favorite places to visit Core Banks are at Portsmouth Island and near Cape Lookout. Portsmouth is accessible by water taxi from Ocracoke. Cape Lookout can be reached either by water taxi or by summer ferry from both Harkers Island and Beaufort. The channels across Core Sounds shallows are relatively well marked, but be cautious in your own boat because sudden rising winds can create sizable waves very quickly in these shallow waters.

Portsmouth Island

Portsmouth Island is the widest part of Core Banks (see figure 27). The mile and a half of low-lying sand at the northeast end of the banks appears to have been built up from sand accumulated in the tidal deltas of Ocracoke Inlet. A walk across the island from the sound traverses extensive salt marshes, low-lying land supporting maritime forest, and the abandoned village of Portsmouth (see figure 31) as well as freshwater marshes in interridge swales and a huge sand flat.

The Portsmouth Island sand flat is very large and unusual. It is almost 1 mile wide and 5 miles long. Extensive sand flats such as this do not normally occur on coastlines with tidal ranges of less than 3 feet, and they are best developed in areas with tidal ranges greater than 6 feet. The presence of this huge sand flat on Portsmouth Island is an enigma, but it is probably explained by the large sand supply built up in and around Ocracoke Inlet. Ocracoke Inlet (just north of the sand flat) is the only inlet on the Outer Banks that has been open continuously throughout recorded history. It was a major entry into North Carolina's coastal sounds and estuaries in colonial times — first for pirates and smugglers (Blackbeard, the famous pirate also known as Captain Teach or Drummond, was killed by British seamen in Ocracoke Inlet in 1718). Later, ships supplying revolutionary war armies used the inlet, and after the war the inlet became important as a transshipment site for materials used for developing the land resources of North Carolina and southern Virginia. The village of Portsmouth was established around Fort Granville in the mid-1750s and, together with Ocracoke, played a major role in the maritime commerce of North Carolina for the next century. The sand built up in the inlet's channel made local pilots essential for oceangoing ships to cross the flood-tide delta. The sand buildup eventually sounded the death knell for

Figure 31. Portsmouth Island salt marshes; marshes within Portsmouth Village. Note maritime forest in the background.

Portsmouth's role in maritime commerce because the tortuous channels through Ocracoke Inlet were quickly abandoned for the clearer channels of Hatteras and Oregon Inlets that were opened by the hurricane of 1846. Some of the sand that made, and still makes, navigating Ocracoke Inlet difficult appears to have come ashore to form the extraordinary sand flat on Portsmouth Island.

The sand flat on Portsmouth supports extensive communities of algae during the warm months. This algae seems not to be heavily grazed by snails and other large herbivores but does support populations of small crustaceans that are fed on by sandpipers and other birds that probe for food in the algae and the underlying sediment. The productivity and ecology of algal mats have been studied by Hans Paerl of the University of North Carolina at Chapel Hill. He finds their rate of photosynthesis to be greater than that of estuarine waters, and in some cases it is as high as that of salt marshes. This is possible because the algae are small, exposed to full sunlight, and supplied by nutrients from underlying sediments and bacterial communities. Thus, these undramatic-looking mats provide considerable amounts of energy-rich organic matter to coastal ecosystems. These mats are complex chemically because they also have the ability to take gaseous nitrogen out of the air and convert it into organic nitrogen compounds. This process is called nitrogen fixation. The fact that both photosynthesis and nitrogen fixation occur simultaneously in these thin mats is surprising because oxygen produced as a by-product of photosynthesis (see Chapter 1) usually poisons the enzymes required for nitrogen fixation. A close look at the mats will show you how this problem is solved. The topmost surface of the mat has green algae carrying out photosynthesis, but just below that surface layer the sand is black, indicating an absence of free oxygen. If you smell a sample of the black sand, you will detect the characteristic rotten-egg smell of hydrogen sulfide, indicating that subsurface bacteria are breaking down sulfate (SO_4) to produce oxygen for metabolism and H_2S as a waste product (see Chapter 1, figure 13). Thus, the sand flat provides good examples of both geological and geochemical phenomena — something to ponder as you hike across it.

Beyond Portsmouth's sand flat there is an oceanside dune ridge that supports a maritime grassland of several plant species. This grassland has extensive stands of American beach grass on the ocean side of the dune.

Probably the most interesting feature of Portsmouth Island for most visitors is the abandoned village. This village is in a special historic zone of the park, as is the Cape Lookout Lighthouse farther south. There are several houses, a church, and an 1896 coast guard station being preserved for visitors to see. Walking among these structures is a little like entering a time warp. One keeps waiting for people in turn-of-the-century clothes to emerge and begin their daily activities. It is worth a trip to Portsmouth for that experience alone.

Cape Lookout

The Cape Lookout area has much to recommend it for nature study. Beach features are well illustrated across a spectrum of wave energy regimes. Some beaches face east toward the high energy of the open Atlantic. Others face west toward lower wave energy behind Cape Lookout. Still others face the low-wave energy waters of Cape Lookout Bight. The dunes near the cape are small but numerous and reasonably well vegetated. There are forests, mostly pine, but with a few oaks beginning to grow among them. Salt marshes are well developed, and sea grass beds and sand flats occur in Core Sound and Barden Inlet (see figure 32). All can be reached by wading. Birding is excellent, as species common at capes, inlets, dunes, forests, marshes, and tidal flats all occur, and many nest on the protected spits and spoil islands of the national seashore. The area benefits aesthetically from the presence of the diamond-painted lighthouse built in 1859.

One of the most interesting aspects of the Cape Lookout area is the cape itself. Here is one of the four places where the sandy Carolina coast makes a right-angle turn (Capes Hatteras, Fear, and Romain are the others). No one knows why they do this, but few, if any, areas in the world are similar. The current shape of Cape Lookout is also interesting, as it illustrates both natural shoreline dynamics and the unexpected impact of human coastal structures. Prior to 1915, Cape Lookout was a long, narrow landform extending more than 3 miles south of the lighthouse, but nowhere wider than ½ mile. In 1915 a rock jetty was built at the widest point to increase the size of the harbor of refuge inshore of the cape. The shoreline changed dramatically as a result. Now Cape Lookout extends less than two miles south of the lighthouse and is over 1.5 miles wide, as Power Squadron Spit continues to extend north of the jetty (see figure 32).

Access. Access to Cape Lookout and other areas of Core Banks is by boat or ferry. The National Seashore grants permission for ferries and will provide a list on request; call (919) 728-2250, or write to them at 131 Charles Street, Harkers Island, NC 28531. Seashore personnel will also send a visitors packet of information and brochures and will do their best to answer questions and help you plan your trip. They asked me to remind readers, however, that they are no better at predicting weather than is anyone else. At the time of this writing, the National Seashore had approved eleven ferry services, two from Ocracoke to Portsmouth, one each from Atlantic and Davis, four from Harkers Island, and three from Beaufort. Many of

Figure 32. Cape Lookout and its elongating spit.

these services provide land tours as well as water transportation; three can transport large vehicles such as campers, pickups, and all-terrain vehicles. Two services even rent cottages on Core Banks for overnight use. All services seem to change frequently, so visitors need to identify the service they need and make reservations for it soon after they can specify the time they wish to come. The ferry services normally operate from April through November, but most require some minimum number of people to justify a trip.

Shackleford Banks

No discussion of natural areas near Beaufort would be complete without a discussion of Shackleford Banks, the latest addition to the Cape Lookout National Seashore. This 8-mile-long south-facing barrier island is easily accessible, has an interesting history, and has the best-developed freshwater marsh, interdune wet slack, and maritime forest habitat in the National Seashore (see figure 33). Until recently I would have said that I had saved the best for last by describing Shackleford at the end of this section. Unfortunately, I cannot quite say that in 1996, because horses have over-grazed the island, and chiggers and ticks are prevalent.

Shackleford became part of the National Seashore in 1976. At that time it was home to sheep, goats, cows, and horses. All had been left on the island by early residents or had been brought there for grazing by local people. The park service proposed removing this livestock so as to return the island to its pre-grazed state. This plan was relatively uncontroversial when applied to the sheep, goats, and cows, but as a professor friend has said, "The horses had a better lobby." Public sentiment clearly favored retaining the horses within the seashore. These horses were not direct descendants of Spanish horses from the colonial era (like the herds of Corolla and Ocracoke farther north) and had been part of Shackleford's ecology only since the 1940s. Nonetheless, they were picturesque; they reminded people of other, more publicized island horses, such as "Misty" of Chincoteague; and they were there when the seashore was established. After several public meetings, the park service decided that the horses could stay. In the mid-1970s there were about 50 horses; by 1996 there were over 240. The good news is that you can see horses whenever you visit the island. The bad news is that if you visit the island interior, you are very likely to take away an unwelcome souvenir in the form of a chigger or tick. My students have taken to calling Shackleford "Chigger Island" in their field trip reports. Chiggers and ticks are not an insurmountable obstacle to nature study on Shackleford. You can reduce the numbers that jump on you by using insect repellent and tucking pant cuffs into your socks; you can find and remove all but the smallest ticks by checking your body periodically while being exposed; and you can rid yourself of chiggers by coating the itching bites they cause with nail polish (clear is best; pink makes you look weird).

The horses are also responsible for overgrazing Shackleford's grass-lands. The evidence is clear: not only are the grasses truncated by having been bitten, but horse droppings contain obvious remnants of dune and forest plants. The park service has confirmed the role of horse grazing by

Figure 33. Maritime forest near the old graveyard on Shackleford Banks.
Photograph by Scott Taylor.

carrying out experiments in which horses were excluded from fenced areas of grassland. Within the fences, the grasses grew taller and were accompanied by a much greater diversity of other plants than occurred in grazed areas outside the fences. The park service is well aware of the overgrazing and insect problems caused by Shackleford's horses and plans to reduce the herd to about 90. When the park service plan is carried out, the interior of Shackleford will once again become as pleasant as it is beautiful to visit.

There is much that is worth seeing on Shackleford. Three types of barrier island habitats (maritime forests, freshwater marshes, and interdune wet slacks) are better represented here than anywhere else in this coastal section. The lasting impact of human use of the land is illustrated by historic evidence of a large dunefield that now occupies an area that was once a maritime forest, the startling differences in plant diversity and abundance inside and outside fenced areas that prevent horses from grazing, and the sand spit elongating into Beaufort Inlet at the west end of the island.

Maritime forests once occupied all of Shackleford. The 1888 chart of the area shows Shackleford Banks as a heavily forested westward extension of Core Banks (Barden Inlet was opened to separate them in 1933 at the urging of Congressman Barden). Maritime forests are now found only on the northern (inland) side of the island, but the forests are mature, well developed, and worth visiting. The grazing horses keep them free of undergrowth and almost parklike in appearance (see figure 33). The vines remain, however, so be on the lookout for the spiny catbrier and rash-producing poison ivy. The three most abundant trees in Shackleford's forests are live oak, red cedar, and American holly, although loblolly pine, other oaks (laurel and willow), sweet and red bay, dogwood, and wax myrtle also occur. Many grasses and other flowering plants occur in the woods, including partridgeberry and nettles. The live oaks are usually draped with Spanish moss and decorated with resurrection fern. A particularly nice place to visit this forest is back from the inshore-facing beach about 1 mile east of the ferry dock. Here the forest is open, well developed, and the site of an old graveyard where inhabitants of the nineteenth-century town of Diamond City are buried. Seaward of the graves, a path leads through the forest, into a thicket, and into the dunes. Other woodland areas are similar and extend for almost 7 of the island's 8-mile northern shore.

Freshwater marshes are interspersed with forests along Shackleford's northern shoreline, but the largest and easiest to visit is Mullet Pond, almost directly inland of the ferry dock. The two most abundant plants are cattails in the open water and rushes along the shore. Other typical freshwater marsh plants such as saw grass, several sedges (*Fimbristylis*, broom, and white top), morning glory, and marshmallow also can be found. Freshwater marshes also occur within forested areas. These are hard to get to, as they are usually surrounded by dense thicket, but botanists have found them to have the richest flora on the island.

Interdune wet slack habitats also occur in many places on Shackleford but are most accessible between the ferry dock and the beach (see figure 34). These level areas form among the dunes when winds blow sand away to expose the top of the water table. The moist sand remains in place and is rapidly overgrown by plants that further protect the sand from wind, even when the water table drops during dry periods. Plant growth and death gradually adds organic matter to the wet slack sediments, creating soil where once there was only sand. When Shackleford was occupied by humans (about 600 people lived there in 1885), these wet slack areas were farmed. Wet slacks differ from freshwater marshes in that they only have standing water during wet periods. You may see the slacks surrounded by a drift line, indicating a recent high water, but usually the slack soils themselves will be dry. The most abundant plants that live naturally in these areas are salt meadow cordgrass, sedges (*Fimbristylis*, broom, three-square, and others), and rushes (black needle and others), although the ubiquitous pennywort and several other herbaceous plants often occur. These plants have been devilishly hard to find and identify in the mid-1990s because of grazing by the horses.

Vegetation on the dunes around the wet slacks is much like that found on Core Banks except for the stumps of "ghost trees" that stick up through the sand. These trees, the nature of the wet slacks, and the extensive dunefield that surrounds them are part of the story that explains why nineteenth-century bankers abandoned Shackleford. The ghost trees are all that remain of the seaward half of Shackleford's forest. The trees were killed when dunes that had been overgrazed by livestock were activated by winds in the major hurricane of 1899. The dunes moved landward, covering what remained of the forests after much had been cut for use in houses, boats, and cooking. The storm surge of the same hurricane flooded both the houses and the fields. Many of the houses had been built to withstand the high water, but the fields could not be used for crops until years of rainfall had flushed out seawater that drained into the wet slacks. The 1899 storm was the worst of several that struck Carteret County in the late nineteenth century and was the final blow for permanent human settlement on Shackleford. Nineteenth-century fishing/farming technology was not able to support a permanent village on Shackleford. One can legitimately wonder if twentieth-century technology can sustain permanent settlement on other southeastern U.S. barrier islands where it is currently being applied.

Figure 34. An interdune wet slack on Shackleford Banks.
Photograph by Scott Taylor.

Inlets

There are three major inlets along the Ocracoke-to-Beaufort section of the North Carolina coast (see figure 27). All have been modified by human intervention. Barden Inlet was dug through Core Banks in 1933, Drum Inlet was blasted open in 1971, and Beaufort Inlet, although old, is regularly dredged to keep the navigation channel open to the state port in Morehead City. There are two, and sometimes more, occasional inlets on northern Core Banks; the named ones are Whalebone and Swash.

Flow through these inlets is controlled by the volume of water driven to and from shore by rising and falling tides — a volume known as the tidal prism. The microtidal setting of the central North Carolina coast generates a relatively small tidal prism. As a result, inlets have an impact on one another because only a finite amount of water flows back and forth through all of them together. Beaufort Inlet channel is dredged to a depth of 40 feet and a width of 400–600 feet. Therefore, most of the tidal water that enters and leaves this coast does so through Beaufort Inlet. Barden Inlet has a narrow channel that shifts laterally and shoals to depths of 6 feet or less in several places. The dredged channel to Harkers Island is less than 80 feet wide and 5½ feet deep. Drum Inlet has shoaled steadily since 1971. It was reported to be only 2 feet deep at low tide in 1975 and remains shallow. Both Drum and Barden Inlets could close completely in a period of rapid sediment movement. Drum Inlet would in all likelihood have already done so were it not for the maintenance dredging. Barden Inlet almost closed in the March storm of 1991, when wind blew from the south at over 60 mph for more than 6 hours. Wind-driven waves and currents moved along the south shore of Shackleford, eroded the southeast tip of the island, and deposited tons of sediment in Barden Inlet.

Some natural features of inlets are observable at all three major inlets. All have elongating spits moving into them from at least one side, all have well-developed flood-tide deltas, and all have some evidence of ebb-tide deltas. My favorite place to observe inlet features is at Barden, in part because lots of other things are observable on the same trip (see Cape Lookout, above), and in part because the inlet is accessible and safe at all tidal stages (Beaufort Inlet has potentially dangerous currents on falling tides that could carry unwary swimmers or slow-moving boats out to sea). Drum Inlet is difficult to get to by any means other than personal boat.

Access. Barden Inlet is accessible by the same methods as Cape Lookout (see above). The lobes of the ebb- and flood-tide deltas at Barden Inlet are readily observable by wading from either Core or Shackleford Banks. The elongating spit is the east end of Shackleford. Barden Inlet is also interesting because it is not very old, and evidence of its antecedents is readily observable as salt marsh peat on the beaches facing each other. Once this peat was part of a continuous salt marsh that extended all the way across the area now occupied by the inlet. Nature seems to favor an inlet in this area, however. Another inlet (called South Core) once occurred just east of the south end of the channel from Harkers Island. The marshes east of the channel are built on the flood-tide delta of that old inlet.

Beaufort through Bogue Sound: A Moderately Developed Shore

The inshore shoreline from Beaufort to Cape Carteret and both shores of Bogue Banks are moderately developed for residential use; by that I mean it is moderately difficult to find a place from which you cannot see evidence of human habitation. Nevertheless, there is much nature still to be observed along this 25-mile stretch of shoreline. The good news is that much of it is easily accessible by car and foot; the bad news is that you are rarely far enough away from civilization so that you cannot see or hear it. Lots of people use this shore for lots of different activities. It remains a startling juxtaposition of cultures to watch recreating jet skiers zip past traditional fishermen raking clams in the shallows of Bogue Sound, but such meetings are increasingly common in the rapidly changing culture of western Carteret County.

The coastal zone in this area is similar to that from Beaufort to Cape Lookout. The zone is made up of a south-facing barrier island at the ocean, backed by a shallow sound, with marsh-bordered estuaries and creeks draining the high land of the interior (see figure 35). The most obvious difference is in human habitation rate. Where Core and Shackleford Banks are essentially undeveloped, Bogue Banks has been developed for residential use from one end to the other. The inland shore of Bogue Sound and the uplands are also developed, although at a density lower than on the beachface. To see nature, not development, you mostly have to go up the creeks or visit nature trails at state parks and on the islands in Bogue Sound.

Five-Star Features. There are five natural sites that I consider of particular note in the Beaufort and Bogue Sound areas. Three of these are in or on the boundary of Croatan National Forest; the fourth is a state natural area. The five sites are (1) Millis Road Longleaf Pine Savanna and its neighboring pocosins; (2) Patsy Pond and the rare coastal fringe sandhill community that surrounds it; (3) the Newport River swamp forest and tidal freshwater marsh; (4) Fort Macon State Park's dune, thicket, and maritime forest communities; and (5) the Theodore Roosevelt State Natural Area and North Carolina Aquarium at Bogue Banks. None of these are seacoast features. None of the seacoast along this coast can be called natural; all of it has been modified to enhance or preserve residential and recreational developments. The description of natural sites begins with a driving tour that includes the Newport River, Millis Road, and Patsy Pond sites, then proceeds to some attractive creek, sound, and Bogue Sound island sites before finishing up on Bogue Banks with descriptions of Fort Macon State Park and Theodore Roosevelt State Natural Areas.

Geologically, the coastal zone west of Morehead City is only superficially similar to that farther north and east. The difference is that the underlying material gets progressively older as you move westward. Land to the east of Pine Knoll Shores and the western edge of Morehead City is built on sedimentary underpinnings that formed less than 5 million years ago. West of Pine Knoll Shores to Indian Beach these underpinnings, known as the Bogue Banks sequence, formed in the late Miocene — 11.5 to 13.5 million years ago. From Indian Beach to Emerald Isle the underpinnings are still earlier; they were formed in the middle Miocene (15 to 16 million years ago). The westernmost portion of Bogue Banks has underpinnings formed 17.5 to 19 million years ago (in the early Miocene). South and west of Bogue Inlet the coastal underpinnings formed in the

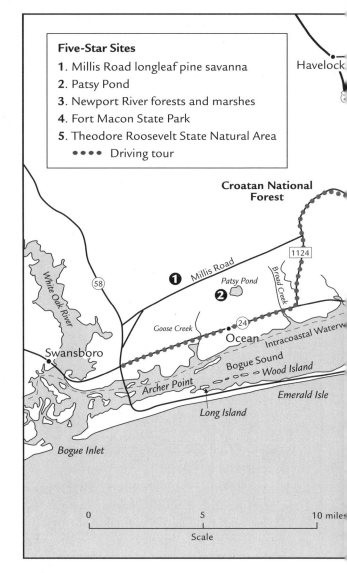

Figure 35. Beaufort through Bogue Sound. Base map from North Carolina Coastal Boating Guide.

Five-Star Sites

1. Millis Road longleaf pine savanna
2. Patsy Pond
3. Newport River forests and marshes
4. Fort Macon State Park
5. Theodore Roosevelt State Natural Area
●●●● Driving tour

Havelock

Croatan National Forest

1124

White Oak River

58

❶ Millis Road

Patsy Pond ❷

Broad Creek

Goose Creek

24

Ocean

Intracoastal Waterw

Swansboro

Bogue Sound

Wood Island

Archer Point

Long Island

Emerald Isle

Bogue Inlet

0   5   10 miles

Scale

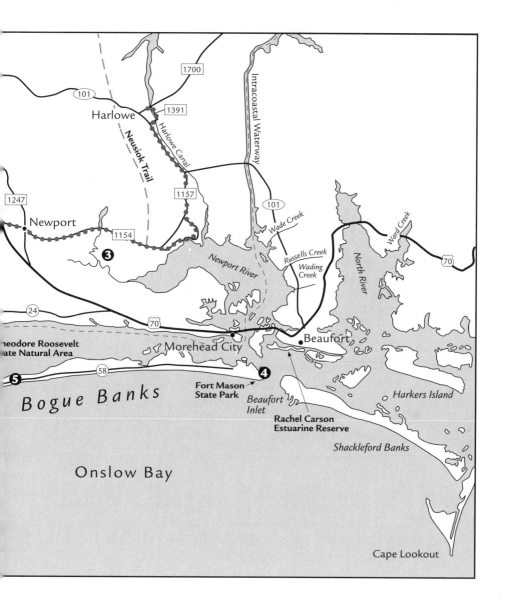

Harlowe

Newport

Harkers Island

Theodore Roosevelt
State Natural Area

Morehead City

Beaufort

Fort Mason
State Park

Beaufort
Inlet

Rachel Carson
Estuarine Reserve

Shackleford Banks

Bogue Banks

Onslow Bay

Cape Lookout

Neusiok Trail

Harlowe Canal

Intracoastal Waterway

Newport River

Wade Creek

Russells Creek

Wading
Creek

Ward Creek

North River

Oligocene — more than 24 million years ago. The differences in the age of underpinnings along Bogue Banks are not obvious at the surface; they can only be detected in geological cores through the island sediments. Sand brought here less than 10,000 years ago covers over the older material and keeps it from being exposed at the land surface. Farther south, the age of the underpinnings is more obvious because the recent sand sheet is not so thick (see figure 2), and Oligocene and earlier materials appear on the beaches.

Another difference is that the recent (Holocene) sand sheet is configured differently on Bogue Banks than in other barrier islands along this coast. The widest parts of Bogue Banks have a ridge and swale topography created by significantly younger beach ridges and the low-lying areas between them. This topography is best expressed in the towns of Pine Knoll Shores and Emerald Isle and resembles that found near Buxton on Hatteras Island. In Emerald Isle the oldest ridge extends beyond Archer Point to form the string of islands extending east to Wood Island (see figure 35). The age of this ridge is in doubt. Some authors say it is as old as 5,000 years; others say no more than 1,400. All agree, however, that successive ridges have built seaward as alongshore sand transport, tides, and collapsing waves brought more sand to the beach, and winds formed some of it into new primary dunes. As each new dune line was added, the island shoreface moved seaward, a process called shoreface progradation by geologists. There is little evidence of such parallel beach ridges on Core or Shackleford Banks because most of Core and Shackleford have stayed in the same place for many years.

Bogue Banks is also unusual in being wider and having more freshwater habitat than either Core or Shackleford. Both features are a function of the successive beach ridges adding dune and interdune habitat as they form. Freshwater habitat develops in the interdune lows, although little remains of it except in the Theodore Roosevelt State Natural Area. The ash-maple swamp forest and interridge salt marsh of this area are described later. Archer Creek in Emerald Isle also drains an interridge low into Bogue Sound and forms the aquatic habitat that separates Archer Point from the main body of Bogue Banks.

A Driving Tour of Carteret County

Harlowe to Neusiok Trailhead Road

A useful way to begin a nature tour of Carteret County is to take advantage of its plethora of roads and drive across the range of habitats found there. The drive is rather indirect because neither roads nor creeks go straight across the habitat spectrum, but a drive from Harlowe to Emerald Isle will take you past all the habitat types and can be done easily, even with stops, in an afternoon.

The tour I recommend begins in the forest and farm uplands at the intersection of highway NC 101 and Adams Creek Road (SR 1700) in Harlowe. Proceed northeast on Adams Creek Road and cross Harlowe Canal — note the tall pine forest on the south side of the bridge and the view north along the canal to the marshes of Clubfoot Creek (a tributary of the Neuse River) in the distance. Continue north for 100 yards and turn right on Ball Farm Road (SR 1391), which parallels Harlowe Canal. If you want to put a boat into the canal, keep your eye out for an open lot beyond houses on the right — it has a ramp at its back right corner. Note also the fields of Ball Farm on both sides of the road. Continue south on Ball Farm Road, turning right where it does, and cross Harlowe Canal again — a kayak or canoe can be launched under the northwest corner of this bridge. Look up and down the canal to see typical upland forest of pine and mixed hardwoods (maple, gum, ash, oak, holly, and others). The forest is not much influenced by proximity to the sea, although at high tide the water near this bridge is often five parts per thousand salt ($\frac{1}{7}$ full-strength seawater).

After leaving Harlowe Canal, continue west to highway 101, turn left, and drive through fields and forest to the next road on the right (Old Wineberry Road — SR 1155). Stop at this intersection to observe the irregularly flooded salt marsh dominated by black needlerush on both sides of the road. If you want to see the transition of upland forest to salt marsh along the canal, park and walk east on highway 101 and look north. To see the same transition from your car, look west from Old Wineberry Road. In both cases you will see black needlerush marsh extending into pine forest with dead and dying trees. The trees are dying because rising sea level and storms flood the upland forest with water too salty for pines to tolerate (at high tide Harlowe Canal near the highway 101 bridge can have a salt content one-half that of seawater).

Continue south on Old Wineberry Road, watching for other examples of the marsh-to-forest transition as you cross creeks along the way. Take the first paved public road to the left. This is Mill Creek Road (SR 1154), but it was unsigned when I last visited (it intersects Old Wineberry Road about 2.3 miles south of highway 101). Follow Mill Creek Road southeast, then southwest, watching first for creeks with the salt-marsh-to-upland-forest transition and second for Dowty Road on the left. Dowty Road leads down to Harlowe Creek south of the canal. It is a good place to observe salt marshes of both irregularly and regularly flooded varieties. There usually are picturesque wooden fishing boats tied up off the beach. You can launch small boats here at high tide, but when the tide is low, there is 100 feet of mudflat between you and the water.

Continue along Mill Creek Road, noting the views to Harlowe Creek and the salt-marsh-to-forest transition when they occur to left and right. The road curves to the right near the mouth of Harlowe Creek and soon opens up views of the mid-reaches of the Newport River on the left. The river is very shallow at this point. Charts show 4–6 feet of water in the middle of the estuary, but those areas are more than a mile from shore. Do not be fooled by observations at high tide; there are large areas of water less than a foot deep, with oysters exposed at a few places and unexposed elsewhere. You will see commercial fishing boats anchored offshore. The captains of these vessels have what navigators call "local knowledge." Shallow draft boats can manage the Newport, but slow speed and extreme caution are needed for those new to the area. The good news is there are several places from which kayaks or canoes can be launched along this stretch of Mill Creek Road as well as at a launching ramp off SR 1156 in Mill Creek Village.

Continue west on Mill Creek Road, exploring roads to the water as you go. Pass the southern intersection of Mill Creek and Old Wineberry Roads at the edge of Mill Creek itself, then watch for the "Neusiok Trail" signs on both sides of the road before you get to the Carteret County waste-handling facility. The Neusiok Trail is a 20-mile-long hiking trail from the Newport to the Neuse River. It was built through cooperative efforts of the U.S. Forest Service, the Weyerhauser Company, and the Carteret County Wildlife Club. It traverses pine timberland, hardwood forest on old beach ridges, cypress-palmetto swamps, and pocosins (see Chapter 1). The swamps and bogs have been bridged by heroic volunteer efforts of the wildlife club members. These boardwalks make hiking through pocosins and swamp forests possible. Usually these boggy areas are almost impenetrable, and many have been drained for use in agriculture and silviculture; however, these habitats are well represented along the Neusiok Trail. The southern end of this trail begins down the gravel road south of SR 1154, just west of the waste-handling facility. The trail is recommended for cool-season walking because biting insects and snakes are less likely to be encountered.

Side Trip: Newport River Marshes
The gravel road to the Neusiok trailhead is worth a side trip even if you are not going to use the trail. Beyond the trailhead parking area there is a road leading through lovely maritime forest to the Newport River. There is a sandy boat ramp here that provides the best views of, and boat access to, the upstream marshes of the river. The water is actually deeper upstream than in the recently viewed mid-reaches of the Newport because sediments accumulate in the mid-reaches after being swept downstream during periods of high flow. Water 4 feet deep is typical of the upstream section that winds through salt marsh, fresh marsh, and swamp forest to the town of Newport (about 6 miles upstream) (see figure 36). The ramp can also be used as a pull-out spot for canoe/kayak trips down the Newport River, as boats of that size can be launched in the swamp forest section of the river near Newport (that is, into Deep Creek at its crossing with SR 1154 and into the river itself at its crossing with SR 1247 about one-half mile south of downtown). There is also a boat ramp where old US 70 (SR 1247) crosses the southwest prong of the Newport River south of town. The trip down the freshwater sections of the Newport River is one of the five-star environmental sites in this section of the coast.

Figure 36. Newport River forests and freshwater marshes.

Neusiok Trailhead Road to Millis Road Longleaf Pine Savanna

The driving tour continues west on SR 1154 from the Neusiok Trailhead Road toward Newport. The road passes through forests, over old beach ridges (note low sandy hills and the road that cuts through them), past an intriguing but heavily posted and fenced millpond, through increasingly dense residential areas, and ends in downtown Newport. Turn left at the T-intersection, go one block, cross the railroad tracks, turn right on old US 70 (now SR 1247), then left after one block onto SR 1124. Follow SR 1124 west, then south on Howard Boulevard, across US 70 onto Nine Foot Road, and follow it through areas of farmland and managed pinelands and across a series of bottomland hardwood forests alongside creeks beyond Holly Springs. Continue left at the intersection with Nine Mile Road past swamp forests and old beach ridges to Millis Road (on the right about 1.4 miles south of the Nine Mile Road intersection).

Millis Road passes through some of the best examples of longleaf pine savanna, pond pine woodland, and pocosin, all within about 3 miles of Nine Mile Road. The longleaf pine savanna begins about ½ mile down Millis Road, and it continues for almost a mile. It is a superb example of this type of community, with all the plants and most of the characteristic animals. Watch for the nesting trees for the endangered red-cockaded woodpecker marked with blue bands (see figure 37). The herb layer here is also representative, with the characteristic wire grass (the primary fuel for the fires that sustain this community) always in evidence. Other typical plants under the longleaf pines include sedges, daisylike wildflowers (composites), orchids, and lilies. The pond pine woodland community begins about 2.5 miles down Millis Road where part of Croatan Forest's pocosin wilderness area extends across the road. The pond pines here have a thick understory of typical pocosin plants such as titi, fetterbush, gallberries, and hollies, as illustrated in figure 37.

Side Trip: Broad Creek/Bogue Sound Sites
After observing the plant communities off Millis Road, return to Nine Mile Road, turn right, then turn right again where Nine Mile Road intersects with NC 24. Broad Creek is about ½ mile to the west. Broad Creek provides easy access to a forest-to-sound habitat transect because the Osprey Oaks Marina south of the highway offers a launching ramp as well as jet ski and small boat rentals. If you are tired of driving, you might consider a "water break" here and travel up and down Broad Creek. The trip is stunning. The creek winds through typical salt marsh north of the NC 24 bridge. Salt marsh cordgrass borders the water, with black needlerush dominating the irregularly flooded areas farther toward land. The land itself supports a surprisingly diverse plant community. A professional botanist living on the creek bank has identified over 118 species of plants on his 40-acre tract—a tract he has willed to the Nature Conservancy so that it will remain a natural area in perpetuity. Upstream the creek bank flora changes with declining salt content, as explained in the description of downeast creeks. Areas of spike grass and glasswort occupy the water's edge as salt marsh cordgrass becomes less abundant. Eventually the salt-tolerant species give way to freshwater marsh dominated by

Figure 37. Longleaf pine savanna with banded nesting trees of red-cockaded woodpecker.

sedges including saw grass, common three-square, and retrorse flatsedge. The creek crosses the official "salt line" that divides responsibility for North Carolina fishery resources between the Wildlife Resources Commission (freshwater areas) and Marine Fisheries Commission. The line is marked with a yellow metal tag on a post. When I visited the Broad River on a high tide that had been forced upriver by a south wind, the salt content at the marker was about one-half that of full-strength seawater. This suggests that seawater encroaches farther upstream than is officially recognized. The impact of saltwater encroachment is seen in the forest, where trees at the marsh periphery are dead and dying.

Downstream from the NC 24 bridge, Broad Creek extends to Bogue Sound and the Intracoastal Waterway that runs through it. On a summer weekend that means lots of boat traffic, but escape can be found in the shallow waters south of the waterway and on the islands within them.

Several of the islands, including one just west of the mouth of Broad Creek, are nesting areas for colonial waterbirds such as egrets, herons, ibises, gulls, terns, pelicans, and black skimmers. An important nesting island is located about two miles south-southwest of Broad Creek. In 1993 this island held over 700 nests of egrets (great, snowy, and cattle) as well as over 600 nests of herons (little blue, tricolored, black crested night, and green) and 40 nests of white ibis. It is best not to disturb the nesting birds, both for their sake and yours (they peck and defecate — sometimes at the same time). There are lots of sandy islands, some with thicket and maritime forest vegetation, near Broad Creek, so you can enjoy the water close up and keep the birds at a distance.

Patsy Pond

On the north side of NC 24 just beyond Broad Creek there are "Foot Travel Only" forest service trails that extend into Croatan National Forest opposite Sandy Shores Road. These trails and the newly signed nature trail opposite the North Carolina Coastal Federation office in Ocean lead through a rare coastal-fringe sandhill community to Patsy Pond. This sandhill community has an open canopy of longleaf and loblolly pine with an understory of drought-resistant scrubby oaks of several species. The paths continue north past some low-lying areas that become ponds in wet seasons to the permanent Patsy Pond, with its water-lily-covered surface (see figure 38).

Patsy Pond is an example of a rare plant community that occurs widely farther south in permanently flooded sinkholes and upland depressions near the coast. The largest examples are the Boiling Springs Lakes in Brunswick County and areas within Carolina Beach State Park in New Hanover County, but Patsy Pond is the most accessible northern example of this community. The pond supports several types of water lily in its deepest areas, with concentric zones of emergent and wetland plants across the seasonally flooded areas that ring the pond itself. Several temporary ponds occur near Patsy Pond. These can be reached by the forest service trails that network the area. The temporary ponds have many of the same emergent and wetland plants that occur around Patsy Pond but, of course, do not support water lilies and other truly aquatic plants. The nature trail across from the North Carolina Coastal Federation Office traverses the same community types as the forest service trails but is newer, less littered, and better signed. I am personally partial to this trail because I saw my first red-cockaded woodpeckers along it in 1996.

Crossing Bogue Sound to Bogue Banks

The driving tour continues west on NC 24 beyond Broad Creek to Cape Carteret, where it turns south on NC 58 and crosses Bogue Sound on a high bridge. The view from the bridge is interesting and worth walking the bridge to see. There are many marsh islands close to the bridge. These islands show the multiply branched watercourses that bring tidal water into and out of marshes (see figure 39). These watercourses appear to most people as drainage systems, and of course they drain high-tide water off the marsh. Drainage is not what forms them, however; tidal flooding does that. As marshes are first established, they flood and drain to the outside. But as the marsh enlarges, extension of indentations in the marsh periphery lengthen by a process called apical growth. This process is driven by tide and wave energy eroding the marsh at the apex of the indentation. Gradually these indentations lengthen, bifurcate, and evolve into the complex watercourses you can see from the bridge.

The bridge also provides an unusual view of dredge spoil islands along the Intracoastal Waterway. Looking down on spoil islands is a little like looking down on someone with thinning hair. There is plenty of cover around the outside, but the substrate shows through at the crown. In this case the substrate is sediment dredged from the waterway. Nowadays this material is pumped to a ponding area surrounded by dikes within which the sand settles while the water that carried it is drained back into the sound. This creates a circumscribed and relatively high spoil island that eventually supports a maritime forest of pines and live oaks. Many of

Figure 38. Patsy Pond.

these islands are visible along the south shore of the waterway. In the bad old days, dredged material was simply pumped into shallow parts of the sound and allowed to settle; many of the marsh islands near the waterway are what remain of that era of uncontrolled disposal.

Finally, the bridge provides a panoramic seaward view of Bogue Banks and the ocean beyond. West of the bridge you can see Bogue Inlet, which is the mouth of the White Oak River. A geographic nomenclature point here: Bogue is the southernmost land mass referred to by North Carolinians as a "bank"; beyond Bogue Inlet, all offshore land masses are called "islands." Thus, common names and geology coincide. North Carolina's Outer Banks are made of relatively thick sheets of recently deposited sand over sedimentary underpinnings less than 5 million years old and separated from the mainland by a mile or more of open water; North Carolina's southern islands are made of thin sheets of recent sand covering sedimentary underpinnings at least 24 million years old and sep-

Figure 39. Complexly drained marsh island at west end of Bogue Sound. Bogue Inlet is on horizon at upper left.

arated from the mainland by salt marsh and/or narrow watercourses. The distant views east of the bridge include Bogue Sound stretching to the horizon. The distant views west of the bridge include Bear Island and the ancient shoreline of the Bogue Scarp. In the middle distance (3–6 miles away) you can make out Archer Point and the remnant beach ridge islands beyond.

Our driving tour concludes by crossing to Bogue Banks, where a sequence of beach ridges and interdune lows are easily seen. Continue to drive south on NC 58, turning east when it does, and turn left onto Lee Street beyond the shopping centers and municipal complex in downtown Emerald Isle. Lee Street leads over two dune ridges separated by the upstream end of Archer Creek and dead-ends at Sound Drive, where there is a public access point to Bogue Sound. The trail to the sound is over boardwalks and steps built over the dune ridge that makes up Archer

Point farther east. It is worth walking to the edge of Bogue Sound here because the view is fine and the dune ridge system shows up beautifully. A quick drive east on Sound Drive will convince you that the old beach ridges really do control the location of Archer Creek—the creek runs between them and you cannot cross it east of Lee Street. Continue south on Lee Street across additional dune ridges and interdune lows until you reach the ocean. Note the primary dune and the beach/berm system beyond, as well as the salt spray clipped forest canopy behind the secondary dune.

Side Trip: Beach Access in Emerald Isle

After completing the driving tour, many readers may feel like a swim or a beach walk. Emerald Isle has many beach and sound access sites. The good news is that almost every street off NC 58 leads to access on the ocean side, and many lead to access on the sound side as well. The bad news is that there are almost no public parking places near the access sites. Emerald Isle must have gotten a whopping volume discount on "No Parking Anytime" signs, as they seem more common than sea oats. Nevertheless, difficult does not mean impossible; persevere and you will find an unsigned verge somewhere where you can park and walk to a marked access site. Once on the beach, you can walk wherever you want within the intertidal zone—that is, on the wet beach. This is much easier on the ocean side than on the sound side, because the tidal range is three times as large on the ocean side, and the intertidal zone on the sound side is mostly salt marsh. The best sound-side option is to sit and observe. The waterfront access site on Cedar Street is well suited for this. It has a pier with benches and (miracle of miracles) at least three (count 'em, three) parking spaces.

Creeks and Rivers in Western Carteret County

There are fourteen creeks as well as the Newport River between Beaufort and Cape Carteret. One of the most natural of these, Broad Creek, was mentioned on the driving tour. If I had to choose one to explore, it would be Broad Creek, but I would also recommend some of the most natural and attractive creeks that can be reached from NC 101 north of Beaufort.

These include Russell Creek and Ware Creek. These creeks show the same type of marshes and marsh/forest transition that has been described for Broad and other creeks crossed on the driving tour. Regretfully, many other creeks along the Bogue Sound coastline have been developed so heavily that their original nature is hard to discern. Calico Creek in Morehead City and Taylor's Creek in Beaufort are used as outfalls by sewage treatment plants. Taylor's Creek is lined by filled land, docks, and dredge spoil islands. In Morehead City, Peletier and Spooners Creeks are lined by marinas and private docks. West of that, Gales Creek is a relatively natural area and is crossed by NC 24 near its upstream end. It provides a good view of the salt marsh/forest transition described in the driving tour.

Bogue Sound

Bogue Sound is a large, diverse, and recreationally heavily used body of water. Its shoreline is almost completely developed residentially, yet its water quality remains good enough for shellfish harvest in most places and good enough for swimming everywhere. Bogue Sound owes its high water quality to its proximity to Beaufort Inlet and the extensive tidal circulation it provides. Although Carteret County is a microtidal coastline, Beaufort Inlet has a large tidal volume that dominates those of Barden Inlet to the east and Bogue Inlet to the west. Maximum tidal current speeds through Beaufort Inlet are over 2 miles per hour and are driven by a tidal range of over 3 feet. This range drops to less than 2 feet at the western edge of Morehead City. This strong tidal current combines with the inshore decrease in tidal range to drive ocean water into Bogue Sound. The driving force is so strong that it replaces much of the water in the sound during each tidal cycle. As a result, pollutants associated with developed shorelines do not build up as they might in slower circulating water bodies. This tidal flushing of Bogue Sound is augmented by winds blowing from the northeast (the strongest winds in this region). Under these conditions, tidal water enters Beaufort Inlet and exits through Bogue Inlet throughout most of the tidal cycle. These conditions convert Bogue Sound into an inshore extension of the coastal ocean.

Bogue Sound has tidal flats and salt marshes. These have all the same characteristics as those described earlier in Core and Back Sounds. Most of Bogue Sound's marshes are along the shore, but some extend far into the sound. The most extensive of these occur just west of the bridge that carries NC 58 between Morehead City and Atlantic Beach. These marshes (see figure 44) have formed on the flood-tide delta sediments of Cheeseman's Inlet (an inlet that closed in the late eighteenth century) and its predecessors (geologic core data show that other inlets preceded Cheeseman's in this location). Other salt marshes and tidal flats occur around spoil islands, along the offshore extension of the Archer Point dune ridge off Emerald Isle, and west of the bridge that carries NC 58 between Emerald Isle and Cape Carteret. The natural marshes in this western Bogue Sound area have developed as a result of tidal prisms from Beaufort and Bogue Inlets meeting and dropping sediment at flood tide. It is an indication of the relative size of the tidal prisms of the two inlets that this nodal point is 20 miles from Beaufort Inlet and only 4 miles from Bogue Inlet.

Bogue Banks

Bogue Banks is 24 miles long and ranges in width from ¾ to less than ¹⁄₁₀ mile. Most of the banks has been developed for residential use. The level of environmental understanding used in this development has varied greatly with time and development goal. Orrin Pilkey, Jr., a geologist at Duke University; his father; and a colleague, William J. Neal, described the range of development on North Carolina's barrier islands in their 1979 book *Currituck to Calabash: Living with North Carolina's Barrier Islands*. These authors deserve credit for publicizing the folly of the most egregious errors of development. But some of the things they complain about can still be seen on Bogue Banks (dredge and fill development on salt marshes; buildings on top of the primary dune — the one that erodes when storms and high tides occur; dredging canals into the island interior to provide new "waterfront" while introducing saltwater into the island's freshwater table; and cutting roads through beach ridges to provide a route for seawater to cut a new inlet as it overwashes into the sound). Most of these practices have now been discontinued. All of us owe the Pilkeys and Bill Neal a debt of gratitude for the often uncomfortably public role they played in changing these practices. Modern development does not disrupt the primary dune or natural island topography. As a result, both the development and the island are protected by natural processes during storms and hurricanes. Unfortunately, much of the best of this new development is in private, gated communities where it cannot be seen by the public, other than as glimpsed from the road between NC 58 and Bogue Inlet.

There are three specific places on Bogue Banks that visitors interested in nature should see. These are Fort Macon State Park, Theodore Roosevelt State Natural Area, and Long Island north of Emerald Isle. Fort Macon State Park is the best place left to observe beach, dune, thicket, and live oak/red cedar maritime forest. Theodore Roosevelt State Natural Area is the best place to observe oak/pine maritime forest, swamp forest, and undeveloped ridge and swale topography. Long Island is the best place to observe a live oak maritime forest on a relict beach ridge. All of these are five-star sites on this section of coast. Visitors should also observe natural systems under and between developments. Bogue Banks was once a fairly diverse habitat. The area east of Hoop Pole Creek was once dominated by bare sand dunes and inlets. The inlets have been filled, but the dunes remain in Fort Macon and under the houses and condominiums of Atlantic Beach. From Hoop Pole Creek to Salter Path the island was, and in many areas still is, heavily forested with live oak/red cedar maritime forests close to the ocean; more diverse maritime forests dominated by laurel oak and loblolly pine on old dune ridges farther back from the ocean; and swamp forests dominated by red ash and red maple in the swales between the dune ridges. Most of the swamp forests have been filled, but remnants of the other two forest types occur along NC 58 and within developments in Pine Knoll Shores and Emerald Isle.

Fort Macon State Park

The easiest access to beach, dune, thicket, and live oak/red cedar maritime forest is in Fort Macon State Park. In addition, the fort is an interesting historic site and provides an unexcelled view of Beaufort Inlet. The first place to visit is the beach parking lot just beyond the park entrance. As you turn into the lot, look carefully at the live oak/red cedar maritime forest on the left. You may want to visit it on foot, but you can see many of its characteristics from your car. Note its low height (10–20 feet), its canopy of closely interwoven branches almost all of which reach to the same height, and the smooth, almost air-foil-shaped top of the canopy. These features are all caused by wind-driven salt spray stunting leaf and branch elongation above the canopy. This creates trees that look as though they have been bonsaied by some Bunyanesque Japanese gardener. This particular forest is quite open, but other forests of this type may have an understory of holly, red bay, and wild olive under the canopy.

The dunes north of the beach parking lot are natural; some are 25 to 30 feet high (see figure 40). Sea oats are abundant, as are beach grass, salt meadow cordgrass, broomsedge, and pennywort. The first three of these were studied here by H. J. Oosting and W. D. Billings in a classic study that showed sea oats to be far more resistant to salt spray than beach grass and broomsedge, and that this difference alone accounted for their distribution patterns. As you look at these dunes, note that sea oats occupy locations exposed to wind-driven salt (on the tops and ocean sides of the dunes) and beach grass and broomsedge are found in somewhat protected areas (behind and between dunes). These dunes also show evidence of blowouts where wind has blown away sand to create crescent-shaped, steep walled, unvegetated areas near the tops of ocean facing dunes. A walk through these dunes will let you observe these features as well as smaller-scale phenomena such as dune sand ripple marks, root and rhizome networks draped over blown-out areas, and pioneer thicket and maritime forest plants growing close to the ground in the wind shadow of the dunes.

The dunes between the parking lot and the beach are mostly man-made (note the sand fences), but they still support a fairly representative flora of sea rocket, pigweed, dune spurge, and sea oats.

The beach near Fort Macon has been nourished many times with dredge spoil from Beaufort Inlet and the state port at Morehead City. As a result the berm is artificially wide, and the natural beach biota is scarce to absent. The dredge spoil deposited on this beach is finer sand than would normally occur, so it tends to be moved offshore fairly quickly. As a result, you still may see mole crabs and coquina clams if you visit after

Figure 40. Fort Macon State Park: maritime grassland, shrub thicket, and dune.

dredge spoil has left the area. You should certainly see ghost crab burrows on the berm.

To complete your tour of Fort Macon State Park, drive to the entrance to Fort Macon itself and park in the lot about a mile east of the beach area. While driving between parking lots, note the hummocked dunefield resulting from low percentage of plant cover, as well as Beaufort Inlet and its erosion-preventing rock jetty. The path between the parking lot and the fort provides access to the Elliot Cones Nature Trail, a well-signed route through a maritime shrub thicket to higher ground where a live oak/red cedar maritime forest is getting started. The thicket is worth seeing because most of these habitats have been destroyed by development elsewhere on Bogue Banks. Note that the shrub thicket off the nature trail is lower than the maritime forest (mostly 5–10 feet high) and that the thicket canopy is neither smooth nor closed (plants grow to different heights, and there are openings in the canopy between them). The shrub thicket is made up of short woody plants such as elders, wax myrtle, and prickly ash (also called Hercules club), as well as young and/or stunted examples of live oak and red cedar. The "impenetrable jungle" aspect of the maritime shrub thicket is enhanced by the abundance of vines, including those of the rash-inducing poison ivy, the spiny greenbrier, and the relatively innocuous grape and pepper.

A visit to Fort Macon itself is worthwhile for the sense of history it evokes and for the view of Beaufort Inlet provided from its ramparts. As you will see, the fort was well designed to control Beaufort Inlet but was nearly defenseless against attack from the opposite side. Guess which side the Federal forces came from when they took the fort from the Confederates on 25 April 1862.

The view of Beaufort Inlet from Fort Macon's ramparts is superb. It is better than it was when the fort was being built in the 1820s and 1830s. Since the fort's construction, Shackleford Banks has elongated to the west, bringing the inlet ever closer to the fort. In 1866 the western tip of Shackleford was located near Mullet Pond, two miles east of its present location. The tip extended only 500 feet between 1866 and 1948 but picked up speed when more extensive dredging deepened the inlet channel after World War II. The tip was extended by more than 1.5 miles of new dune-field between 1948 and 1995. The westward movement of Shackleford caused Beaufort Inlet to move toward Fort Macon, a move now held in check by the rock jetty along the east-facing shore of Bogue Banks. As you look at this scene, imagine the shallow but almost 2-mile-wide natural inlet that existed from before 1708 (the earliest record of Beaufort Inlet) to 1866 and compare it with the ½-mile-wide inlet containing the 600-foot-wide, 42-foot-deep channel you see before you today. More water flows through here now than before, affecting current patterns, tidal regimes, and inlet flow patterns from Bogue to Barden Inlets.

Theodore Roosevelt State Natural Area

The Roosevelt natural area is a 290-acre tract on the west side of Pine Knoll Shores. Twenty-five acres are devoted to the North Carolina Aquarium; the remaining 265 acres are held in their natural state. Visitors are discouraged from entering the natural area, although special arrangements can be made if there is a professional purpose for the visit. There is an excellent, publicly accessible nature trail that illustrates many of the natural features of this area. It and the larger natural area it represents make this a five-star feature of this coast. The trail now begins inside the aquarium, but staff will usually let you reach it without paying an admission fee if you ask them to do so. The trail begins on an old dune ridge beside a salt marsh filled swale and winds east, providing views of the loblolly pine/laurel oak maritime forest and swamp forest between the ridges (see figure 41). About ¼ mile from the trailhead there is a spur trail that leads down to a salt-marsh-bordered pond on the edge of Bogue Sound. The main trail winds back to the trailhead over a series of beach ridges and swamp forest filled swales. Dominant trees in the swamp forest are red ash and red maple, although more than eighty different plant species occur in and around the swamp forests of the natural area. The trail was closed because of downed trees after Hurricane Fran. No doubt the evidence of damage will remain for some time.

Wood and Long Islands

Wood and Long Islands are worth visiting, each for different reasons. The obvious reason to observe Wood Island is for its importance as a colonial waterbird nesting area (see description in the Broad Creek side trip of the driving tour, above). Wood Island is directly offshore of the water access site at Twenty-third Street in Emerald Isle. The sound is shallow for the ³/₁₀ mile that separates the island from the access area, so you can wade closer if you want to. There are two good reasons not to set foot on this island, however. One is that you might disturb the nesting birds; the other is that Wood Island was once a bombing range and is posted to warn of potentially unexploded ordnance still buried there. Wood Island is managed by the Audubon Society, and they, for both reasons described above, discourage visitors.

Long Island, on the other hand, is an engaging place to visit. It is a remnant of an old beach ridge, so it has an almost triangular cross-sectional topography. In most places the island is about 100 feet wide and 20–30 feet high. It is covered with an open maritime forest dominated by live oak (see figure 42), although botanists who sample it can find over seven-

Figure 41. Nature trail at North Carolina Aquarium in Theodore Roosevelt State Natural Area. Note ridge and swale topography under swamp forest.

ty species in an hour. The island is bordered by salt marsh everyplace other than the southwest corner and the east end, where there are sandy beaches. Unfortunately there is a 4- to 6-foot-deep channel that separates Long Island from Bogue Banks, so either a swim or a boat are involved in visiting it. There are apparently unregulated but remarkably clean campsites in several places. A ridge crest trail runs the length of the island (about 500 yards).

Figure 42. Long Island in Bogue Sound. Note wedged canopy and marsh, shrub, forest sequence of communities.

The White Oak River: An Extraordinary Estuary

The entire White Oak River should qualify as a five-star environmental site. The river is only about 35 miles long from its headwaters in the White Oak Pocosin to its mouth at Bogue Inlet. Most of the river's course is through undeveloped or protected land. The headwaters and upstream 10 miles are in Hofmann State Forest; 9 additional miles of the freshwater section flow through Croatan National Forest; the freshwater-saltwater transition occurs in an area of undeveloped fresh and salt marsh; and the lower 12 miles flow through a mile-wide, open-water section, before entering extensive salt marshes and flood-tide delta deposits behind Bogue Inlet (see figure 43). There are only three towns near the river—Maysville, Stella, and Swansboro—but only the last of these has more than a few hundred residents. I will, however, choose some extra-special places as five-star features of this river.

Five-Star Features. If you cannot tour the White Oak by boat, I urge you to visit the following three sites: (1) Haywood Landing, where tidal fresh-water marsh, maritime swamp forest, bottomland hardwood forest, and 20-million-year-old fossil shell deposits can be seen; (2) the Tidelands Trail in the Cedar Point Recreation Area of Croatan National Forest; and (3) Bear Island in Hammock's Beach State Park. These three sites are representative of freshwater, estuarine, and marine habitats, respectively, but to visit these alone will leave a visitor uninformed about the gradual changes that take place as natural systems of these salinity regimes grade into one another.

The natural habitats along the White Oak include all the major ones that occur in the southern North Carolina coastal zone. The Haywood Landing road passes through sandy ridges that are occupied by typical pine and hardwood forests. Between these ridges the forests give way to pocosins and pond pine on organic-rich, poorly drained soils. Along the river itself, the Haywood Landing site allows visitors to view cypress and other types of swamp forest, bottomland hardwood forests farther inland, and wildflower-filled marshes along the stream bank. Near the ocean the streamside habitats are replaced by the salt marshes, tidal flats, grass flats, oyster reefs, and estuarine fringe forests that can be observed from the Tidelands Trail. Hammock's Beach State Park has accessible and excellent examples of all the natural barrier island habitats shown in figure 6.

One can visit White Oak habitats by car or boat. Those who use cars alone will get only snapshots of the habitats because only four roads cross the upper 25 miles, and the downstream shoreline is mostly private. The real lesson to be learned from the White Oak is one of environmental transitions along its course. If you plan to visit any part of the southern coast by boat, I urge that it be the White Oak. The upstream river is easily runnable by canoe or kayak, as are most of the tributary creeks and the salt marshes behind Bear Island. Even the open-water sections between Stella and Swansboro are safe most of the time, although waves and headwinds can make them difficult when winds are from the south. Those who tour the White Oak in boats may wish to have a copy of *A Paddler's*

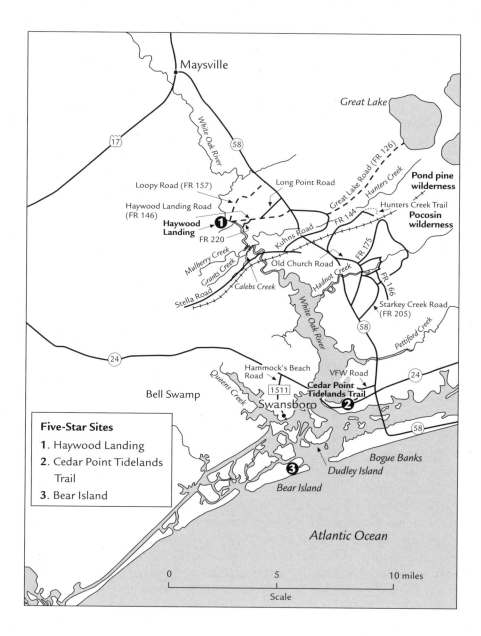

Maysville

Great Lake

17

White Oak River

58

Loopy Road (FR 157)

Long Point Road

Great Lake Road (FR 126)

Hunters Creek

Pond pine wilderness

Haywood Landing Road (FR 146)

Haywood Landing

1

Hunters Creek Trail

FR 144

Pocosin wilderness

FR 220

Kuhns Road

FR 175

Mulberry Creek

Grants Creek

Old Church Road

Hadnot Creek

FR 166

Calebs Creek

Stella Road

White Oak River

Starkey Creek Road (FR 205)

58

Pettiford Creek

24

Bell Swamp

Queens Creek

Hammock's Beach Road

1511

Swansboro

VFW Road

Cedar Point Tidelands Trail

2

24

58

Five-Star Sites

1. Haywood Landing

2. Cedar Point Tidelands Trail

3. Bear Island

3

Dudley Island

Bogue Banks

Bear Island

Atlantic Ocean

0   5   10 miles

Scale

Guide to Eastern North Carolina, by Bob Benner and Tom McCloud (Birmingham, Ala.: Menasha Ridge Press, 1987). These authors describe two sections of the White Oak, one from highway 17 near Maysville to Hayward Landing, the other from Hayward Landing to Stella (see figure 45). Those who do not feel comfortable in boats may wish to tour with a guide and a rental boat. This can be arranged through the North Carolina Coastal Federation, whose headquarters is on NC 24 east of Cape Carteret. The federation's educational staff leads "Coastal Adventures" of several types and can arrange trips guided by knowledgeable naturalists to every type of habitat within the White Oak watershed. The federation's address is 3609 Highway 24 (Ocean), Newport, N.C. 28570 (919) 393-8185.

Freshwater Sections

Upstream of Maysville the freshwater sections of the White Oak are easy to visit by car or bicycle. Upstream the river is narrow and shallow but is crossed by three bridges. I recommend visiting it on a 15-mile road trip from Maysville as a way to see pocosins, pond pine, and swamp forest habitats. Depart Maysville to the northeast on NC Bike Trail 3 (Fourth Street, SR 1116). Turn left on Gibson Bridge Road after about 1.2 miles (SR 1118). Cross the river and turn right on White Oak River Road (SR 1332). This road more or less parallels the river through field and forest. Follow it for about 4 miles and turn right on Emmett Lane (SR 1333, Forest Road [FR] 3004). Follow Emmett Lane about 1.1 miles, cross the mighty river (here about 20 feet wide), and turn right at the T-intersection with SR 1116 and follow it back to Maysville about 8.2 miles to the east. Those with kayaks and courage may want to run this upper section of the river. I have never done it; but I am told it was possible before Fran, and the three bridges in 8 miles of river make for easy logistics.

Boating downstream from the US 17 crossing south of Maysville is relatively easy any time of the year, although there are two rock ledges and five small lakes that must be navigated before reaching the river's main

Figure 43. White Oak River area. Base map from North Carolina Department of Transportation.

channel (see figure 44). If you have some time, turn into the triangular lake just west of the main channel. It is surrounded by an almost pure stand of large bald cypress trees that produce both the feeling and the echoes you experience in a Gothic cathedral. Farther downstream the river widens and deepens and is bordered by swamp forest dominated by cypress, gums (tupelo and black), willow oak, and red maple, but with an occasional pine. Benner and McCloud describe the section from US 17 to Haywood Landing as 8.8 miles long with zero drop and taking 3.5 hours to paddle. For those less logistically challenged than I, a one-way trip is possible; but for those who travel alone, all of the significant habitats can be seen in a round-trip up and down the river from Haywood Landing.

Haywood Landing is a must-visit site for both automobile and boat tourers. It is reached from NC 58, most easily from the aptly named Loopy Road (FR 157) but also by Haywood Landing Road, reached by Point Road. Loopy Road is 11 miles north of the NC 24/58 intersection in Cape Carteret and 7.2 miles south of the NC 58/US 17 intersection in Maysville. The road is marked with "Haywood Landing" signs and passes through managed loblolly pine forest to its junction with Haywood Landing Road. Haywood Landing Road is built close to the edge of a sandy ridge that drops down to a bottomland hardwood forest to the north. Bottomland hardwood forests differ from swamp forests in frequency of flooding and are usually dominated by willow oak, red maple, and, sometimes, white cedar. Unlike swamp forests they have a shrub flora of swamp magnolia and swamp bay that is well represented in the example found north of Haywood Landing Road. Typical shrub and vine species in this particular forest also include ironwood and buckeye and vines such as greenbrier and poison ivy. If you stop about 125 yards east of Haywood Landing (where a resurrection-fern–covered live oak limb extends almost across the road), you will see a path leading down to the bottomland. Look to your right as you descend the path and look into the holes in the bankface. The back of these holes is fossil shell material about 20 to 25 million years old (late Oligocene to early Miocene). There are two other holes that expose these fossils to the right and left of the path, and another exposure of the fossiliferous layer lies on the east bank of the river near the boat ramp (reached by a path at west edge of picnic area). The fossils do not seem

Figure 44. White Oak River: swamp forest between Maysville and Haywood Landing.

very dramatic; they are mostly small clamshells with a few small snail shells. Close examination of this material has shown that these shells represent a relatively diverse assemblage with six species of bivalves and four species of snail being common. By fossil standards these are also very good specimens, termed "the best preserved fossil molluscs for their age along the Atlantic Coast of North America" by J. G. Carter and his colleagues who authored *Fossil Collecting in North Carolina* in 1988 (bulletin 89 of the North Carolina Geological Survey). They may not look terribly well preserved to untrained eyes such as mine, but we would probably have been well served by our funeral director if our remains were to look as good 20 million years from now.

Hayward Landing itself is about 200 yards west of the fossil site. There is a cement ramp for launching boats, a picnic area with chemical toilets, a trail along the river, and excellent views of typical swamp forest habitat (see figure 45). Haywood Landing is on the tidal freshwater section of the river. If you visit at anytime other than dead high tide, you will see the high-tide line above the water. The maximum range here is about 1 foot, so high tides regularly flood the forest floor, eliminating plants that cannot tolerate complete immersion. These include most of the shrub and vine components of the hardwood bottom forest as well as most of the oaks, ash, and sycamores. Red maple and willow oak occur in both swamp forests and hardwood bottoms. Tidal freshwater marshes also occur near Haywood Landing. These are dominated by cattails and saw grass but also include numerous wildflowers that bloom in spring and summer. The swamp forest here is dominated by bald cypress, tupelo, and black gums.

A boat trip up and down the river from Haywood Landing is a great way to see the diversity of swamp forests, freshwater wetlands, and the ecological transition that occurs where freshwater meets saltwater. Most of these features can be seen by a round trip extending about 1 mile upstream and 2 miles downstream. Upstream the significant observations are of the swamp forest and freshwater marshes along the river. The swamp is impressive with the size and diversity of trees. The marsh is not as diverse but is impressive for its annual production of plant material. All these plants die back each winter, so all the vegetative matter in the 9-foot-tall plants that are packed densely on the marsh surface grows in one season. These marshes are also notable for their wildflowers. The most spectacular of these include iris and spider lilies in the spring; cardinal flowers, marshmallows, morning glories, and swamp roses in the summer; and asters and marigolds in the fall.

A trip downstream from Haywood Landing passes extensive swamp forest and marsh habitats and two osprey nests. It demonstrates the transition from tidal freshwater habitat to salt marsh. Observers should look for evidence of plant adaptation to the nutrient-rich but oxygen-poor soils of these productive communities. The tall grasses and rushes of both

Figure 45. Freshwater habitats along the White Oak River: cypress swamp near Haywood Landing.

fresh and salt marshes have open-air channels to supply oxygen to the roots and rhizomes in the soil. Bald cypress and tupelo gum have "knees" that grow upward from their roots and reach the air. Red maples, cedars, and several other swamp forest trees have unusually shallow root systems. This keeps their roots close to air but makes them susceptible to being blown down.

In areas closer to the ocean, plants must adapt not only to low oxygen in the soil but also to increasingly frequent immersion with water that contains salt. The immersion frequency varies with location and tidal range. At the officially designated separation between fresh and coastal water, measured salt content of the water can range from 0 to over 10 parts per thousand, depending on whether tides are high or low and neap or spring (see Chapter 1). Roots of plants growing in water-saturated soils are not exposed to this full range, however, because water in the soil moves so slowly that it takes a long time to change in response to variations in salinity of overlying waters. Soil salinity does change, however, and in periods of rising sea levels, salt-sensitive plants close to rivers gradually die back as tidal flooding exposes them to increasingly salty water. This die-off occurs along the White Oak and can be observed within 2 miles of Haywood Landing. Farther downstream the trees are stunted from salt exposure and restricted to areas well back from the river itself.

Tributary Creeks

There are many tributary creeks that enter the White Oak. Exploring these creeks by small boat is easy and fun. Some creeks can also be visited by car. My favorite is Hadnot Creek, which crosses NC 58 between Cape Carteret and Kuhns. This creek is traversed by two bridges and a culvert in its 4-mile course from the White Oak River to its headwaters in the Pocosin Wilderness of Croatan National Forest. It can therefore be seen repeatedly in a figure-8 circuit. Be warned, however, that my wife says this is not worth doing.

Boat access to Hadnot Creek can be found from the bridges that cross it. The easiest access point is on NC 58, where boats can be launched both south of the bridge and 50 yards farther south along the west side of the causeway. The mouth of the creek is about 1.25 miles downstream of NC 58. The creek enters the White Oak after cutting through sand ridges about 30 feet high. These are part of North Carolina's ancient shoreline system (see Chapter 1, figure 4). The mouth faces across the White Oak (now over 1 mile wide) to the high land of Holland Point on the west bank. The plant communities that border the creek mouth are typical salt marsh with cordgrass at the creek edge, black needlerush farther back, and estuarine fringe forest on the high land behind the marsh.

Forests

There are several types of forest that occur on the upland away from the banks of the White Oak River. The largest acreage of forest is managed for production of timber from loblolly pines. Forests managed by forest products companies, private landholders, the U.S. Forest Service, and the state's Division of Forest Resources occur within the White Oak basin. Croatan National Forest is the largest single tract of forest in the White Oak, but Hofmann State Forest is also large. Almost all of the loblolly pine forests in the watershed have been modified from pond pine and pocosin habitat by extensive systems of drainage ditches. The canals to which these ditches connect can be seen all along the freshwater sections of the river. This drainage system lowers the groundwater table in the ditched areas, allowing loblolly pines to grow in habitat previously too moist for them. Runoff from these modified areas reaches the river much more rapidly than would normally be the case. Oystermen and clammers claim that shellfish catches have gone down as the drained area has expanded, but there is no scientifically established relationship between the two.

If you want to see the natural forest types of the upland region of the White Oak watershed, you will need to get fairly far off the beaten track. You, like my wife, may question whether a visit to pond pine and pocosin is worth the effort, but for the sake of completeness as well as the author's compulsion, here are some directions.

The two best places I have found to visit pond pine stands are along the gravel road to Great Lake and on the east end of Hunter Creek Trail. Both areas are within Croatan National Forest. The road to Great Lake branches off SR 1100 — a loop east of NC 58 between Kuhns and Long Point. The road is well signed from NC 58 but not where it joins SR 1100 as paved SR 1101 for about ½ mile before becoming the gravel FR 126 for the remaining 6 miles to Great Lake. This road passes through the Pond Pine Wilderness, although, as you will see, it is not very scenic to the north and west, as a recent forest fire has left it scarred and dead. To the south and east of the road the pond pine and pocosin habitats remain largely untouched. You will note that pond pine differs from loblolly in being smaller, with a less straight trunk and a smaller (about 2½") cone without spikes. On a larger scale you will note that the pocosin habitat understory is extremely dense. Enter it at your peril. In 1991 it took 100 searchers three days to find a lost hunter *even with* the assistance of a helicopter. You will be pleased to know there are over 30,000 acres of designated wilderness in Croatan National Forest; one can find lots of places to get lost in such an area.

A pond pine experience intermediate between the car window view from Great Lake Road or the uncharted wilderness view available to those who plunge into the dense vegetation is found on Hunter Creek Trail. This clearly marked and easily walked 2-mile trail is near the end of Hunters Creek Road. Hunters Creek Road (FR 144) branches off east of NC 58 just south of the railroad crossing south of Kuhns (see Figure 43). The trail itself has been used by off-road vehicles and has deep depressions that fill with water in damp weather. The best pond pine habitat is about one-third the distance along the loop from the trailhead farthest from NC 58 (about 5 miles in—where FR 144 ends at the railroad crossing). The remainder of the loop is pleasant but not essential, even by the author's compulsive standards.

If pond pine habitat is difficult to reach, pocosin habitat is even more so. Unfortunately some of the best examples burned in the forest fire near Great Lake. That area is still worth visiting because the pocosin vegetation is recovering and the peaty soil is easily seen north of the Great Lake boat ramp. Walking here is strenuous as a result of downed trees and ruts created by firefighters. You can see, however, where and why the soil itself caught fire. Its high concentration of organic-rich peat leads any observer to understand why very hot fires are such a threat to eastern North Carolina forests. Pocosin habitat can also be seen from Catfish Lake Road that extends from NC 58 2 miles south of Maysville to US 70 at Croatan (4.5 miles north of Havelock). This road is too far north to appear on figure 43 and too small to appear on North Carolina transportation maps, but it does exist and can be navigated in two-wheel-drive vehicles by those with the time and patience to do so.

The Mid-Reaches of the White Oak

The mid-reaches of the White Oak—the eight miles that separate Stella from Swansboro—are bordered by salt marshes. Often these marshes occur between the water and the base of the 30-foot sandy ridges that characterize this area's ancient shoreline. The mid-reaches of the river itself are wide and shallow, in keeping with its origin as a river floodplain recently inundated by rising sea level. If the White Oak were a bigger river and/or had a higher sediment load, its mid-reaches would be filled with salt marshes—just as it is in the upstream areas close to the riverine sediment supply. The mid-reaches remain open water, however, as sea level is rising at a rate faster than sediment can be provided to fill it. The bottom of the mid-reaches grades from mud and silt in the freshwater-to-saltwater transition zone to sand-size particles close to Swansboro. There do not seem to be many intertidal or grass flats within the mid-reaches, although the estuary floor has an extensive shellfish biota similar to that described above for mud and sand flats near Beaufort. Oyster reefs are rare, perhaps because of increased freshwater drainage from the surrounding forests, perhaps because of reduced tidal exchange caused by the man-made causeway between Swansboro and Cape Carteret, or perhaps because of mechanical harvest of clams, which dredges much of the bottom and spreads sediment throughout the river's midsection. Whatever the reason, White Oak oysters—once locally renowned—are now rare and only marginally profitable to harvest.

Salt marshes are the habitat to visit in the mid-reaches of the White Oak. There are many great places to observe them. One of the best is the Cedar Point Recreation Area and its Tidelands Trail. This trail and the habitats along it make this site one of the five-star features of this section.

The Cedar Point Recreation Area is a left turn off VFW Road—the road leading west 0.6 miles north of the intersection of NC 24 and 58 in Cape Carteret. The Tidelands Trail leads north from the picnic area parking lot. It is an easy 1.4-mile trail that crosses salt marsh on six boardwalks and is equipped with two permanent shelters from which to view wildlife of the marsh and estuary. Many of the boardwalks were destroyed by Hurricanes Bertha and Fran in 1996, so the trail will not be as easy to use until they are rebuilt. One of the surprising aspects of the salt marsh here is the range of plants outside their normal habitats. You will find all the expected salt marsh plants (sea ox-eye, spike grass, glasswort, black needlerush, and salt marsh cordgrass), but you will also find high marsh species scattered through a poorly developed estuarine fringe loblolly pine forest on islands in the marsh and growing on spoil piles surrounded by regularly flooded stands of cordgrass. The latter is fairly common and represents an irregularly flooded high ground artificially introduced into an area that is normally flooded on every high tide. The distribution of salt marsh plants in the herbaceous layer of the forest is unusual. It may represent a transition under way from forest to marsh as increasingly frequent flooding with saltwater kills back the forest and extends the salt marsh. This marsh extension is not occurring in the higher forested area surrounding the last 0.3 miles of the Tidelands Trail. The forest in this upland is a well-developed estuarine fringe loblolly pine forest dominated by pine and hardwoods (red maple, sweet gum, and tupelo gum), with thickets of wax myrtle, marsh elder, and yaupon.

Both the Tidelands Trail and the picnic area at Cedar Point provide excellent places to sit quietly and watch marsh wildlife. I have seen eight egrets at a time feeding over the flooded salt marsh at Cedar Point (see figure 46).

Other delightful places from which to observe marsh biota are the Swansboro Town Park and the restaurants on the north side of NC 24 nearby. The view up the estuary is stunning from any of these vantage points, but you will have to bring your own food and shade to the park. The restaurants provide food, drink, and shaded outdoor dining. I watched an osprey holding a captured fish in perfect aerodynamic position fly past the White Oak Cafe while I dined on ziti and sausage. Who said fieldwork always had to be uncomfortable?

The Mouth of the White Oak:
Bear Island and Hammock's Beach State Park

The mouth of the White Oak holds one more great place to visit. Bear Island is home to Hammock's Beach State Park and has all the habitats typical of barrier islands (see Chapter 1, figure 6). There are excellent exam-

Figure 46. Cedar Point Tidelands Trail: salt marsh and estuarine fringe forest.

ples of salt marsh, dunefields, thickets, and maritime forest on the way to one of the most reliably gentle, energy-dissipating beaches along our coast. Most visitors concentrate on the beach, but there is much to discover on a walk through the dunes, thickets, and forests. The island is only about 3.5 miles long, so one can walk down the beach and back through the dunes in an hour or two. If you have the time, I recommend the walk. The dunescapes and maritime forests are truly stunning.

The island is reached by ferry, water taxi, or private boat. The mainland ferry dock is at the park headquarters reached from NC 24 via Hammock's Beach Road (SR 1511) about 2 miles west of Swansboro. The ferry runs daily between Memorial Day and Labor Day and on weekends in May, September, and October. At other times the island can be reached by small boats that can, with permission, be launched from the park headquarters. There is also water taxi service from Swansboro; the best way to obtain a list of water taxis is by calling the park at (910) 326-4881. Park personnel are very accommodating and genuinely anxious for visitors to see and enjoy the superb natural area they oversee. They will help you get to the island in any way they can.

The marked channel to Bear Island passes through salt marshes typical of those from this point south but quite different from the open waters that typify back-barrier habitats from here to Virginia. A ready supply of fine-grained sediments in the island's ancient geological underpinnings and a tidal prism sufficient to erode and move these sediments account for the marshes developing where they do. Most of these marshes have internal drainage channels, but marshes also border the island itself (see figure 47).

The highest land on Bear Island is in or on the north shore of the island (the shore where the ferry lands). In some places this shoreline supports a maritime forest; in others the dunes extend almost to the back-barrier salt marsh (see figure 47). The dunefield on Bear Island is the most extensive in southern North Carolina. It is large, active, and moves inexorably into and over maritime forests, thickets, and grasslands.

Some of the dunes are stabilized by plant growth. Although these plants look unsubstantial, they held most of the dunefield in place during both Hurricanes Bertha and Fran in 1996. Both grasslands and thickets develop in interdune areas, especially where seaward dunes offer some protection from ocean-derived salt spray. Note that sea oats dominate the most exposed location, with salt meadow hay, bluestem, broomsedge, and thickets found in less-exposed habitats.

The dunefield on Bear Island is not only as extensive and diverse as any along the southern North Carolina coast; it also has as many interesting artifacts as any. In the open dunes south of the paved beach access trail, you will find areas where whole clam and scallop shells are abundant. These are what the park personnel call "seagull microwaves." Gulls collect the living shells on the beach, carry them into the dunes and wait until time and hot sun cause them to open. Those seagulls are no dummies. Have you ever tried opening a raw clam? How about one that has been warmed slightly? The warmed one was easier, right? What every shellfish eater needs is a nice, convenient dune suitable for warming clams.

Figure 47. Dunes and marshes on Bear Island. Photograph by Scott Taylor.

There are other shell piles in the dunes that were built by humans, not seagulls. These piles are kitchen middens that Native Americans made when they occupied the island from precolonial times through the mid-eighteenth century. Park personnel asked me to remind readers that these midden shells are artifacts and are not to be removed from their resting places.

The dunes also contain the remains of a pre–Civil War fort, a whaling station, a wooden boat building yard, and a menhaden fish camp. The last three of these all are found in the area recently occupied by the group campsites just west of the bathhouse. The fort is near the northwest corner of the island near the highest point on the island.

The beach at Bear Island is a classic example of the dissipative type—a beach that dissipates the energy of breaking waves over a broad, relatively flat surf zone. The diagnostic feature of such beaches is that they have at least three waves breaking in the surf zone at any one time. I have never seen surf at Bear Island without three simultaneous breakers, and I have been there when eight to ten waves were breaking at one time.

Waves that break on energy-dissipating beaches still move sand around. In some cases they move sand onto the beach from offshore bars. Usually this sand moves as a sand wave or migrating bar to form the ridge and runnel systems described in Chapter 1. At other times these seemingly gentle breakers may erode sand from beach and dunefield, creating cliffs where sand has been removed and undermining and washing away thicket plants that seemed to be effectively stabilizing the seaward fringe of the dunefield. This type of erosion and the washover of sand into dunes and salt marsh by hurricanes is well illustrated on the eastern end of Bear Island facing Bogue Inlet.

The eastern end of Bear Island can be reached by boat or by walking along the beach. The trip is worth the effort because you can see Bogue Inlet's tidal delta, and extensive series of a washover fans behind the beach, salt marsh habitat, and a dune ridge being eroded out from under a maritime forest by currents in Bogue Inlet. The maritime forest is especially worth visiting. It can be entered from the east behind the beach or by sliding down the dunes on the northeastern edge of the dunefield. Either entry brings you to a fine, and increasingly rare, example of an undeveloped maritime forest. This forest is open and easy to walk through. I recommend it as a way to end your visit to the White Oak River.

Camp Lejeune and the New River: The Off-Limits Shore

The Camp Lejeune Marine Corps Base occupies over 160,000 acres of coastal land between Swansboro and Sneads Ferry. The military reservation extends along both shores of the New River from just south of Jacksonville to the ocean on the east bank and to Sneads Ferry on the west bank. Access to this large area is strictly controlled to preserve public safety and avoid interference with military training. As a result, it is fair to classify this part of the coast as "off limits," even though highway NC 172 (Bike Trail 3) passes through it and navigable waters along the New River provide boat access to other parts of it.

Rules for road access through Camp Lejeune on NC 172 provide one hour for the trip and preclude stopping in transit. The road is closed when firing or military training is taking place near the highway. The 14-mile trip across Camp Lejeune is still worth taking, however, because it provides a glimpse of the base's extensive natural areas and offers food for thought about the role of wildfire suppression in altering natural habitats along the southern coast.

The other way to see this section of the North Carolina coast is by boat. Navigable waters of the New River and its tributaries are open to boats of all sizes. As a result, canoeists and kayakers can see more of Camp Lejeune's natural areas than can motorists. Not all navigable waters within the base are open, however. Those at the eastern end are restricted along the Intracoastal Waterway from Bear's Creek to Onslow Beach.

I have not designated any five-star features within Camp Lejeune, even though there are many that would be so designated were they publicly accessible. There are wonderful longleaf pine savannas, mixed southern forests, pocosins, and pond pine wilderness. Currently these can only be glimpsed by visitors transiting the base by boat or car.

A trip through Camp Lejeune by boat along the Intracoastal Waterway shows that Shackleford Island (sometimes called Brown Island)—the easternmost landmass along the shoreline—is similar in size and topography to Bear Island, its neighbor to the north. Shackleford Island is more extensively vegetated than Bear and, unlike Bear, shows impact craters from artillery and mortar shells. Access to Shackleford Island and the waters surrounding it is prohibited by the marine corps. The central and western part of the Camp Lejeune shoreline is occupied by land that would not be an island were it not for the man-made Intracoastal Waterway. The shoreface is a beach—Hurst Beach and Onslow Beach are named portions of it—and there are now salt marshes landward of its eastern and western extremities; for about two miles, however, the waterway cuts through land that once extended all the way to the beach. This is the beginning of a section of coastline over the Cape Fear Arch (see figure 2) in which the younger sediments that form the natural barrier islands along this coast have been eroded away by rising sea level. The land along this 11-mile stretch of shoreline has dune ridges like Bear and Shackleford Islands in the east, lower and flatter areas like ancient shoreline supporting NC 172 in the center, and low and overwash-prone areas like North Topsail Island on the west. This transition is typical of habitats found along the coastline between Cape Lookout and Cape Fear. East of Onslow Beach and extending all the way to Cape Lookout, the shoreface islands have high dunes and large sand volumes. West of Onslow Beach the islands are low and have few high dunes and small sand volumes. Why this occurs is not clear. It may have something to do with the sand supplied to the coast by the ancestral channel of the Neuse River. This channel extended south from Havelock to the middle of Bogue Banks—about the center of the 40-mile stretch of high-sand-volume barrier islands. It is unfortunate that the transition between high-and low-volume barrier islands occurs within Camp Lejeune because the attention-getting concept of "undetonated ordnance" is likely to inhibit the coring and drilling projects needed to obtain data on geologic underpinnings.

A trip through Camp Lejeune by automobile on NC 172 does not provide access to the extensive natural areas that occur within the base. The land that extends inland from the shoreface supports some of the most unusual and unaltered plant communities known in North Carolina. Surprising as that statement may seem, it becomes less so when one considers three things. First, Camp Lejeune has not been developed for farming, forestry, or housing as has most land in the coastal area. Second, the history of fire suppression that has led hardwoods and thickets to take over longleaf pine savannas and pond pine habitats has not been practiced in Camp Lejeune. Third, the base has active Forestry and Fish and Wildlife Divisions within its Environmental Management Department that manage land on the base to sustain populations of endangered species of plants and animals and their historical habitats. These three facts combine with knowledge generated from a biological inventory of Camp Lejeune carried out by scientists from the North Carolina Natural Heritage Program to produce the startling result that Camp Lejeune contains some of the most important and best-known natural areas that still exist in coastal North Carolina. The 1994 reports on the rare species, natural communities, and critical areas of Camp Lejeune published by Richard La Blond, John O. Fussell, and Alvin Braswell are available from the Natural Heritage Program in Raleigh. These reports document that over fifty-five species of plants and fifteen species of animals recognized as rare by federal or state officials occur within Camp Lejeune's fourteen natural communities. One of these species—the Lejeune goldenrod—is found nowhere else in the world, and Camp Lejeune populations of seven other species are a significant fraction of the known global populations. The Camp Lejeune Fish and Wildlife Division is particularly proud of their knowledge and restoration of red-cockaded woodpecker populations. The camp's ornithologist has developed a technique for providing man-made nesting sites within the heartwood of longleaf pines, a technique that was used to provide new nests for the woodpecker population in Francis Marion National Forest after the original nesting trees were blown down during Hurricane Hugo.

The role of fire in the natural communities of the southeast has been badly misrepresented by Smokey the Bear. Fire is a natural feature of southeastern habitats. Frequent fires keep communities from developing heavy understory thickets and reduce the threat of hot, forest-destroying fires fueled by thicket plants. A regimen of controlled fires is carried out on Camp Lejeune to maintain the longleaf pine savanna habitat of the red-cockaded woodpecker and several species of insectivorous plants. Even more frequent fires are started in the impact areas of the camp's artillery and mortar ranges. A number of the rare plants found in Camp Lejeune flourish in the frequent fire regimes near these impact areas.

Camp Lejeune from NC 172

Unfortunately, very little of Camp Lejeune's extraordinary natural habitat is visible from NC 172. Only four of the fourteen described habitats are encountered as one crosses the camp. These four are (1) maritime evergreen forest, (2) mixed hardwood forest, (3) longleaf pine savanna, and (4) coastal plain small stream swamp (blackwater subtype). These communities are quite easy to identify as you drive along, although the types mix as they grade into one another. There are several bird species that are common near NC 172 and might be seen. These include wild turkey, quail, dove, osprey, red-tailed hawk, and American kestrel. Mammals you might see include white-tailed deer, black bear, fox squirrel, gray squirrel, raccoon, red fox, gray fox, river otter, and bobcat.

Topsail Island Area:
Developed Beach with Natural Back-barrier Systems

The Topsail Island area stretches about 25 miles between the mainland towns of Sneads Ferry and Hampstead and the inlets at New River and New Topsail. Topsail Island, a low and narrow barrier island, extends along the ocean for the 24 miles between the two inlets. There were few natural areas left on Topsail Island itself before the hurricanes of 1996. Almost all the island had been developed residentially with condominiums, duplexes, and single-family cottages. Much of that development was destroyed by storm surge and washover. What will replace it had not been determined when this book went to press.

Behind the island, however, there are exceptional natural areas, salt marshes, sounds, inshore islands, creeks, hardwood bottomland forests, longleaf pine savannas, pond pine woodlands, and pocosins, all of which are readily accessible to interested visitors. The best examples of the last four of these habitats are found in the Holly Shelter Game Management Area, which is managed by the North Carolina Wildlife Resources Commission, and in the Great Sandy Run area of Camp Lejeune. Holly Shelter communities are accessible year-round, although vehicle access is limited to September 1 to March 1. Camp Lejeune areas are off limits (see above), but many of the habitats listed can be seen from NC 50 or US 17 (see figure 48).

Five-Star Features. Predictably enough, neither of the two five-star natural features I would mention on this stretch of coast is on the ocean shoreline. One, Stump Sound, is between the Intracoastal Waterway and the landward side of Topsail Island; the other, Holly Shelter Game Management Area, is on the landward side of US 17.

The waters of Stump Sound are surrounded by natural salt marshes and support dense populations of fish, shellfish, and wading birds. Stump Sound's oysters are regionally famous, and they command a premium price when they are available. Stump Sound supports numerous shellfish "gardens" where enterprising "farmers" grow oysters and clams. It cannot help but be environmentally encouraging that such enterprises can continue to exist while new, high density housing projects have been built nearby.

The habitats in the Holly Shelter game lands are very similar to those not accessible to the public in Camp Lejeune. Access routes to them are indicated on figure 48 and are described below.

The inland habitats behind Topsail Island make this stretch of coast more interesting to naturalists than would be the case were the island the only attraction. Residential development on Topsail was initiated in the 1930s, and its characteristics were established well before the Coastal Area Management Program set current guidelines. A major pulse of development began soon after the U.S. Navy abandoned its Operation Bumblebee missile range in the late 1940s. Ominously enough, the range was abandoned (eventually to be reinvented at Cape Canaveral) because storms and hurricanes repeatedly destroyed buildings and equipment during the mid-1940s and early 1950s. The potential for hurricane damage was realized during Hurricane Fran in 1996, when almost all of the construction on the North Topsail oceanfront was destroyed or severely damaged by flooding, dune overwash, and new inlet formation.

The island's low elevation and paucity of natural dunes or other sand supplies make it particularly susceptible to beach erosion and dune overwash. In addition, its history does not inspire confidence. Over 90 percent of the houses at New Topsail Beach were destroyed by Hurricane Hazel in 1954, and the normal storms have chewed up the shoreface such that the road to North Topsail has been relocated twice during the last 20 years. Topsail Island, like New York City, may be a nicer place to visit than to live. Most landowners seem to agree; most Topsail residences seem to be

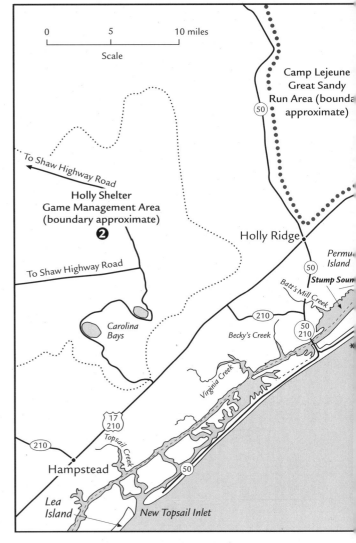

Figure 48.
Topsail Island area.
Base map from North
Carolina Department
of Transportation.

0   5   10 miles

Scale

Camp Lejeune
Great Sandy
Run Area (bounda
approximate)

50

To Shaw Highway Road

Holly Shelter
Game Management Area
(boundary approximate)
❷

To Shaw Highway Road

Holly Ridge

Permu
Island

50

Stump Soun

Batt's Mill Creek

210

Becky's Creek

50
210

Carolina
Bays

Virginia Creek

17
210

210

Topsail Creek

Hampstead

50

Lea
Island

New Topsail Inlet

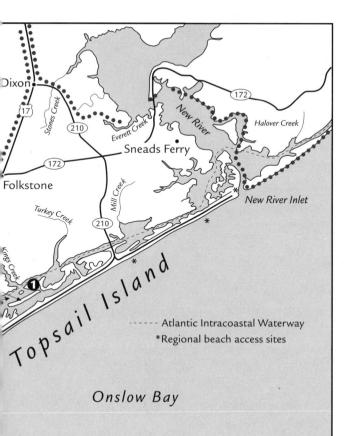

----- Atlantic Intracoastal Waterway
*Regional beach access sites

Onslow Bay

Five-Star Sites
1. Stump Sound
2. Holly Shelter Game Management Area

second homes or vacation cottages. The island's beaches attract fair-weather visitors, but as permanent housing is built on the mainland, more people seem to be settling inland rather than on Topsail itself. Living *near* the beach has more to recommend it than living on a low, narrow island like Topsail. Recent construction with Coastal Area Management funds has even provided improved beach access for island visitors. The access sites have been built with public funds, the same source that has repeatedly nourished Topsail's beaches and rebuilt its dunes. Four regional beach access areas have been developed; three are north of the NC 210 high bridge to North Topsail Beach, and one is just north of Surf City. There are also numerous local access points at the beach end of most cross-streets in Surf City and Topsail Beach. Unlike the situation on Bogue Banks (see above), most of these access sites have some designated parking, and other cars are permitted to park nearby as long as they are off the pavement and not blocking access to homes or fire hydrants.

Holly Shelter Game Management Area

The Holly Shelter Game Management Area was established in the 1930s on 48,000 acres of low-lying peatland on which property taxes were not paid during the depression. Such lands reverted by state law to the North Carolina Board of Education, but the Carolina Bays, pocosins, and assorted wetlands of Pender and Duplin Counties were viewed as of little value for anything other than game preserves. Thus the board of education transferred them to the North Carolina Wildlife Resources Commission, which developed Holly Shelter and Angola game management areas. Federal funds for this purpose were obtained from excise taxes on hunting and fishing supplies under provisions of the Pittman-Roberson Act for Federal Aid in Wildlife Restoration. The first major project supported by these funds in Holly Shelter was construction of a ditch bank road across the area in 1939–41. About 80 percent of the original area was peatland pocosin and pond pine woodland, with the remaining 20 percent longleaf pine savannas and upland sand ridges associated with ancient shorelines. These habitats are well represented in Holly Shelter today (see figure 49).

Figure 49. Pocosin community with pond pine in Holly Shelter Game Management Area.

The best way to appreciate the extent and diversity of Holly Shelter is to drive across it. The sand roads in the management area are open from September 1 through the end of February. These roads are passable in two-wheel-drive vehicles during dry weather, although the roads can get rutted during hunting season and impassible to non-four-wheel-drive vehicles during periods of heavy rain. Holly Shelter's roads are reached from US 17 just north of Topsail Baptist Church (between Hampstead and Holly Ridge near Belvedere Plantation), and from Shaw Highway Road that runs between NC 53 and 210 east of the Northeast Cape Fear River. There are only a few roads within Holly Shelter. The main ones are illustrated on figure 48, but a complete map and a report on current road conditions can be obtained from the area management office by calling (910) 259-5555. The drive across the area allows one to see some of the wetter habitats in the area — saturated soil pocosins with no pond pine and managed freshwater marshes.

Hunting is allowed in Holly Shelter on Mondays, Wednesdays, Saturdays, and holidays. If you expect to wander along the extensive hunting trails within the area, I suggest you pick other days to do it. Most hunting in Holly Shelter is for deer, although squirrel, rabbit, fox, bobcat, and black bear occur there along with dove, quail, wild turkey, and ducks. Much of the area is managed to enhance deer density, and like other areas of the state, deer have increased dramatically in the last three decades. According to the Wildlife Resources Commission, the statewide deer population has quintupled since 1950.

It is unlikely that naturalists will ever outnumber deer in Holly Shelter, but those that do visit have a chance to see one of the most extensive natural areas remaining in the state. I recommend visiting even when the roads are closed. Visitors on foot are encouraged at all times. The best place to walk into Holly Shelter is at the US 17 entrance north of Topsail Baptist Church (see above). Within 2 miles you will pass through longleaf pine savannas. Keep your eye peeled for red-cockaded woodpeckers in this old-growth forest. You will also see pine woodlands with pocosin plant understory. If you leave the road, you can find areas with numerous wildflowers and pure pocosins with few, if any, pond pines. The latter are most abundant in the Carolina Bays (distinctive, oval-shaped areas of low-lying peat — the processes that cause the shape have yet to be identified). Two of these Carolina Bays occur relatively close to US 17 as illustrated in figure 48.

Old Shoreline Sand Ridges

The shoreline sand ridge under Hampstead, Holly Ridge, and Sneads Ferry was formed more than a million years ago. Its well-drained sandy soils are more productive than the peaty organic soils of pocosins and pond pine woodlands. As a result, highways, railways, farms, and towns were built upon it. The sand ridges were also the preferred living sites for Native Americans, as evidenced by the extensive shell mounds, gravesites, and artifacts found in the coastal sand ridges of Pender County. Many Native American artifacts have been found in sand ridge fields, and evidence of extended habitation has been found on Permuda Island in Stump Sound (see figure 48). Much of the old shoreline sand ridge was converted from field and forest to residential developments and golf courses as Pender County developed economically. A few natural areas remain, mostly along small creeks.

The freshwater marshes, creeks, and bottomland hardwood forests of the old shoreline sand ridge can be seen where roads cross wetlands, but they are best observed from small boats. Many creeks drain into Stump Sound. Those most recommended for exploration are Virginia Creek, off Sloop Point Road; Becky's Creek west of NC 50/210; and Kings Creek inland from Permuda Island. These creeks appear to be relatively unaffected by human development, but appearances can be misleading. The sandy soil is very porous, so fertilizer from lawns and golf courses, as well as septic system water from homes and businesses, drains into the creeks along with the groundwater. Many of the creeks have bacterial levels too high to allow oyster harvest. Others have nitrogen and phosphorous levels high enough to cause abnormal algal blooms and, recently, fish and crab kills as well.

Stump Sound, Islands, and Marshes

The inshore open-water areas between the two highway bridges to Topsail Island are collectively known as Stump Sound, although many subsections have other names as well. All of these waters have a long history of supporting productive fisheries for finfish and shellfish. Stump Sound oysters are well worth trying if one is an oyster fancier. They normally have a relatively deep shell filled with delicious and unusually salty soft parts. The North Carolina Marine Fisheries Commission has identified all of Stump Sound as a primary nursery area, a place where "initial post larval development takes place." This identification means that it is unlawful to use trawl nets in the area unless it is opened after biological sampling shows it to contain only adult animals late in the season. As a result, Stump Sound teems with algal blooms, small fish and shrimp, and the larger animals that prey on them. This abundance of aquatic life is the basis for citing this area as a five-star natural feature.

There is no better place to see the abundant wildlife of Stump Sound than in the waters near Permuda Island (see figure 50). Here the Stump Sound oyster is cultivated in extensive shellfish leases, while shrimp scatter across the surface to escape predators or boats, and mullet leap clear of the water for reasons known only to them. Wading birds, ospreys, and fish predators are abundant and active. That this abundance of seafood is no recent development is amply demonstrated by the shell mounds made by Native Americans on Permuda Island. These extensive mounds provide mute testimony to the fact that these waters have supported extensive shellfish harvests since precolonial times. Permuda Island itself was designated an area of environmental concern by the North Carolina Coastal Resources Commission. This action, taken in 1985, and the subsequent purchase of the island by the North Carolina Nature Conservancy, was based mainly on preserving archaeological sites on the island, although its preservation to assure continuing oyster harvests was the major reason why many proponents supported the action. Obviously, the designation serves both purposes and pleases naturalists, archaeologists, and fishing enthusiasts. Permuda Island formally became part of the Estuarine Research Reserve System in 1987 when the state purchased the westernmost 50 of its 62 acres from the Nature Conservancy. The conservancy retains possession of areas with Native American gravesites and other remains. The state's portion is available for hiking and camping, although, much as I hate to say this, the island is currently heavily overgrown with catbrier and dense thickets and has a local reputation of being densely populated with rattlesnakes — forewarned is forearmed.

Stump Sound has numerous islands other than Permuda. Many of these occur on the south side of the Intracoastal Waterway and are formed of sediment dredged from this channel. Surprisingly, few of these islands are nesting sites for colonial waterbirds, although many of these birds can be seen feeding in the salt marshes and creeks that surround the

Figure 50. Ocean side of Permuda Island in Stump Sound. Note crab pot, signs for oyster leases, and wedged shape of canopy.

spoil islands. Perhaps they nest farther east and west, as many nesting sites have been identified east of the NC 210 bridge and west of New Topsail Inlet. The absence of nesting colonies of waterbirds enhances Stump Sound's islands for human visitors. Most of the spoil islands are forested, many have sandy beaches, and some are open enough for comfortable camping and picnicking. Boat access is easy and safe, as there are many ramps and marinas on the mainland shore, and the waters are protected enough so that waves rarely become big enough to be dangerous.

Salt marshes abound in Stump Sound as well as along the Alligator and Chadwick Bays northeast of the NC 210 bridge and in Topsail Sound southwest of Surf City. The extent of these marshes is easily seen from the two highway bridges. The marshes are typically zoned, with black needlerush in the irregularly flooded areas and salt marsh cordgrass dominating in areas that are regularly flooded. The usual succulent glassworts, grasses, and composite shrubs occur at the upland fringe (see Chapter 1). Extensive salt marshes without much upland are also found southwest of Topsail Island behind the low sand spits of islands farther south.

Topsail Island

As mentioned above, there are few natural areas left on Topsail Island itself. The two largest publicly accessible areas are the regional beach access sites north of NC 210 and in Surf City.

The access site closest to NC 210 is located between developed sections of the island where some dune, maritime grassland, and maritime shrub habitat existed before Fran. Parking space at these locations was provided on an earlier road that had already been destroyed farther north.

The other beach access sites north of NC 210 are in the community of North Topsail Shores. The first of these has parking on the sound side of the road. Sound-side salt marshes are easily viewed from the parking area. The beach here has been maintained by periodic beach nourishment projects (the latest in the early 1990s added sand that was dredged from the nearby New River Inlet) and even more frequent bulldozing of sand from low to high in the intertidal area. In theory, the beach steepening that results from bulldozing sand from low on the beach to the high-tide line should steepen the beachface and result in increased erosion. The basis for this theory is that waves in deep water dissipate little of their energy over the low-tide beach and concentrate more of it on the high-tide beach, thereby eroding the bulldozed sand and moving it back out to sea. There is no doubt that the bulldozed sand does eventually move back to sea; but the rate of movement is slow during nonstorm periods, and repeated bulldozings between storms keeps a sand supply available to nourish the beach and reduce its rate of landward retreat. No one believed that this system would prevent erosion, overwash, and residence destruction during a major hurricane, and that belief was confirmed by both Bertha and Fran in 1996. Prior to 1996, however, beach sand bulldozing worked surprisingly well when exposed to the less intense storms experienced in the 1980s and early 1990s.

The northernmost regional beach access area on Topsail Island is at New River Inlet at the northeastern end of the island. This site was also heavily damaged during the hurricanes of 1996. Condominiums were built almost on the berm behind the inlet beach even though evidence of the inlet eroding into back-barrier salt marshes was found all along the inlet. An inlet dredging project in the early 1990s straightened and deepened the inlet mouth but was already beginning to meander and erode before the hurricanes.

The beaches along the inlet and ocean continue to be interesting places to visit because meandering channels erode old fossil-bearing sediments, providing lucky visitors with a chance to find 30-million-year-old sharks' teeth and 10-million-year-old clamshells. The fossils can be distinguished from modern, similar-looking examples by their dark gray to black color. This color develops when objects made of calcium carbonate are buried in sediments that have no free oxygen (see see Chapter 1). The occurrence of these fossils along Topsail's beaches is evidence that ancient sediment layers on the flanks of the Cape Fear Arch (see Chapter 1) are close to the surface along this stretch of the North Carolina coast. A word of caution about tidal currents is needed here: the beach at this access area is exposed to strong currents on both ebb and flood tides. Even the strongest swimmers can be carried away by these currents. Be cautious if you enter the water, and watch closely any children or pets who might not realize how dangerous the currents of tidal inlets can be.

The fourth regional beach access site on Topsail Island is located just northeast of Surf City. There is parking on both sides of NC 210 and a short nature trail with views through maritime shrub habitat on the sound side. These facilities essentially filled the space once occupied by dunes and maritime grasslands. The beach is moderately wide and extends almost a full block. The parking areas provide a nice view across the marshes and open waters of Stump Sound.

Much of the rest of Topsail Island has been developed for residences. The entry drives to the sound-side houses provide useful observations of what botanists call fragmentation of maritime shrub and forest communities. As is obvious to all observers, the growth and resultant canopy shape of these communities is controlled by wind and salt spray exposure. Natural communities are "wedged," with a ground-hugging canopy on the ocean side gradually becoming taller as seaward plants absorb the brunt of the spray impact while protecting the plants farther back. Some of Topsail's low-density sound-side development had preserved this natural canopy shape by building tunnel-like driveways under it. Most of the recently constructed access roads have cut through the natural vegetation and sliced open the forest canopy. When this happens, the plants on the side of the new opening are exposed to high levels of salt spray and die back. Eventually a new wedged canopy will develop around the canopy opening; but the process takes years, many trees die unnecessarily, and the protection of the undisturbed canopy is lost. All phases of this process and the communities' recovery from it are observable during a drive along Topsail Island.

The final natural area worth visiting on Topsail is the extending sand spit at its southwestern end. There is a local beach access area just before the end of the road. If you park off the pavement, you can walk to the wide beach and the elongating sand spit that extends into New Topsail Inlet at the end of the island.

The benefit derived from an extending sand spit by residents of Topsail is not shared by property owners to the southwest. From the western beach access area on Topsail, you can see Lea Island across the inlet. This island is accessible only by boat and is low and even narrower than Topsail. Lots are available on this island, although at least five of them are now under the waters of the migrating inlet. One of these lots had a house built on it that became known locally as "Glump's Folly," as the inlet moved to claim it. Other lots and houses have suffered the same fate since, providing more food for thought about the wisdom of residential development of low-lying barrier islands.

East of Wilmington:
Natural Beaches, Dunes, and Grasslands

New Hanover County and the city of Wilmington are booming. Although the population in North Carolina's southeasternmost county increased *only* 26 percent between 1980 and 1993, the area is locally touted as the fastest growing in the United States, and the assessed value of real property has increased fivefold since 1980 to a level of over $6.1 billion. Anyone visiting Wilmington is viscerally aware of this upscale expansion. It is everywhere. What is great for the economy, however, is not always so good for natural areas. Many sites once visited by naturalists are now paved, converted to golf courses, or covered with condominiums. Wilmington remains twice blessed, however. Not only does it have wonderful natural rivers on its west and north; it has a coastal zone to the east that has some amazingly diverse areas preserved in parks and other natural areas.

The rivers of New Hanover County are described in other books. Benner and McCloud's *A Paddler's Guide to Eastern North Carolina* devotes 104 pages to the Cape Fear Basin, including fourteen pages to the Cape Fear River itself, eight to the Northeast Cape Fear, and four to the nearby Black River. Together these describe twenty-eight river sections that can be traversed by canoe or kayak. Local paddlers tell me that there are many other creeks, streams, and swamps that can be paddled from almost any of hundreds of access sites at road crossings and boat ramps.

The natural areas of the coastline east of Wilmington are not secret, but they have not been described together elsewhere. The gem of these eastern natural areas is Carolina Beach State Park. It has over 5 miles of nature trails that lead into some of the most interesting plant communities along the southern North Carolina coast. The North Carolina Aquarium at Fort Fisher provides access to unspoiled beach, dune, and salt marsh habitats, as does the adjoining Zeke's Island component of the National Estuarine Research Reserve. Zeke's Island stretches 3½ miles along the shore to New Inlet. Another component of the estuarine reserve system begins only 3 miles north of Carolina Beach State Park, on Masonboro Island. This component extends 8 miles along the shoreline between

Carolina Beach and Masonboro Inlets. Not to be outdone by state preservation programs, New Hanover County has developed a park on the north shore of Snow's Cut, which provides access to a fossil-rich outcrop of coquina rock in which clams and oysters nearly 1 million years old are available for observing and collecting. Rarely are sites of present and past eras so easily and conveniently accessible as they are in the coastal zone east of Wilmington. These areas are identified and located on figure 51.

Five-Star Features. All the areas east of Wilmington are worth visiting, and their proximity to one another makes it convenient to visit them all. There are two sites that stand out for their habitat diversity, size, and ease of access. These five-star features are (1) Carolina Beach State Park, for its forest and riverfront natural areas, and (2) Zeke's Island Estuarine Research Reserve, for its maritime forest and grasslands as well as its extensive tidal flats and accessible beach.

Carolina Beach State Park

Carolina Beach State Park is located in the town of Carolina Beach off US 421 about 10 miles southeast of Wilmington. The park entrance is just west of US 421 on Dow Road, which bypasses downtown Carolina Beach and rejoins US 421 in Kure Beach about 3.5 miles to the south. The park occupies 1,773 acres on the northwest corner of the island created when Snow's Cut was dredged in 1929 for the Atlantic Intracoastal Waterway. The U.S. Army Corps of Engineers gave 135 acres along Snow's Cut to the park and leases additional land to it. North Carolina purchased a core holding of 437 acres to preserve the habitat and provide public access to shores of Snow's Cut and the lower Cape Fear River.

The park provides areas for family camping, youth group camping, and picnicking, and a marina with both slips and a launching ramp. The main attraction for those interested in nature, however, is the more than five miles of trails laid out through forest and lowland plant communities. One of these trails—referred to as "Nature Trail" on signs and as "The Fly Trap Trail" in park literature—is the only one I know of that explicitly identifies areas where you can find the often-poached Venus flytrap and other insectivorous plants. A stop at the park office to obtain trail maps is a good idea because all sand ridges look alike and many existing roads and walkways are easily confused with official trails. The descriptive brochure for the Fly Trap Trail even provides drawings of sixteen plants typical of the three major forest types in the park and discusses animals — including the endangered red-cockaded woodpecker — that are found in the forests.

Carolina Beach State Park contains representative areas of at least nine different plant communities. Three of these — longleaf pine savanna, pond pine woodland, and pocosin — are seen from the well-marked Fly Trap Trail (see figure 52). An additional six communities are found along the 2.25-mile Sugarloaf Trail, reached from the southeast corner of the marina parking area. The Sugarloaf Trail gets its name from a 50-foot-high relict sand dune whose unvegetated top rising above the forest canopy has been used as a landmark for ships in the Cape Fear River since it first appeared on navigational charts in 1738. The trail reaches Sugarloaf along the banks of the Cape Fear River after passing through a short section of estuarine fringe loblolly pine forest. The bank of the river is occupied by salt marsh plants, with salt meadow cordgrass located between the upland and the taller, smooth cordgrass at the water's edge.

The trail continues to Sugarloaf itself, then swings back through sand ridges supporting a forest community with an open canopy of longleaf pine and a distinctive understory of turkey oak sometimes interspersed with yucca. This community is called Xeric Sandhill Scrub by plant ecologists, although park literature refers to it as the dry sand ridge community. The trail continues past three more communities located on low-lying depressions within the sand ridge area. These areas support freshwater wetland communities that range from seasonally flooded grasslands to a permanent lily pond much like Patsy Pond (described above) and a rare cypress savanna (see figure 53).

The Sugarloaf Trail returns to the marina after crossing the paved road to the Fly Trap Trail and a section of bottomland hardwood forest. There is also a cutoff called the Swamp Trail that branches off to the west just south of the paved road. The Swamp Trail passes through the youth group camping area, near the edge of the Fly Trap Trail area, and comes back to the Sugarloaf Trail on the bank of the Cape Fear just south of the trailhead at the marina parking lot.

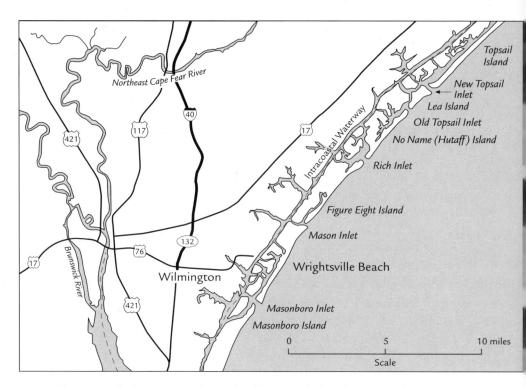

Figure 51. Wilmington area. Base map from North Carolina Coastal Boating Guide.

Carolina Beach State Park has a remarkably diverse flora. A 1990 study by David Sieren and Karen Warr of the University of North Carolina at Wilmington reports over 240 species present, including 30 that are described as rare to North Carolina by the state's Natural Heritage Program. This diversity and presence of rare species is partially a function of the diverse soil types, topography, and hydrology of the park lands. There are four distinct soil types distributed in a complex mosaic over a topography that ranges from high dune ridges, through organic-rich muds in pocosins, to limesink depression ponds and grasslands. The ridge, swale, and depression topography produces complex freshwater drainage patterns of

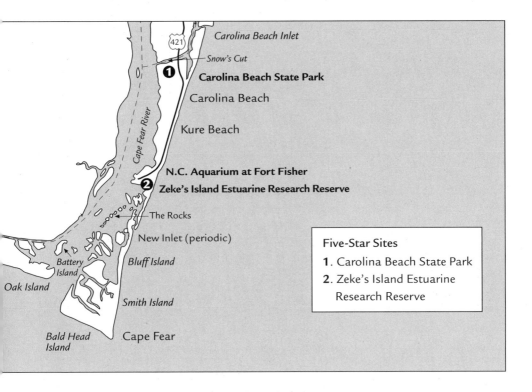

creeks, seeps, swamps, and ponds. The Cape Fear River and Snow's Cut provide brackish tidal water that floods the west and north sides of the park property. The natural communities that occur within this mosaic are rarely classic examples of the types they represent. In most cases they are transitional examples with plants occurring together that usually exist in different communities when large areas of uniform soil type, topography, and hydrology are available for colonization. Plant distributions in Carolina Beach State Park support the hypothesis that southern coastal plants are distributed in response to nothing more than physiological characteristics and chance. The plant combinations found in Carolina Beach State Park are quite different from those described as natural communities by Schafele and Weakley (see Chapter 1).

Figure 52. Carolina Beach State Park: pond pine woodland and longleaf pine savanna along the Fly Trap Trail.

North Carolina Aquarium at Fort Fisher and Zeke's Island Estuarine Research Reserve

The North Carolina Aquarium at Fort Fisher is about 5 miles south of Carolina Beach State Park on US 421. The entrance to the aquarium is south of Kure Beach and Fort Fisher State Historic Site. The natural areas around the aquarium and in Zeke's Island Coastal Research Reserve are excellent examples of beach, dune, maritime grassland, and salt marsh communities. There is also a maritime forest along the nature trail that extends south from the aquarium parking lot. The nature trail passes through the maritime forest, continues past some artificial ponds sur-

Figure 53. Carolina Beach State Park: cypress savanna along the Sugarloaf Trail.

rounded by freshwater marsh plants, then enters an extensive area of maritime grassland and salt marshes stretching away to the south and east (see figure 54). About ¾ mile from the parking lot there is a side trail that leads to a World War II–era bunker in which Robert Edward Harrell — known as the Fort Fisher Hermit — lived from 1955 until his death in 1972. Harrell was a colorful character who developed a considerable following among those who found his philosophy and lifestyle fascinating. The circumstances of his death remain controversial, even though two coroners found no evidence of foul play. He is buried near Fort Fisher, and his epitaph reads, "He made people think" — a kind of immortality he earned by his conversations with thousands of visitors who sought him out.

The Zeke's Island component of the Estuarine Research Reserve occupies 1,165 acres of beach, dune, maritime shrub, maritime forest, salt marsh, intertidal sand flat, and tidal basin habitat immediately south of

Figure 54. Maritime grassland and salt marsh habitats of Zeke's Island Estuarine Research Reserve.

the North Carolina Aquarium at Fort Fisher. In fact, most of the nature trail described above is within the Zeke's Island complex. Additional access to these habitats is by way of an off-road vehicle road behind the dunes and by private boat from the state-maintained launching ramp at the south end of US 421.

One very unusual feature of the Zeke's Island reserve is a 3-mile-long stone breakwater that forms its western boundary. This breakwater, known locally as "The Rocks," was built by the U.S. Army Corps of Engineers to close off New Inlet and keep sand from its flood-tide delta from filling in the Cape Fear River channel. It succeeded in achieving both those goals and now offers waders a unique opportunity to see algae and animals that live attached to this artificial island of rocky substrate. Oysters, mussels, sea anemones, starfish, and sea urchins can all be found, along with hundreds of other smaller and less conspicuous forms. Un-surprisingly, this feature is much used by sport fishermen and by birds that prey on the fish that prey on the animals that live on the rocks. The breakwater protects the tidal basin to its east from waves and wakes of the Cape Fear River. Thus this basin is a great place to use boats smaller than would be prudent in the river itself. You will find johnboats, canoes, kayaks, windsurfers, and inner tubes plying these waters in abundance whenever the weather permits. Access to The Rocks is provided from the public boat ramp at the end of US 421 just south of the state ferry terminal.

The most extensive habitats in the Zeke's Island area are salt marsh, maritime shrub, maritime forest, dune, and beach communities, de-scribed in Chapter 1. In addition there are tidal flats on the river side of the estuarine preserve (see material on tidal flats earlier in this chapter for a description of the kinds of organisms you will find here).

The habitats at the aquarium and Zeke's Island make the southern end of US 421 a good destination for naturalists and make this one of the five-star features of this coastline. A very full day can be spent hiking along the beach or back dune road; tramping across sand dunes, maritime grass-lands, and tidal flats; wading the shallow tidal creek to North Island; and climbing The Rocks, which separate these natural areas from the Cape Fear River. Your activities can be extended by visiting the exhibits at the aquarium, boating in the protected tidal basin east of The Rocks, or, if you have an interest in human as well as natural history, touring the near-by Fort Fisher State Historic Site — the most visited historic site in North Carolina.

The Fort Fisher Historic Site includes a museum that explains the fort and the battles fought there, the remains of the earthworks and bunkers of the fort itself, and the Underwater Archaeology Laboratory of the North Carolina Division of Archives and History. The staff of the labora-tory have spent the last 20 years exploring shipwrecks and other under-water artifacts of archaeological interest. Some of their finds are on dis-play in the museum. The historic site also has some exceptionally picturesque live oak groves that have been cleared of undergrowth and ap-pear silhouetted against the sky. For naturalists, however, one of the most interesting features of Fort Fisher State Historic Site is the exposure of offshore "hardground" habitat that can be seen off the beach at low tide (see figure 55).

Hardground habitats like those exposed at Fort Fisher are rarely seen above the sea surface but are more extensive offshore, where they support a community of algae, soft and encrusting coral, sea anemones, sea whips, and recreationally important finfish. These rocky outcrops are oases of seafloor life that support a northern extension of the snapper-grouper complex of fish as well as habitat for predators like mackerel and bluefish. These fish are preyed on by anglers of all species. The rocks off Fort Fisher are the nearshore edge of a series of sandstone and mudstone ledges that occur all across the continental shelf and along the topographic change in seafloor slope known as the shelf-slope break (see figure 1). The shelf break feature is under the nearshore edge of the Gulf Stream and is populated by a northward extension of a subtropical soft coral community, some members of which (sea whips and conical coral heads) can be found washed up on the beaches south of Cape Lookout.

The eroded beach at Fort Fisher is also interesting for its status as an exception to North Carolina's sensible policy not to harden beaches to prevent erosion. The exception was granted in an attempt to protect Fort Fisher's earthworks from further destruction. The effectiveness of this measure and its impact on the downdrift beach at the Fort Fisher State Recreational Area and the already catastrophically eroded beach updrift of the construction will be interesting to observe in the post-construction period.

New Hanover County Park at Snow's Cut

The natural rock ledges exposed at low tide at Fort Fisher are also exposed on both sides of Snow's Cut. Snow's Cut was dredged in 1929 for the Atlantic Intracoastal Waterway. It made an island (sometimes called Pleasure Island in tourist and real estate brochures) out of the southern part of New Hanover County's coastal peninsula. Some of these rocks can be seen from the Snow's Cut Trail in Carolina Beach State Park, but the best exposure is on the north shore at Snow's Cut Park, a unit of the New Hanover County Parks and Recreation Department system. Snow's Cut

Figure 55. Outcrops of coquina rock ledges off Fort Fisher. Note pieces of this hardground material on beach and the ongoing construction of a hardened structure designed to protect Fort Fisher's earthworks from further damage by beach erosion.

Park is reached from US 421 from River Road—the southernmost road to the west, just north of the high bridge over the cut. River Road parallels US 421 west of the bridge abutment, then turns west with NC Bicycle Trails 3 and 5 to parallel Snow's Cut. The park entrance is about 0.2 miles after the turn.

The late Pleistocene outcrop of fossil-rich sandstone is at the western end of the park. You reach it by descending a multi-switchbacked handicap access ramp. The rock is a yellowish-orange to grayish-orange coquina made of sand grains and shells cemented together by a calcium carbonate (limestone) matrix. Coquinas of this sort form currently and thus are common farther south but are relatively rare in North Carolina. North America's first European house in Saint Augustine, Florida, was constructed of blocks of this material. At Snow's Cut Park the rock outcrop is about 2 feet thick and overlain by about 10 feet of fossil-rich sand (see figure 56). The fossils in both the rock and the sand are slightly less than 1 million years old and consist of at least eight species of clams and two species of snails. Most of these shells look quite similar to those living now. You will recognize oysters, hard clams, stout razor clams, and mud snails.

Masonboro Island

Another major natural site east of Wilmington is the Masonboro Island component of the North Carolina Estuarine Research Reserve System. This 5,000-acre tract of shoreline is the largest natural area along North Carolina's southern coast. It contains an 8-mile-long beach and dune complex that fronts a salt marsh and a complex of intertidal and subtidal habitats. The island is accessible only by boat. There are public boat ramps in the towns of Carolina Beach and Wrightsville Beach, at both ends of Masonboro Island. There are also small, publicly accessible ramps at Trails End Road and some other, apparently private ramps at the end of other roads that extend seaward from Masonboro Loop Road and Masonboro Sound Road. There is a small mainland part of the reserve where the University of North Carolina at Wilmington is to build a marine research center, but there is no public water access there at present. There are companies that rent kayaks and other small boats near Masonboro Island (consult the telephone book yellow pages for an up-to-date listing), but at the time of this writing there were no water taxi services.

The natural communities of Masonboro Island are quite similar to those described above for the Zeke's Island component of the estuarine reserve system. One hundred and thirty-nine plant species have been identified. Most of these are distributed among beach, maritime grassland, maritime shrub thicket, and salt marsh communities, although there is a developing maritime forest near the middle of the island. The maritime grassland communities are less diverse and complex than those of Zeke's Island, although they are extensive in some areas where low oceanside dunes reach back to intertidal salt marsh on the sound side. There are dredge spoil islands on the inland side of the island.

Figure 56. Outcrop of late Pleistocene coquina rock at Snow's Cut Park.

Masonboro Island is a good place to visit if you have a private boat. The island will be more valuable to the general public when more services are developed to make it accessible. In the meantime, go if you can; it is a large, underutilized area with good marsh habitats and great beaches.

Other Islands East of Wilmington: Wrightsville, Figure Eight, No Name (Hutaff), and Lea

The islands directly east of downtown Wilmington are either heavily developed (Wrightsville Beach) or determinedly private (Figure Eight). The salt marshes inshore of these islands are worth exploring by boat, as they are large, natural, and accessible by an extensive network of navigable tidal creeks. Those behind Figure Eight Island are particularly scenic, as they provide views of some of the most interesting residential architecture on the North Carolina coast. Figure Eight has high dunes and maritime forests that homebuilders have used effectively to site houses that take excellent advantage of both water and marsh views.

Two less-developed and lower barrier islands occur between Figure Eight and Topsail Islands. The southernmost of these is listed in some books as No Name Island, a landmass that is listed elsewhere and known locally as Hutaff Island. This island is low, undeveloped, and privately owned. It is about two miles long and extends southwestward into Rich's Inlet just north of Figure Eight. Lea Island is also privately owned but has been platted into more than forty lots, some of which have been built on, even though there are no public electricity, telephone, water, or wastewater disposal systems. Several houses on the northeastern edge of Lea Island have been destroyed by the southward migration of Topsail Island. The most famous of these — known locally as "Glump's Folly" — was the first to go.

The marshes and intertidal beaches of Hutaff and Lea Islands are accessible by boat from Topsail Island, Hampstead, or Scott's Hill — all towns with public boat ramps. Like the islands farther south, the marshes and navigable creeks are worth visiting, but they do not differ greatly from the more easily accessible ones in Zeke's Island Estuarine Research Reserve.

Brunswick County: The Swamp-backed Shore

Brunswick County occupies the southernmost coastal area in North Carolina. It stretches from the Cape Fear River to South Carolina (see figure 57). With a land area of 855 square miles, Brunswick is North Carolina's fourth largest county. It is also among the richest from an environmental and biological standpoint. Richard J. LeBlond, a natural scientist with the North Carolina Natural Heritage Program, describes the county as follows on page 43 of his 1995 *Inventory of the Natural Areas and Rare Species of Brunswick County, North Carolina.*

Brunswick County contains not only some of the most biologically significant areas in North Carolina, but along the entire U.S. Atlantic

Coast. It supports more Federally Endangered or Threatened plant and animal species — 15 — than any other county in the state. It has the greatest diversity of natural communities in the state with 36 community types and subtypes. Brunswick County has the second highest number of rare species occurrences among North Carolina counties, and the second highest number of natural areas (sites). The county is a center of species diversity along the Atlantic Coast, with several species globally restricted to Brunswick County or adjacent areas. Some of the county's pine savannas have among the highest species richness of any similar-sized area in temperate North America. The concentration of Coastal Plain ponds is the largest along the Atlantic Coast between Massachusetts and Florida.

The thirty-six natural communities that LeBlond identifies in his inventory include all twelve described in Chapter 1 of this book. Some of these communities can be seen from almost anywhere in the county, but the most efficient way to see them is to visit a few exceptional sites that support several different communities in close proximity to one another. LeBlond identifies eleven natural areas of national significance in the county. Several of these are off limits in the Military Ocean Terminal at Sunny Point, others are privately owned and posted to prohibit trespassing, but at least nine excellent sites remain accessible to the public and are well worth visiting.

Five-Star Features. There are five sites in Brunswick County that are five-star environmental events: (1) Green Swamp north of Supply; (2) the Waccamaw River between NC 130 and 904; (3) Boiling Springs Lakes west of NC 87; (4) the Lockwoods Folly River estuary between Varnamtown and NC 211; and (5) Bald Head Island. Together these sites contain all the communities covered in Chapter 1 and some others that are not described but are well worth visiting. These five sites provide extraordinary examples of these communities, but good examples of the same types of communities can be found elsewhere. To provide these options, this section is organized by habitat type, with several sites of representative communities described in each section. Specific sites from which to view these habitats are included on the map (figure 57).

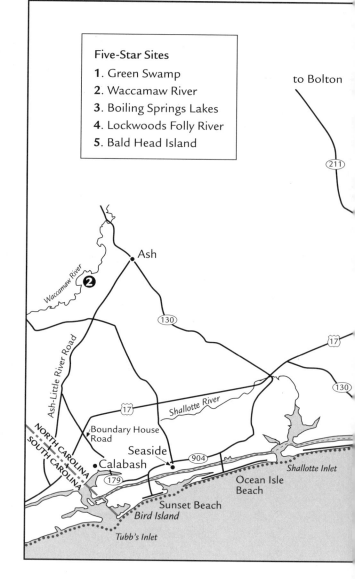

Figure 57. Coastal Brunswick County. Base map from North Carolina Coastal Boating Guide.

Five-Star Sites

1. Green Swamp
2. Waccamaw River
3. Boiling Springs Lakes
4. Lockwoods Folly River
5. Bald Head Island

to Bolton

Ash

Waccamaw River

Ash-Little River Road

NORTH CAROLINA
SOUTH CAROLINA

Boundary House Road

Shallotte River

Seaside

Calabash

Ocean Isle Beach

Shallotte Inlet

Sunset Beach

Bird Island

Tubb's Inlet

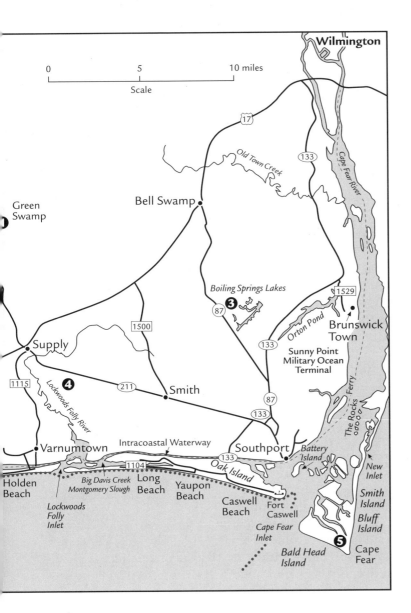

Wilmington

0   5   10 miles
Scale

17

133

Cape Fear River

Old Town Creek

Green
Swamp

Bell Swamp

Boiling Springs Lakes

1529

Orton Pond

Brunswick
Town

87   ❸

1500

133

Sunny Point
Military Ocean
Terminal

Supply

1115

❹   211   Smith

87

133

Lockwoods Folly River

The Rocks

Intracoastal Waterway

Varnumtown   Southport

Battery
Island

New
Inlet

133

1104   Oak Island

Holden
Beach

Big Davis Creek
Montgomery Slough

Long
Beach

Yaupon
Beach

Caswell
Beach

Fort
Caswell

Smith
Island

Bluff
Island

Lockwoods
Folly
Inlet

Cape Fear
Inlet

Bald Head
Island

❺

Cape
Fear

Swamps and Wooded Wetlands

Green Swamp

Much of northern Brunswick County is swampland. Some of it has been drained to enhance forest production of loblolly pine, but several areas remain in their original state. The most accessible of these is in Green Swamp, where the Nature Conservancy has preserved 15,722 acres of longleaf pine forest and pocosins. Management of this area is supported by the estate of Henry Patrick Gold and Erma Green Gold. The habitats here are among the best of their kind anywhere in the world—a fact recognized by Great Britain's David Attenborough, who filmed Venus flytraps here for his documentary "The Private Life of Plants."

The easiest entrance to the Green Swamp Nature Conservancy tract is off NC 211 about 7 miles north of Supply (or 15 miles south of Bolton, if you come south on 211 from US 74 and US 76). The entrance lies just south of Driving Creek, where Atlantic white cedars can be seen along the banks, and just north of an extensive longleaf pine savanna in which club mosses can be found in the herb layer.

The parking area for the Nature Conservancy tract is between a borrow-pit pond and some white boundary markers on the east side of NC 211. Trails lead back into the preserve from the parking area. The main trail leads along the pond, then veers southeast through a loblolly pine plantation for about ¼ mile to reach a pond pine woodland with pocosin plant understory. The trail diminishes in size but leads east across a boardwalk through the pocosin to a magnificent longleaf pine savanna (see figure 58), where pitcher plants and other insectivorous plants are not only present but common. Note that the Green Swamp preserve allows the taking of deer in accordance with state rules and seasons but prohibits the taking or disturbance of any plants.

The trails in Green Swamp preserve extend for many miles through high-quality communities of pine savanna, pine flatwoods, pond pine woodland, and pocosin. The longleaf pine savanna community is one of the richest in number of plant species of any in the country. LeBlond's inventory identifies twenty-six rare plants and sixteen rare animals that occur here. Clearly, Green Swamp is a must-visit site for naturalists in Brunswick County.

Figure 58.
Longleaf pine savanna
in Green Swamp.

Other Swamps

Green Swamp is by no means the only noteworthy example of swamp and forested wetland habitats in Brunswick County. LeBlond lists all of the Waccamaw River wetlands from Juniper Creek (on the northern border of the county) to South Carolina as a nationally significant natural area. Unfortunately, most of this area is hard to visit without a four-wheel-drive vehicle with high ground clearance. Swamp roads tend to have deep puddles with soft, muddy bottoms. Nonetheless, any passable-looking side road that extends through northern Brunswick County is a good bet for seeing swamps, pocosins, pond pine woodlands, and longleaf savannas as well as other freshwater wetland communities. Some of these communities found in Brunswick County but not described in Chapter 1 include bay forest, coastal plain small stream swamp, cypress-gum swamp, oxbow lake, sand and mud bar, and coastal plain levee forest. A full description of these communities can be found in Schafele and Weakley's 1990 *Classification of North Carolina Natural Communities* and in LeBlond's *Inventory of Natural Areas of Brunswick County*. Both are available from the North Carolina Natural Heritage Program in Raleigh.

Other Wooded Wetlands

Another area where longleaf pine savannas, pond pine woodland, and pocosins are found is east of Boiling Springs Lakes off NC 87. The lakes themselves are man-made, but extensive grassy wetlands like those of naturally occurring, seasonally flooded topographic depressions are found along their edges. To reach the best place to see this spectrum of wetlands in the Boiling Springs Lakes area, go west off NC 87 just north of the lake on west North Shore Road. Although dirt, the road is well maintained and easily passable in two-wheel-drive vehicles. About ⅒ mile down this road there is a road to a dam on the left. This area provides a good place from which to see the wetlands both within and beside the lakes. Driving farther along west North Shore Road and others with which it intersects will lead you through pocosins, pond pine woodlands, and longleaf savannas in great profusion and past many areas where plant combinations transitional among these communities occur. The same communities and transitional areas are found along highways NC 133, 87, and 211 in the eastern end of the county.

Rivers

Brunswick County's eastern and western boundaries are rivers, and several other rivers drain southward through central areas of the county. The most significant river is, of course, the Cape Fear, which borders the county on the east. There are wonderful brackish water marshes along the creeks that enter the Cape Fear at many places along its passage through the county. Juniper Creek and the Waccamaw River form the county's northwestern border. Aquatic and bank habitats along both are regionally significant natural areas.

The Waccamaw River is easily accessible from both NC 130 and NC 904 (see figure 57). There are launching ramps at both crossings, and the river between the highways can be navigated with no risk other than that provided by downed trees. The crossing at NC 130 has a cypress-gum swamp immediately upstream. The crossing at NC 904 leads upstream through cypress-gum swamp into coastal plain bottomland hardwood and coastal plain levee forest (blackwater type) communities.

Cypress-gum swamps, sometimes known locally as back swamps, are dominated by the tree species that give the community its name — cypress of the genus *Taxodium* and tupelo gums of the genus *Nyssa*. Red maples, Carolina ash, and water elm also are present. These plants occur in broad areas that are frequently flooded by high-river levels or along cutoff river channels known as sloughs.

Coastal plain bottomland hardwood communities along the Waccamaw River (see figure 59) are unusual as they are among the few areas in the state where Atlantic white cedar is an important constituent. Otherwise the community along the Waccamaw is relatively similar to the general description in Chapter 1 — a community dominated by oaks, maples, and loblolly pine, with hollies, red bays, and mayberry (*Vaccinium elliottii*) in the understory. These communities can be dense or surprisingly open.

Coastal plain levee forest (blackwater type) communities are made up of many of the same trees that occur in bottomlands, but they grow closer to the river channel and are therefore more frequently flooded. The shrub layer is usually more open and less bound together by vines than that of bottomland hardwood communities.

Other areas of bottomland hardwood and cypress-gum communities occur along ponds and streams throughout the county. Two of the easiest places to observe these communities by car are on NC 211 where it crosses the Lockwoods Folly River just east of Supply and in Orton Pond off NC 1529 between Orton Plantation and Brunswick Town.

Figure 59. Forests along the Waccamaw River.

Estuaries

Although the Cape Fear River is the largest estuary in North Carolina, its size makes it hard to observe by any means other than a cruise along it in a substantial vessel. For this reason, I recommend estuarine tours up smaller and more manageable streams such as the Lockwoods Folly or Shallotte Rivers. My personal favorite is the Lockwoods Folly River. There are three reasons for this: (1) there is relatively little housing constructed along its banks; (2) it cuts through eight old beach ridges, thereby demonstrating beautifully the relationship between topography and plant communities; and (3) Varnamtown is a picturesque fishing village with a publicly accessible boat ramp.

The launching ramp in Varnamtown is at Dixon Point, just down Varnamtown Road from Stone Chimney Road (NC 1115). Follow Varnamtown

Road until you see the Lockwoods Folly River down the hill straight ahead of you. The road leads to the ramp at Dixon's Landing, where there are several fish houses and their associated boats. The salt marshes here are extensive and boast almost a pure stand of smooth cordgrass.

Upstream from Varnamtown, the Lockwoods Folly River cuts through old sand ridges (see figure 60). This creek bank erosion has exposed Pleistocene outcrops similar to those at Snow's Cut along the foot of the cliff. Erosion has also brought oaks down from the ridgetop forests. These make good resting areas for egrets. Between the upstream sand ridges, the marsh becomes increasingly diverse through addition of black needlerush, salt grass, and glassworts along the upland margin. Upstream, the forest margins also show signs of dieback associated with saline water encroachment.

Even farther upstream the riverbank supports cypress-gum forests like those along the Waccamaw. Lockwoods Folly River remains navigable for at least 10 miles upstream. It is 100 feet wide where it is crossed by NC 210 and continues at least another 5 miles, where one branch of it passes under old US 17 at Piney Grove. These upstream areas are surrounded by cypress-gum swamps and bottomland hardwood forests.

There are other river estuaries worth visiting. The Shallotte River stretches 5 miles north from its inlet between Ocean Isle and Holden Beach. There is more residential construction along its shores than there is along Lockwoods Folly River, but that makes it easier to see by automobile. There are some excellent examples of freshwater marsh and black needlerush marsh north and south of the Main Street (US 17 Business) Bridge in downtown Shallotte. Note the state sign marking the line between inland and coastal fish management areas just south of this bridge.

Calabash Creek in (you guessed it) Calabash is also worth observing. There are well-developed salt marshes near the mouth (just west of the charter boat dock) and at the upstream end that, although surrounded by golf courses, still provide nesting habitat for rare wood storks, a species generally found farther south.

The best examples of freshwater tidal marshes in Brunswick County are along Town Creek (see figure 61). LeBlond rates these as of national significance in his Brunswick County inventory. Town Creek is easy to visit

Figure 60. Old dune ridge along the Lockwoods Folly River.

by both car and boat, as it is crossed by roads in three places and there are launching ramps near two of these. Town Creek empties into the Cape Fear River about 7 miles south of Belville. The creek's lower reaches can be observed from NC 133, where a boat can be launched beside the highway bridge or at a concrete launching ramp about 100 yards upstream on the north shore. The ramp is reached by an unposted dirt road at the south side of an abandoned store on the west side of NC 133. The habitat in this area has a tidal freshwater marsh near the creek, with some cypress and gum trees on the creek bank levee. The marsh here is occasionally flooded by saltwater and is dominated by saw grass, cattails, and giant cordgrass. Farther upstream these grasses are replaced by lanceleaf arrowhead, spider lilies, and pickerel weed along the creek and backed by cypress-gum swamps. The upper reaches of the creek can be observed from US 17 about 2 miles south of Bishop. Here the cypress-gum trees are incorporated into a typical swamp forest as described in Chapter 1. The middle reaches can be accessed by boat from a ramp 1.4 miles down Governor's Road (SR 1521), the road that leads east from the crossroads just south of the US 17 bridge. Those with kayaks or canoes can launch them down the shoulder of a dirt road north of the US 17 bridge. Turn west on Mount Zion Road, immediately left toward a house, then right onto Benson Road. The launch site is less than 0.1 mile up Benson Road.

The Shoreline of Brunswick County

Bald Head Island is unquestionably a five-star natural feature of Brunswick County. It is expensive to visit but worth the price. Bald Head itself is being developed for residential and recreational use, but much natural area remains. The most striking habitat is the evergreen maritime forest, which is unarguably the finest example in the state. It is rated as nationally significant by the North Carolina Natural Heritage Program. In addition to this extraordinary forest, Bald Head also has dune, beach, and marsh communities that are almost as good. Together these communities sustain eight species of animals and two species of plants that are ranked as rare nationally and another four animal and ten plant species that are rare in North Carolina.

Much of the remaining Brunswick County coastline has been developed in such a way that few natural areas remain, and none save those on Bird Island can even come close to matching those on Bald Head.

Bald Head and the Smith Island Complex

Bald Head Island is the most recently formed and southernmost of three separate islands shaped by old shorelines left behind as the east shore of the Cape Fear River extended to the south. The other islands created by this southward elongation of the shoreline make up what geographers call the Smith Island complex. Much of this complex is undeveloped and essentially pristine. Together these shorelines and the extensive salt marshes that separate them make up the awkwardly named Bald Head–Smith Island complex.

Bald Head and Smith Island are reached by boat or by private toll ferry

Figure 61. Town Creek.

from the Indigo Plantation development at the end of Ninth Street in Southport. The landing is well marked by signs that call it the "Ferry to Bald Head Island." The fare is $15.00 round trip, with bicycles or boats extra. The ride to Bald Head is pleasant and scenic, as you pass excellent marsh habitat, the waterfront of historic Southport, and Battery Island in transit. Battery Island is owned and maintained by the National Audubon Society because of its importance as a nesting area for colonial water-birds. Nine different species occupy the island, and over 10,000 nesting pairs were in residence in 1993 (the most recent reporting period). Ninety percent of these nesting pairs were white ibis, a species frequently seen from the Southport waterfront. Across the shipping channel to the south of Battery Island is the town of Caswell Beach, with its Oak Island Light-house and Fort Caswell. Fort Caswell was built in 1826 and was used until World War II to guard the entrance to the Cape Fear River. The site is now owned by the North Carolina Baptist Assembly, which runs workshops, classes, and camps there throughout most of the year. The assembly allows visitors onto the site for a modest fee designed to offset the cost of insurance required by this public access. Both Battery Island and Fort Caswell are worth visiting, although Battery Island is off limits during the waterbird nesting season.

Arrival at Bald Head Island is much less picturesque than departure from Southport. The ferry enters the yacht basin through a bulkheaded and riprapped channel cut through a man-made protective dune. Once off the ferry, you can rent bicycles or golf carts from the transportation office just south of the ferry dock. I recommend renting some means of transport because the best natural areas are 1 to 5 miles from the ferry landing. You can, however, easily walk to, and laboriously climb, the nearby privately maintained 1817 lighthouse known as "Old Baldy."

The natural areas on Bald Head are quite far removed from the residentially developed part of the island. The best natural habitats are north and west of the developed area. The most spectacular natural habitat is the 435-acre maritime forest tract owned by the state and overseen by its Division of Coastal Zone Management. This tract is reached by Federal Road (follow the signs to Middle Island). The forest reserve begins about 1.5 miles from the ferry landing. This forest is the least-disturbed evergreen maritime forest in the state, although its canopy has been opened in several areas where trees have been downed by hurricanes. Nevertheless, large live oaks with diameters up to 6 feet remain. These are found along a trail into the reserve marked by a small sign with a tree silhouette. Other trails have boardwalks to indicate their presence, but still others are unmarked except by openings in the vegetation. It is certainly worth taking the time to explore these trails. They lead to huge oak trees and unusual wetlands and pass the most unusual trees in this forest—the cabbage palm, *Sabal palmetto*. Many of these are hard to see fully because they grow up through the live oak canopy (see figure 62). Other trees found in this forest include loblolly pine, laurel oak, red bay, wild olive, Carolina laurel-cherry, and dogwood. The vines and underbrush typical of undisturbed maritime forests are here as well, but trails through the preserve circumvent the densest thickets.

Figure 62. Deciduous maritime forest on Bald Head in the Smith Island Complex. Note the Sabal palm extending above the live oak canopy.

There are several other natural areas on Bald Head and Smith Islands that are worth seeing. One of these, the Kent Mitchell Nature Trail, begins on a boardwalk crossing the marsh north of Federal Road between the forest preserve and the ferry landing. This trail was built by the Bald Head Island Conservancy and is both imaginative and informative. It is imaginative because it combines crooked trails and boardwalks in ways that repeatedly bring you to new and surprising vistas of salt marsh, vegetated hammock, and creek. The trail is informative because most of the dominant plants are discreetly identified with elegant wooden signs. This is the kind of trail that delights both the eye and the mind; it is a treat not to be missed. The marshes through which the trail leads separate Bald Head and Middle Island. There is a tidal creek that drains the marsh and its associated uplands. The marsh here is typically zoned with smooth cordgrass close to the creek and black needlerush, saltgrass, glasswort, and sea ox-eye along the upland fringe. The plants on the hammocks include those often found in maritime shrub communities, including a few examples of cabbage palm.

The northernmost island of the Bald Head–Smith Island complex is sometimes called Bluff Island. This island has the least-disturbed upland area in the complex and is located about a mile north of the gazebo and parking area for East Beach. Most of Bluff Island is in the Bald Head Island State Natural Area, but some is still in private hands. The island contains a pristine maritime forest on its central sand ridges, a rare interdune pond between ridges on the central and eastern part of the island, maritime shrub on the island flanks, and salt marsh, salt flat, and dune communities on the periphery. LeBlond's Brunswick County inventory lists nine plants and the loggerhead sea turtle as rare and threatened species that occur in Bluff Island habitats. The most unusual community on the island is that of the interdune pond, mainly because such ponds are quite rare along North Carolina's southeastern coast. Readers will be familiar with plants found there. They include the common reed, black needlerush, and cattail, along with less familiar bulrush and spike rush species. The oceanside dune habitat is unusual in having more bitter panic grass than most communities.

Another must-visit natural site on Bald Head is the point at Cape Fear (see figure 63). This is one of three places where North Carolina's seacoast changes direction by over 90° (Cape Hatteras and Cape Lookout are the others). Cape Fear Point is reached most easily from the old lighthouse keeper's cottages called Captain Charlie's House. The well-signed entrance road leads south just west of the Bald Head Island Conservancy building on Federal Road.

The most striking oceanic features of the North Carolina capes are the wave interactions and the long offshore sandbars that result from convergence of waves and alongshore currents from the northeast and southwest. Evidence of both features is easily observed at Cape Fear Point. Wave trains approach from both sides of the point, and individual waves that comprise them smash together, throwing spray into the air in a process called *claptois*. Currents that move in the same direction as the wave trains

Figure 63. Cape Fear Point at southeastern tip of Bald Head Island.
Note the greater than 90° angle made by the shoreline at this point.

meet off Cape Fear Point and carry sand offshore to form Frying Pan
Shoals—the sandbar complex that stretches more than 20 miles offshore
and that, together with comparable shoals off Capes Hatteras and Lookout, trapped sailing ships and gave the North Carolina coast the fearsome
nickname "Graveyard of the Atlantic" among early mariners.

Cape Fear Point is also interesting geologically because the beach shows
signs of the shoreline accretion that formed the sequence of islands in the
Bald Head–Smith Island complex. Northeast or southwest winds (the
two most frequently prevailing winds in coastal North Carolina) blow
sand along the beach to the point, where it settles on the wet beach on the
downwind side of the point (see figure 64). In addition, sand brought onshore by alongshore currents and collapsing breakers (see Chapter 1) accumulates in beach ridges with steep landward sides. Together these

Figure 64. Beach accretion at Cape Fear Point. Wind-driven sand (note "fuzz" of windblown sand above the berm) depositing on the wet beach.

processes of wind and water cause sand to accumulate on the southeastern corner of the island. Over time, this sand is spread along the beach to extend the island southward, thereby creating a series of progressively younger beach ridges and islands in a sequence stretching from north to south—Bluff Island, Middle Island, and Bald Head Island.

Other Natural Areas

The ocean shoreline of Brunswick County is over 40 miles long. Almost all of it consists of low, relatively narrow barrier islands that have been developed for recreation facilities and residences. The beaches are good and, with a few exceptions, publicly accessible. The beach towns and their public access areas are well described by Glenn Morris in his 1993 book, *North Carolina Beaches: A Guide to Coastal Access* (Chapel Hill: University of North

Carolina Press). I will not repeat that information here; rather, I will focus on the relatively few areas that remain natural along this coast. Quite frankly, there are not a lot of natural areas left on these barrier islands. Bird Island, west of Sunset Beach and extending into South Carolina, is the only undeveloped island remaining, although patches of maritime grassland communities exist on Holden Beach, and patches of maritime forest, maritime grassland, and salt marsh remain on Oak Island.

Bird Island: A Publicly Loved Private Holding

Bird Island, at the southwestern corner of Brunswick County, is partially owned by a Greensboro family, but the south end of the island is owned by the U.S. Army Corps of Engineers. The island has long been used by the public as an accessible natural area and beach. Controversy has resulted from the conflicts between private ownership and public use, but most of the owners now say they want the island preserved in its current state for public use. In 1996 the North Carolina Coastal Resources Commission voted to prohibit construction of a bridge across Mad Inlet, thereby further discouraging prospects for development. The controversy has no bearing on the natural habitats of Bird Island, although private property rights can be invoked to enforce trespassing laws on land above the high-tide line at the north end of the island. Therefore, I suggest that readers stay on the wet beach, salt marsh, or southern dunes if they visit Bird Island.

Bird Island is accessible by boat from Little River and by wading Mad Inlet at the west end of Sunset Beach (see figure 65). There are several boat launching ramps in Calabash and across the state line, in Little River, South Carolina. Access to Sunset Beach is via state road 1172. Parking in west Sunset Beach is not easy, as there are only four obvious spaces, but it can be done if you get off the pavement in an area unmarked by "No Parking Anytime" signs. There is a public beach access ramp near the western end of state road 1177. The walk up the beach is unremarkable, but note the obvious westward extension of the Sunset Beach sand spit and the resultant erosion of the easternmost portion of Bird Island's oceanfront

Figure 65. Mad Inlet and Bird Island beach and dunes. Note incoming tide with a surge wave.

dune (see figure 65). LeBlond lists the communities of Bird Island as salt marsh, beach, dune, and maritime shrub and notes two rare animals (loggerhead turtle and black skimmer) and one rare plant (seabeach amaranth) as occurring there. The communities are all visible from below the high-tide line. When I visited in October, the maritime shrub community was host to an amazingly large flock of tree swallows. These birds overwinter along the southeastern coast after nesting in northern states. They were eating berries from the wax myrtle bushes on the island. Their presence certainly reinforced the appropriateness of Bird Island's name.

Figure 66. Holden Beach maritime grasslands with immature white ibises feeding on fiddler crabs.

Maritime Grasslands and Irregularly Flooded Communities on Holden Beach

Holden Beach has a man-made dune on the ocean side, spoil islands on the inland waterway side, and maritime grassland, salt marsh, and sand flat communities in between. Earlier phases of development have converted irregularly flooded intertidal habitats to residential lots, but some of the natural communities remain. White ibises (*Endocimus albus*) use these areas to feed on fiddler crabs and other abundant salt marsh animals (see figure 66). Beyond the maritime grasslands there are extensive areas of salt flats and irregularly flooded salt marsh. These areas are particularly well developed between Swordfish Drive and Sand Dollar Drive. The eastern end of Holden Beach is being eroded by Lockwoods Folly

Figure 67. Salt marsh and maritime forest on Oak Island.

Inlet moving west. This situation makes dramatically clear why inlets are classified as areas of environmental concern by the North Carolina Coastal Area Management Program.

Maritime Forest and Grassland on Oak Island

Oak Island is the largest barrier island along the Brunswick County shoreline. It is home to the towns of Long Beach, Yaupon Beach, and Caswell Beach. Most of Oak Island is platted for house lots, and many have houses on them. There are a few that are not built upon, and these sustain remnants of the maritime forest community that once occupied this area. Seaward of the maritime forest areas are dunefields that support maritime grassland communities. Some of these communities are diverse, with common reed and other plants indicative of habitat disturbance occurring among the natural plant assemblage. Most of the maritime grassland and salt marsh habitats are along the northern edge of Oak Island. These extensive marshes are easily seen from the high bridge that carries NC 133 to the island. Maritime grasslands develop between dune and forest in Yaupon Beach here. Farther west, this interdune low expands to form Montgomery Slough and Big Davis Creek (see figure 67). These tidal watercourses are flanked by salt marshes, and the town of Long Beach has developed a canoe trail through them. The easiest access point is at the western end of the island, although canoes and kayaks can be launched at many places when the tide is high.

HUMAN USE OF THE SOUTHERN COAST

Population, Land Use, and Economic Development

Anyone who has visited the southern coast recognizes that the natural processes and habitats described in this book are increasingly influenced by human activities. Fifty years ago no one would have had to write a field guide to natural areas of southern North Carolina—almost all of it was natural. Startling as it may seem, when the U.S. Navy began using Topsail Island as a missile test range during World War II, they could not find people to whom rent payments were due because the island was used as common grazing lands and few people cared enough about ownership claims to pay the property taxes required to maintain them. Today any land on barrier islands is valuable. This value was established shortly after World War II and has been increasing ever since. The value of land near the ocean, like the missiles once tested on Topsail Island, is heading toward the sky.

For at least two decades the human population of North Carolina's coastal zone has been increasing at a rate roughly twice that of the state as a whole. This population began expanding in three areas: New Hanover and Brunswick Counties near Wilmington, Onslow County near Camp Lejeune, and Dare County near Virginia. In the last decade, however, growth in these areas has been joined by that in areas between them. Recently Pender County had the fastest population growth in the state. Between 1980 and 1993 the number of permanent residents in North Carolina's coastal counties increased by more than 35 percent. The seasonal population has grown even faster. In Carteret County the summer population is at least three times as large as the permanent population. Substantial seasonal increases occur in Pender and Brunswick Counties as well. Military personnel and urban populations swell the base populations of Onslow and New Hanover Counties, so percentage change is less there than elsewhere; but anyone who visits the coast recognizes that "summer people" and tourists flock in during warmer months.

Both permanent and seasonal populations have invested in coastal real estate. As a result, the value of existing homes has increased, and new construction has added dramatically to the total appraised value of real property. The value of real property in the five coastal counties covered in Chapter 2 rose from $3.4 billion in 1980 to $15.9 billion in 1993. This is an increase of 363 percent during the period. These and other data obtained from official census and population projections available on the Log In North Carolina system are presented in figure 68. The striking divergence between rate of population increase and rate of real estate values has three causes: (1) the increase in size and amenities of recent residential construction; (2) the increase in value of existing homes resulting from increasing demand on a finite supply; and (3) economic inflation and changes in appraisal rules. The relative contribution of these factors to the increases varies from area to area, but the inescapable conclusion applies everywhere — an increasing number of people are making increasing investments in coastal real estate along the southern coast.

The new residents of the coastal zone are using it quite differently than the earlier residents did. Where once there were fields and forests, there are now golf courses and gated communities of luxury homes. Where once there were fishing grounds and intertidal marshes, there are now marinas and condominiums. Where once there were seasonally used beach cottages, there are now million-dollar mansions on the strand. All this makes clear that new residents are using coastal resources more intensely than their predecessors did. Early stages of heavier use were accommodated by making buildable lots on salt marshes and oceanfront dunes, but these practices have been curtailed by regulations put in place after more than one-eighth of North Carolina's original salt marsh acreage had

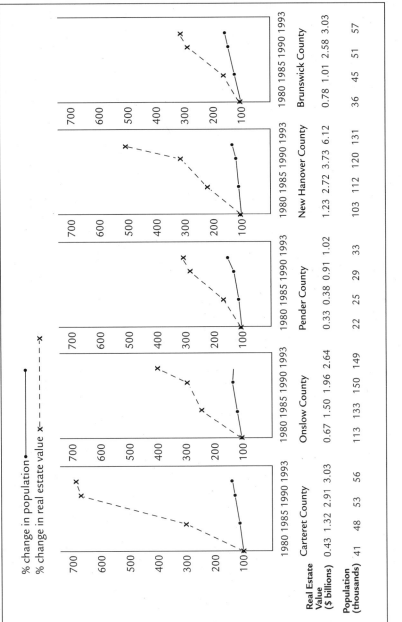

Figure 68. Development of coastal counties, 1980–1993.

been filled. Even now, road berms on some barrier islands continue to be widened in such a way that high marsh is covered with fill and subsequently sold as roadsite lots. Road maintenance activities are exempt from the definition of "development" that is regulated by North Carolina's Coastal Area Management Act.

Barrier island dunes and salt marshes are by no means the only wetlands lost to development. The Division of Environmental Management (DEM) estimates that fully 34 percent of North Carolina's original coastal wetlands have been impaired by development. Of that total, 52 percent have been affected by agricultural development, 10 percent by urban development, and 38 percent by forestry. Much greater changes have taken place in the region's forests as harvest and catastrophic fires resulted in the replacement of longleaf pine savannas by southern mixed forests and pine flatwoods. In North Carolina the acreage of longleaf pine savanna decreased from over 3.5 million to 28,000, while the acreage of mixed pine-hardwood forests increased to over 2.2 million between 1770 and 1970. Thus change in coastal zone habitats is not exclusively a product of recent development.

Coastal habitats change constantly and have been doing so for over 200 million years. The mid-continent desert that was flooded by the opening of the Atlantic Ocean has never been seen again, and the land that is now coastal has repeatedly been seafloor and upland forest as sea level has changed to flood or expose it (see Chapter 1). Thus we cannot claim that change in coastal habitats is unnatural. Change is what characterizes these areas.

But it *is* fair to say that today's changes are as rapid as any in the past. Numerous academic treatises have been written to document the easily reached conclusion that the rate of change in modern society continues to accelerate. No one with a multiyear exposure to the southern coast will doubt that for a minute. The only question is how much change is acceptable, and how do we assure that change can be managed to keep it within the limits we think appropriate.

One of the fundamental changes we might consider is how much change in economic activity do we wish to encourage by further development of coastal resources. Surprisingly enough, economic analysis shows that coastal zones of southern states have not been a major generator of the gross national product (GNP) in the United States. Only the coastal zones of Virginia, Florida, and Louisiana have contributed more than the national average of 31 percent of the GNP generated by their states. The coastal zones of other southeastern and Gulf Coast states have generated an average of only 10–13 percent of their state contribution to the GNP. Michael I. Luger of the University of North Carolina at Chapel Hill has shown that this situation has begun to change. Luger has developed an innovative technique for calculating the economic value of the nation's coastal zones based on a system of "national income accounting." The technique involves classifying activities that create value into three coastal sectors: (1) coast-dependent activities—those that must be performed in the coastal zone (such as marina services and ocean transport); (2) coast-linked activities—those that use coastal habitats for their production but do not have to be located in the coastal zone (such as fishing equipment manufacture and marine science research); and (3) coastal services—those that provide services to coastal residents (real estate agencies and retail stores).

When Census Bureau employment data are evaluated in these categories, they provide a measure of state coastal GNP and a percentage of total state GNP based on coastal economic activity. For southern states facing the Atlantic (other than Florida), the coastal GNP has more than doubled between 1978 and 1985, and the percentage of total state GNP produced by coastal activities in these states increased by an average of 4.5 percent. For states facing the Gulf of Mexico (Florida and Louisiana excepted), the coastal GNP increased by 167 percent between 1978 and 1985, but the coastal percentage of total state GNP declined by 0.6 percent. Luger has analyzed 1990 census data for North Carolina and has shown that the state's coastal GNP increased another 48 percent between 1985 and 1990. This last increase puts North Carolina's percentage of total state GNP at about 11 percent—about one-third that of the average coastal state.

Impact of Development on
Coastal Resources and Water Quality

It is now clear that development of the southern coast puts large demands on coastal resources. Land resources are heavily used. Stable shorefront building lots have always been in limited supply, but the construction boom of the late twentieth century clearly has exhausted that supply and moved on to construct houses on lots that are not stable. Stable building lots on some southern barrier islands (Topsail, Wrightsville, and Sunset Beaches) are essentially all occupied, even though these and other islands still have lots for sale. The coastal building boom has begun to move onto inland land resources. Other resources are also under stress. Living resources are frequently harvested at unsustainable rates. Coastal fish resources show unmistakable signs of overharvest. About one-third of the economically valuable seafood species in North Carolina are classified as overfished at any one time. The most worrisome aspect of the increase in coastal population and economic development, however, is its impact on coastal water quality. This impact attacks the fundamental coastal resource — safe, clean water — and has the potential to threaten the base of the new coastal economy.

The negative impact of coastal development on water quality has a long and ugly history. Early development of coastal land was undertaken with little regard for the impact of that development on the nearby waters. Wetlands were ditched and drained with no regard for changes the more rapid runoff would have on estuaries and lagoons. Communities were built at the upstream limit of navigation, where environmental processes characteristic of the freshwater-saltwater interface would trap and concentrate wastes in the river bottoms. Factories were located on small, slow-flowing creeks where oxygen-consuming wastes created anaerobic zones that were lethal to native animals and plants. Communities and factories used flowing waters as waste removal systems and followed the dictum "The solution to pollution is dilution," by dumping waste materials in whatever watercourse was nearby. When the problems of that approach became obvious to anyone with a nose, new techniques were developed to remove the most obvious and dangerous pollutants. Specifically, wastewater was treated to remove agents of human disease and reduce the amount of oxygen-consuming material. These techniques were adopted relatively slowly in the coastal zones of southern states. Inadequate waste treatment technology created increasing problems through the 1960s and 1970s with occasional crises and repeated calls for action. Water quality crises in coastal North Carolina in the late 1970s created newspaper headlines such as "Algal Bloom Colors Area of Neuse River," "Lack of Money, Manpower Hamper River Protection," "Extensive Neuse Probe Set to Find Pollution Source," "State Fines City of Raleigh for Pollution of Neuse River," "Chowan Clean-up May Aid Neuse," and "Fishermen Want All Rivers Cleaned Up."

Water quality was not the only environmental problem in U.S. coastal zones in the middle years of the twentieth century. The population rush to the coast was accompanied by development that went forward with little attention to preserving either the environment or existing property use and value. Toxic chemicals used for pest and weed control produced increasingly adverse impacts on songbirds and predators such as pelicans, ospreys, and eagles. These broad problems of the environment were documented during the 1960s, most notably by Rachel Carson in her 1962 book *Silent Spring*. The problems, the books, and public concern galvanized by the first Earth Day in 1970 led to a spate of federal and state legislation designed to regulate use of the coastal zone. The major federal laws passed in this period are listed and summarized in table 3.

The legislation listed in table 3 has done much to control and improve land use practices and limit dumping of many types of pollutants in the coastal zone. These changes have established new procedures for protecting the environment, but the size of coastal development has continued to create problems with coastal water quality. This is particularly true in areas where summer temperatures are high and where tidal currents and river flow interact to hold water in the coastal zone for long periods. Where such conditions occur, nutrients such as phosphorous and nitrogen build up (see Chapter 1 description of estuarine nutrient traps) and stimulate rapid growth and photosynthesis of algae. The algae and animals that feed on them combine with other oxygen-consuming organic

Table 3. Major Federal Statutes Regulating Use of the Coastal Zone

Act	Description
Clean Water Act	Includes many functions such as dredge and fill permits, National Pollution Discharge Elimination System, oil and hazardous substance spills, pretreatment of toxic pollutants, ocean discharge, nonpoint source pollution control, combined sewer outflows, remedial action, and estuarine management.
Coastal Zone Management Act	Supports comprehensive state programs to balance development and coastal protection. Amendments in 1990 included a mandatory nonpoint source pollution program and enhancement grants for national priorities such as wetlands. Establishes the National Estuarine Research Reserve System.
Marine Protection Research & Sanctuaries Act (MPRSA)	Title I issues ocean dumping permits and designates sites for ocean dumping. Title II establishes a monitoring program. Title III establishes the National Marine Sanctuaries. Title IV establishes regional research programs.
Fishery Conservation & Management Act	Conservation of fish stocks in a 200-mile U.S. Fishery Conservation Zone; development of fishery management plans by eight regional fishery management councils.
Fish & Wildlife Coordination Act	Interagency consultation to give fish and wildlife resources equal consideration with other projects.
National Ocean Pollution Planning Act	Reviews each agency's pollution budget request and prepares a comprehensive plan for federal ocean pollution research and monitoring.

Table 3. Continued

Act	Description
National Sea Grant College Act	Promotes research, education, and advice related to ocean and coastal resources.
Comprehensive Environmental Response Compensation & Liability Act (CERCLA)	Natural resource damage assessment program. Recovers damages or seeks funds from superfund for natural resources injured, destroyed, or lost by releases of hazardous substances into the coastal or marine environment.
Shore Protection Act	EPA regulates waste-handling practices to minimize waste in coastal waters. Handles permitting of vessels that transport waste in coastal waters.
Marine Mammal Protection Act	Prohibits/strictly regulates taking, harassing, or importing marine mammals.
Endangered Species Act	Regulates any action related to a federal agency that could jeopardize endangered or threatened species or the habitat of such a species.
Coastal Barrier Resources Act	Restricts federally subsidized development of under-developed coastal barriers along the Atlantic and Gulf Coasts.

matter to cause depletion of dissolved oxygen in the water, resulting in fish kills and other adverse impacts in the affected habitats. These conditions are regrettably common in the areas described in Chapter 2 and caused a coastal water quality crisis in North Carolina in the summer of 1995. Headlines much like those in the late 1970s dominated newspapers again: "Pollution Taking Its Toll on Once Pristine Neuse," "Presence of Fecal Bacteria Closes Vast Areas to Shellfish Harvesting," "Heat, Low Oxygen Causing Large Fish Kills in Pamlico," "Nutrient Overload Cause Fish Kills in State Rivers," "Dramatic Fish Kills Trouble Scientists," "Fish Kills May Make People Ill," "Scientist in Midst of Fish Controversy," and a fine example of an attempt to kill the messenger of bad news, "Hewitt Asks Officials to Silence Scientist."

The water quality crisis of the summer of 1995 was the result of conditions that have impaired coastal water quality for decades. This fact has been officially recognized in a series of reports required by section 305B of the federal Clean Water Act. These biennial reports assess the water quality of the whole state and document areas where waters do not support the uses normally expected of them. The state's 1995 Environmental Indicators Report notes that only 35 percent of streams and rivers had water quality that fully supported their designated uses, with "most impairment . . . in the slow-moving reaches of the Chowan, Pasquotank, Roanoke, and White Oak Basins"—that is, coastal rivers and estuaries. The distribution of coastal zone streams that either fail to support or only partially support their designated uses is shown in figure 69. Note that these include almost all the miles of streams that drain into coastal lagoons and estuaries as well as the upper reaches of the state's large estuaries.

The data presented in figure 69 give the impression that most coastal water quality problems occur upstream of the lower estuaries and large lagoons. Regrettably, that impression is only partially correct. North Carolina has almost 2 million acres of tidal saltwater. Most of this is in large lagoons along the northern coast, in Albemarle, Pamlico, Core, Back, and Bogue Sounds. Together these large open-water areas make up 48 percent of the state's tidal area. The water quality of these large tidal water bodies remains good (99.4 percent of these waters fully support their designated uses). The remaining 52 percent of tidal saltwaters are not in such good shape; only 81 percent of them fully support their designated uses, and when rainfall brings polluted water downstream and/or off the land, the percentage supporting use as shellfish harvest waters can drop to zero. State waters are frequently closed to shellfish harvest after heavy rainfalls

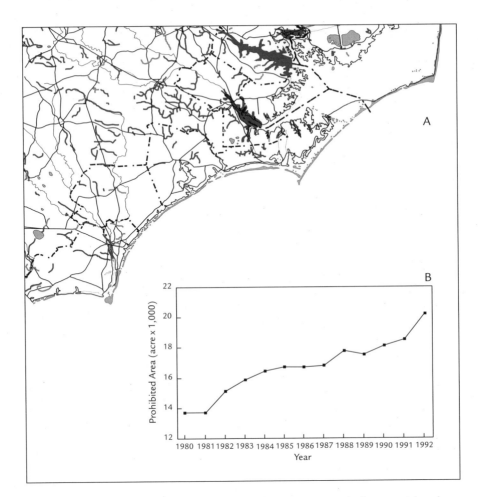

Figure 69. Southern North Carolina coast. (A) Use support: dark areas either do not support or only partially support their designated uses. (B) Annual change in area prohibited from shellfish harvest in the North Carolina region from Cedar Island to the South Carolina border, 1980–1992. Data from the Cape Fear and the New River areas have been removed. From R. Ohrel, ed., "Why We Are Convinced That Traditional Strategies for Wastewater Management Are Not Working," proceedings of a workshop on Integrated Coastal Wastewater Management in North Carolina, N.C. Coastal Federation, Newport, N.C. (1994).

because under these conditions all tidal waters have been shown to have higher numbers of fecal bacteria than is permissible under state and federal law. Thus, while it is technically true to say that 90 percent of North Carolina's tidal saltwater areas support their designated uses (as was stated in the state's 305B report submitted in 1994), informed readers will recognize that the percentage underemphasizes water quality problems in small water bodies and the lower portions of the state's estuaries.

Coastal water quality problems are of two general types. In some areas the major problems are caused by excess nutrients that reach rivers and estuaries from farmers' fields, urban areas, and septic tanks. In other areas the worst problems are commonly caused by fecal bacteria that reach the rivers from animal husbandry operations, sewage treatment plants, poorly performing septic systems, and wildlife. The two types of problems have different adverse impacts on coastal environments. Excess nutrients stimulate levels of plant growth that cannot be sustained (see Chapter 1). Rivers become clogged with plants, dissolved oxygen drops to lethally low levels, and fish and bottom-dwelling animals are killed. Recently we have learned through studies by JoAnn Burkholder of North Carolina State University that toxic algae flourish in high-nutrient waters, adding their killing power to that of lowered dissolved oxygen.

The problems caused by fecal bacteria contamination are usually less visible than those caused by excess nutrients, but the risk to human health is probably greater. Fecal bacteria in natural waters indicate a risk of transferring diseases from one human to another. In coastal areas such transfers are known to occur through shellfish. Oysters and clams eat bacteria of all types, and humans eat these shellfish without benefit of cooking. If the raw shellfish eaten by one human contains a disease organism from another human, the disease may be transferred from one person to the other. The fact that diseases may be transmitted by eating shellfish has caused state and federal governments to pass laws requiring that waters with low levels of fecal bacteria be closed to shellfish harvest. Shellfish harvest is prohibited in waters with only 7 percent of the concentration of fecal bacteria that can occur in water used for swimming. Bacteria from humans enter the water from faulty waste treatment systems (municipal and septic) as well as from boats and storm sewers that receive human wastes. Fecal bacteria of the same species found in humans can come from several other types of warm-blooded vertebrates (cows, horses, pigs, sheep, dogs, cats, birds, wildlife, and waterfowl). The test used to close waters cannot tell the difference between human and nonhuman fecal bacteria. As a result, waters may be closed when they pose little or no threat of disease transmission, but the rules, as they should be, are conservative. Unfortunately, the area in southern North Carolina not affected by major sewage treatment systems that has been placed under prohibition for shellfish harvest has gone up steadily since 1983 (see figure 69). Additional areas are closed provisionally and opened occasionally. Still other areas are considered open, even though they are closed whenever significant rainfall occurs. All temporarily closed areas are classified as partially supporting their designated use by the DEM, but since all state waters are closed when major rainfall occurs, no state shellfish waters fully support their designated use at all times.

Environmental Management

Coastal water quality problems do not originate in the water itself; they originate with land use and are transferred to watercourses by waste disposal systems and runoff. These two sources are termed "point" and "nonpoint," respectively. A point source is something like a pipe or canal that you can point to and say, "That's a source of pollution." A nonpoint source is harder to identify and measure, as it refers to pollutant materials that run off fields, forests, roads, golf courses, septic system drain fields, and paved areas. As you would expect from the definitions, point sources of pollution have proven easier to regulate than nonpoint sources. The national Clean Water Act requires that all facilities that discharge wastes into natural waters must have a National Pollution Discharge Elimination System permit. In North Carolina these permits are managed by the DEM and are overseen by the Environmental Management Commission. Nonpoint source pollutants have no permit system; they are identified by the DEM on the basis of chemical and biological monitoring of water quality in streams and tidal waters, land use patterns where problems occur, surveys of stream-bottom animals, citizen complaints, and "best professional judgments."

Regulation of both point and nonpoint pollution sources has developed to respond to identified problems, federal legislation, and economic realities. Both types of regulations continue to be a "work in progress" in coastal areas of the Southeast. In North Carolina more than $1.1 billion has been spent to upgrade municipal wastewater treatment plants in the last 20 years, but many plants continue to operate under "special orders of consent" when they fail to keep pace with population increases or technological improvements. Similarly, more than $52 million has been spent in the last decade to help farmers reduce pollutant runoff from their fields, but little state or federal effort has been focused on other sources of nonpoint source pollutants. The summer of 1995 made it clear that more needed to be done if coastal water quality was to be maintained while coastal populations, economies, and recreational amenities developed further. North Carolina's general assembly responded in 1996 by passing new legislation to control waste spills from animal producers, establish natural wetland buffers along streams, and assist municipalities in improving their waste treatment systems. Altogether, this multi-million-dollar commitment of public funds was a major step toward cleaner coastal water for the future.

Coastal Management and the Future

Government programs focused on coastal area land use planning and management were created in response to the 1972 passage of the federal Coastal Zone Management Act (CZMA) (see table 3). These programs supplemented those already in place to deal with specific issues. For example, the involvement of the U.S. Army Corps of Engineers in wetland dredge and fill permits and other matters related to construction in navigable waters traces to the 1899 Rivers and Harbors Act. Subsequent to passage of the CZMA, federal and state statutes have been passed to establish regulatory control over other aspects of coastal development. The major federal acts of this sort are summarized in table 3, but others not listed there are also important. For example, in 1973 the U.S. Congress changed the definition of "flood" to include flood-related erosion hazards along the nation's coastlines, thereby qualifying beachfront property owners for the National Flood Insurance Program so they could obtain mortgage loans from federally backed programs (such as the Veterans' Administration or Farm Home Administration) or federally insured lending institutions (such as banks or savings and loans). A full description of the complex of federal and state regulations that interact with one another in an evolving program of coastal regulations is beyond the scope of this book. For those interested in these details, I recommend a 1994 book by Timothy Beatley, David J. Brower, and Anna K. Schwab, *An Introduction to Coastal Zone Management*, published by Island Press of Washington, D.C. Chapters 4, 5, and 6 provide overviews of federal and state agency responsibilities and programs in coastal management. Overlapping responsibilities, interagency agreements, and even the results of case law make an interesting but confusing network of programs that the book's authors politely call "a fragmented management framework."

The fragmentation of North Carolina's system for managing coastal resources was made starkly apparent in a 1994 report to the governor by a distinguished coastal futures committee appointed to assess the management of the coastal area, celebrate North Carolina's coastal resources, and chart a clear course of action for the future of the coast. This committee worked through 1993 and 1994 under the leadership of chairman L. Richardson Preyer and produced an important eighty-page report titled "Charting a Course for our Coast" in September 1994. This report provided 230 recommendations relating to six topics: (1) land use and growth management; (2) coastal water quality; (3) protection of natural areas; (4) regulatory programs and organization; (5) environmental education; and (6) the coastal economy. A striking feature of this report is that these recommendations had to be addressed to a total of twenty-one different units of government and six different statutorily established councils, commissions, and advisory groups. The fact that the Coastal Futures Committee found it appropriate to frame 230 separate recommendations and necessary to address these to twenty-seven different government entities speaks volumes about how responsibility for coastal environmental matters has been fragmented. I am reminded of the old adage, "When everyone is in charge, no one is in charge."

The crucial questions facing the southern coast are What level of development should be achieved? and What public and private arrangements are needed to achieve and sustain that level of development?

It is clear that modern technology can create and sustain intense levels of development on coastal barrier islands. Atlantic City, New Jersey; Ocean City, Maryland; Miami Beach, Florida; and Galveston, Texas, are a few examples. This level of development intensity has not yet been created in southern North Carolina, although Wrightsville Beach appears headed in that direction. Obviously there is nothing inherently wrong with high-density development. Citylike amenities and services can be made available in coastal settings if enough money and planning goes into their development. The nature of the coastal zone must be taken into account, however, if the development is to be safe and sustainable and retain the environmental amenities that brought people to the coast in the first place. The natural phenomena that need to be considered are now clear. Many of these can be accommodated by appropriate local arrangements for transportation, sanitation, utility systems, and the like. Other phenomena require broader involvement. For example, we know that current environmental conditions (such as rising sea level and strong winds during storms) cause beaches to erode and tidal inlets to migrate. If high-intensity development is likely to disrupt the natural system that allows moving sand to bypass an inlet (see figure 6) or sustain a beach (see figure 10), a regional sand management plan should be developed to avoid damaging nearby beachfronts and islands. Still other phenomena require action at river basin, state, or national levels for effective management. Coastal water quality is an example. Coastal counties can manage waste perfectly and still have unacceptable water quality as a result of pollution from upstream sources.

Coastal Area Management Programs have made a good start toward environmentally responsible development of the southern coastal zone. The worst excesses of barrier island and shoreface developments have largely been controlled. The need for control of regional and river-basin scale environmental processes is appreciated but not yet realized. All those with an interest in the southern coast have a stake in finding solutions to these problems. We need to express our opinions about the level of coastal development that should be achieved and help develop the public and private arrangements needed to sustain it. To do less is to consign the southern coast to a future of environmental deterioration.

INDEX

Page numbers in italics refer to figures within the text.

area, 150; Tidelands Trail, 151, 161–62,
   163
Croton (*Croton punctatus*), 51, *54*
Currents, alongshore, 14, 27–28, 211–12
Cypress-palmetto swamps, 133

Davis, N.C., 99
Davis Island, 105
Deep Creek (Newport River), 133
Deltas, tidal, 15, 18–19, *21*, 125, *126*; of
   Carteret County, 143
Diamond City (Shackleford Banks),
   121
Dixon Point, 204–5
Dogwood (*Cornus florida*), 60, *62*
Downeast mainland, 97–112; creeks
   of, 100–105; forests of, 103; bays
   of, 103–7; access to bays, 105, 107;
   sounds of, 107–12
Dredge spoil islands: of Carteret
   County, 138–39, 145–46, 161; of
   Stump Sound, 179
Drum Inlet, 112; tidal effect on, 19, *21*;
   sand flats of, 108; opening of, 125
Dune broomsedge, 32, 164
Dunefields: vegetation of, 33; ecologi-
   cal conditions in, *36*; of Shackleford
   Banks, 147; of Bear Island, 163, 164–
   65, *165*; of Zeke's Island, 189
Dune grass communities, 50–51, *52*
Dunes: vegetation of, 30–35, *32*, 50–51;
   primary, 31, 50, 51; secondary, 51; ter-
   tiary, 51; migration of, 60, 61; of Core
   Banks, 112, 114; of Fort Macon State
   Park, 144, 145; of Bluff Island, 211; of
   Brunswick County, 215
Dune spurge (*Euphorbia polygonifolia*),

50, *52*; of Core Banks, 114; of Carteret
   County, 145

Earthquakes, 2, 23
Eel grass (*Zostera marina*), 104, *106*
Elliot Cones Nature Trail, 146
Emerald Isle (N.C.), 130, 131, 140–41;
   beach access in, 141
Estuaries, 13, 35; water circulation in,
   14; nutrients of, 38, 40, 225; sedimen-
   tation of, 43, 47–48; filtering effect
   of, 44; of Brunswick County, 204–7;
   excess nutrients in, 225, 230; water
   quality of, 228, 230
Estuarine fringe loblolly pine forests,
   65, 68, 69, 83; of Carolina Beach
   State Park, 185. *See also* Loblolly pine
Estuarine Research Reserve System: of
   Zeke's Island, 56, 60, 183, 184, 188–92;
   of Rachel Carson, 111; of Permuda
   Island, 178; of Masonboro Island, 194

Fetterbush (*Lyonia lucida*), 82, *84*, 88,
   135
Field study, guidelines for, 91–94
Figure Eight Island, 195–96
Fimbristylis spp., 51, 56
Finger grass (*Chloris petraea*), 51, *54*
Fire: and plant communities, 45; in
   estuarine fringe forests, 65; in bottomland communities, 78; in pine
   savannas, 79; in pond pine woodlands, 82–83; in pocosins, 89; controlled, 169
Fire-wheel (*Gaillardia pulchella*), 51, *55*
Fish: of downeast mainland, 102; of
   downeast sounds, 109–10; of inter-

Salt meadow cordgrass, 32–33; of Core Banks, 114; of Carolina Beach State Park, 185

Salt meadow hay (*Spartina patens*), 50, 51, *53*, 56; of Bear Island, 164

Salt-pannes, 65

Salt spray: toleration by plants, 32, 33, 34, 46; in dune grass communities, 50–51; in shrub communities, 57, 182; in evergreen forests, 60–61

Saltwater, 35–39; conductivity of, 38; in tidal marshes, 68; in maritime forests, 137; in freshwater tables, 143; of White Oak River, 158; water quality of, 228, 230. *See also* Freshwater-saltwater transitional areas

Sand: drainage patterns of, 3; erosion rate of, 5; stabilization of, 14, 22, 30–35; in inlets, 18; transportation of, 22, 23–30, *31*; alongshore transport of, 27–28, 130, 211–12; overwash deposits, 28, 30; in maritime plant communities, 56

Sandbars, offshore, 27–28, 166, 211

Sand flats, 15, 22; of downeast mainland, 105; of downeast sounds, 108–10; food chain of, 110; of Portsmouth Island, 115, 116; of Core Sound, 118

Sand Island, 112

Sand-sharing systems, 22, 27–28, *29*; of Core Banks, 112

Sawgrass (*Cladium jamaicense*), 68, *70*, 136

Scarps, 10–11, *12*

Schafele, Michael P., 45, 46, 57, 68, 72

Seabeach amaranth, 114

Sea grass beds: productivity of, 104–5;

of downeast sounds, 112; of Cape Lookout, 118

Sea grasses, *106*

Sea level changes, 2–12, 222; in downeast mainland, 100–101; and economic development, 234

Sea oats (*Uniola paniculata*), 30, 32, *53*; in dune grass communities, 50; in Fort Macon State Park, 145; of Bear Island, 164

Sea ox-eye (*Borrichia frutescens*), 64, *66*, 102; of White Oak River, 162; of Bald Head Island, 211

Sea rocket (*Cakile harperi*), 50, *53*; of Core Banks, 114; of Carteret County, 145

Seaside goldenrod (*Solidago sempervirens*), 51, *55*

Sedimentation: of South Atlantic coast, 2–4; depth of, 4–5; supply of, 18; effect of freshwater runoff on, 37, 38, *39*; estuarine, 43; of lagoons, 47–48; of salt marshes, 61, 64–65, 104; riverine, 64; of tidal freshwater marshes, 68; of downeast sounds, 108; of Bogue Banks, 130; fossil-bearing, 181

Shackleford Banks, 97, 98, 119–24; beach accretion on, *27*; grassland communities of, 56; shrub communities of, 60; dune migration on, 61; marshes of, 111; habitats of, 119–20; maritime forests of, 120, *121*, 122; interdune wet slacks of, 120, 121, 122–23, *124*; horses of, 120–21, 122, 123; freshwater marshes of, 121; westward movement of, 147

Shackleford Island (Brown Island), 167
Shallotte River, 204, 205
Shelf-slope break, 192
Shoal grass (*Halodule wrightii*), 104, *106*
Shoals, 28, 212
Shoreface progradation, 130
Shorelines, ancient, 5, *12*, 46–47; scarps of, 10–11; at White Oak River, 158, 161; of Camp Lejeune, 168; sand ridges of, 176–77
Shrubs. *See* Maritime shrub communities
Smith Island complex, 207–14
Smooth cordgrass, 102, 104; of Core Banks, 114; of Bald Head Island, 211
Smyrna Creek, *101*, 102–3
Snakes, 92–93
Sneads Ferry, 166; sand ridge of, 176
Snow's Cut, 11, 184, 187
Snow's Cut Park, 192–94
Snyder, Steve, 11
Soft coral communities, 191
Sounds, 13; water circulation in, 14; of downeast mainland, 107–13
South Core Inlet, 126
Southern coast: development of, xiii–xiv, 91, 219–24, *221*; environmental processes of, xiv, 1, 13–14, 219; geology of, 1, 2–12; stratigraphy of, *8*; effect of sea level on, 12; field study of, 91–94; weather hazards of, 93–94; sedimentation of, 139–40; population growth of, 219–20, 225; economic importance of, 223, 233; water quality of, 228, *229*; environmental management of, 231–35
Southport (N.C.), 208

Spike grass (*Distichlis spicata*), 64, *67*, of downeast mainland, 100; of Core Banks, 114; of Carteret County, 135; of White Oak River, 162
Spooners Creek, 142
Spring tides, 16–17
Stella, N.C., 150
Storm surges, 17–18, 23; on maritime shrub communities, 57; on Shackleford Banks, 123
Stump Sound, 170–71; wildlife of, 177–78
Suffolk Scarp, 10
Sugarloaf Trail (Carolina Beach State Park), 185
Sulfate, 43
Sundew (*Drosera capillaris*), *87*, 89
Sunset Beach (N.C.), 214, 224
Supercontinents, 3
Surf City, N.C., 181
Swamp bay (*Persea borbonia*), 76; in pond pine woodlands, 82; in pocosins, 89
Swamp dogwood (*Cornus foemina*), 72, *75*
Swamp forests. *See* Maritime forests
Swamp magnolia (*Magnolia virginiana*), 76, *77*, in pond pine woodlands, 82; in pocosins, 89; of White Oak River, 154
Swamp Trail (Carolina Beach State Park), 185
Swamp tupelo (*Nyssa biflora*), 68, *69*, 72; of Brunswick County, 203
Swansboro, N.C., 150, 161; tidal range of, 15; Town Park, 162
Swash Inlet, 112, 125